SOLIDARITY IN CONTINGENCY

Solidarity in Contingency

Rorty's Constructive Project

Edited by
Elin Danielsen Huckerby and Marianne Janack

https://www.openbookpublishers.com

©2025 Elin Danielsen Huckerby and Marianne Janack
Copyright of individual chapters are maintained by the chapter author(s).

This work is licensed under the Creative Commons Attribution-NonCommercial 4.0 International (CC BY-NC 4.0). This license allows you to share, copy, distribute and transmit the text; to adapt the text for non-commercial purposes of the text providing attribution is made to the authors (but not in any way that suggests that they endorse you or your use of the work). Attribution should include the following information:

Elin Danielsen Huckerby and Marianne Janack (eds), *Solidarity in Contingency: Rorty's Constructive Project*. Cambridge, UK: Open Book Publishers, 2025, https://doi.org/10.11647/OBP.0487

Further details about CC BY-NC licenses are available at
https://creativecommons.org/licenses/by-nc/4.0/

All external links were active at the time of publication unless otherwise stated and have been archived via the Internet Archive Wayback Machine at
https://archive.org/web

Digital material and resources associated with this volume are available at
https://doi.org/10.11647/OBP.0487#resources

ISBN Paperback: 978-1-80511-709-4

ISBN Hardback: 978-1-80511-710-0

ISBN Digital (PDF): 978-1-80511-711-7

ISBN HTML: 978-1-80511-713-1

ISBN Digital ebook (epub): 978-1-80511-712-4

DOI: 10.11647/OBP.0487

Cover image: Photo by James Wainscoat, a whale in the sky (starling roost at Otmoor UK), January 20, 2018, https://unsplash.com/photos/a-large-flock-of-birds-flying-over-a-field-b7MZ6iGIoSI

Cover design: Jeevanjot Kaur Nagpal

Contents

Contributor Biographies	vii
Abbreviations for Key Works by Richard Rorty	xi
1. Introduction: From Explication to Application *Elin Danielsen Huckerby and Marianne Janack*	1
2. Rorty's Interpretations and the Possibility of Social Change *Marianne Janack*	11
3. Tenderness as the Norm: Rorty on 'Intense Mental Pain' *Paul Giladi*	25
4. Actually (Anti-)Utopian? Levitas, Rorty and the Conditions of Utopianism *Elin Danielsen Huckerby*	57
5. Pragmatist Eirenism in Post-Truth Society *Michela Bella*	93
6. Creative Doubts against Authoritarian Certainty: Rorty through Reparative Critique *Heidi Salaverría*	123
7. Rortyan Irony as Civic Virtue in Our Myside Society *Martin Müller*	147
8. Irony as Hope and the Future of the Humanities *Bryan Vescio*	175
Works Cited	201
Index	221

Contributor Biographies

Michela Bella

michela.bella@unimol.it

Michela Bella is a postdoctoral research fellow in the Department of Humanities, Social Sciences, and Education at the University of Molise, Italy. She is the author of *Ontology After Philosophical Psychology: The Continuity of Consciousness in William James's Philosophy of Mind* (2019). She works on American pragmatism and the philosophy of mind, and a range of related issues.

https://orcid.org/0000-0002-0000-5261

Paul Giladi

pg30@soas.ac.uk

Paul Giladi is Reader in Philosophy at SOAS University of London. Paul has published extensively on German Idealism, American Pragmatism, philosophical naturalism, critical social theory, critical social epistemology and critical social ontology. He is one of the co-creators of the world's first Decolonising Philosophy Curriculum Toolkit and Handbook.

https://orcid.org/0000-0002-8934-3602

Elin Danielsen Huckerby

elin.d.huckerby@uib.no

Elin D. Huckerby is a postdoctoral fellow at the Department of Foreign Languages at the University of Bergen, Norway, where she works on affects and agency in 'Brexlit'—contemporary British literature responding to Brexit. She is also writing a book on Rorty's uses of literature, reconstruing his pragmatism as poeticism, and has published articles and chapters on this topic. Before becoming an academic, Huckerby worked for a number of years as a computer engineer.

https://orcid.org/0000-0003-1990-0204

Marianne Janack

mjanack@hamilton.edu

Marianne Janack is the John Stewart Kennedy Professor of Philosophy at Hamilton College, and has published extensively on pragmatism, philosophy of science, philosophy of mind, feminist philosophy, and philosophy and literature. She is the author of *What We Mean By Experience* (2012) and the editor of *Feminist Interpretations of Richard Rorty* (2010).

https://orcid.org/0000-0001-9338-6077

Martin Müller

martin.mueller@ggi.uni-tuebingen.de

Martin Müller is an airline pilot and lecturer in philosophy at the University of Tuebingen and at the Munich Volkshochschule. Müller has published a range of contributions and books on American Pragmatism and Rorty in particular, existentialism, discourse theory and current debates in political philosophy, amongst other topics. He is the editor of *Handbuch Richard Rorty* (2023).

https://orcid.org/0009-0004-7769-8811

Heidi Salaverría

heidi.salaverria@medicalschool-hamburg.de

Heidi Salaverria is a philosopher and Chair Professor for Art Theory and Artistic Practice at the Medical School, Hamburg. She is a philosopher, art theorist, and cultural worker, living in Hamburg, Germany. She is working on an Aesthetics of Doubt. She has published widely on ideas of non-identitarian subjectivity and critical common sense, the problems of recognition, the intersection of aesthetics and politics, and the question of agency.

https://orcid.org/0000-0002-4522-7730

Bryan Vescio

bvescio@highpoint.edu

Bryan Vescio is Chair and Professor of English at High Point University. He is the author of *Reconstruction in Literary Studies: An Informalist Approach* (2014), as well as numerous articles on American authors including Thoreau, Twain, Faulkner, Steinbeck, West and McCarthy. His philosophical work applies pragmatist philosophy and philosophy of language to literary and aesthetic theory, to redefine the role of literary study in higher education today.

https://orcid.org/0000-0003-0499-0163

Abbreviations for Key Works by Richard Rorty

AOC   *Achieving Our Country: Leftist Thought in Twentieth-Century America* (Cambridge, MA: Harvard University Press, 1998).

CIS   *Contingency, Irony, and Solidarity* (Cambridge: Cambridge University Press, 1989).

CP   *Consequences of Pragmatism: (Essays: 1972–1980)* (Minneapolis, MN: University of Minnesota Press, 1982).

EHO   *Essays on Heidegger and Others: Philosophical Papers, Vol. 2* (Cambridge, New York: Cambridge University Press, 1991).

ORT   *Objectivity, Relativism, and Truth: Philosophical Papers, Vol. 1* (Cambridge, New York: Cambridge University Press, 1991).

PCP   *Philosophy as Cultural Politics: Philosophical Papers, Vol. 4* (Cambridge, New York: Cambridge University Press, 2007).

PMN   *Philosophy and the Mirror of Nature* (Princeton, NJ: Princeton University Press, 1979).

PSH   *Philosophy and Social Hope* (New York: Penguin Books, 1999).

TP   *Truth and Progress: Philosophical Papers, Vol. 3* (Cambridge, New York: Cambridge University Press, 1998).

1. Introduction:
From Explication to Application

Elin Danielsen Huckerby and Marianne Janack

This collection originates from a conference held at the Centre for Research in the Arts, Social Sciences and Humanities (CRASSH) at the University of Cambridge, UK, in September of 2019, convened to mark the thirtieth anniversary of the publication of *Contingency, Irony and Solidarity* (1989, hereafter CIS). Our meeting was motivated by a desire to highlight the affirmative and constructive aspects of Richard Rorty's work. Once called 'the man who killed truth', Rorty was for a while infamous for insisting that we must give up the idea of language as a 'mirror of nature' and, with it, the idea of philosophy as able to provide us with foundational truths.[1] While the negating or dismantling aspect of Rorty's work has been intensely debated, the conference commenced from the belief that Rorty's vision of a culture which no longer understands truth as correspondence between word and world might offer epistemological, rhetorical and practical strategies of help to foster a well-functioning democratic culture in a fragmented era.

Then came the Covid-19 pandemic: work on this collection halted as the world locked down. Eventually, the desire to come together to discuss the constructive sides of Rorty's project compelled us to take it back up. In the meantime, some conference contributors had moved on to other

---

1   Stuart Jeffries, 'Richard Rorty: The Man Who Killed Truth' (BBC). Recorded off-air from BBC4 on 16/12/2003. Repeat: original airing date 04/12/2003. See also 'Stuart Jeffries: How to Make Philosophers Telegenic', *The Guardian*, 3 November 2003, https://www.theguardian.com/media/2003/nov/03/broadcasting. artsandhumanities; Richard Rorty, *Philosophy and the Mirror of Nature* (Princeton, NJ: Princeton University Press, 1979). Hereafter PMN.

endeavours. Others familiar with the project have now been included. But the collection continues to centre CIS, and the premise that Rorty's positive project still deserves further exploration and development. We also became convinced that, as Rorty's work and its significance are undergoing steady consolidation, and Rorty scholarship continues to produce informed an-d insightful explications, there is a growing need to focus on application. What is Rorty's philosophy useful for today?

Given the precarious nature of our current moment, this question is vital. Still, it might seem incongruous to turn to Rorty for insights about how to deal with the present. Rorty studies is a vibrant and remarkably friendly field of scholarship, but it should not be underplayed that his thoughts still provoke vocal criticisms. The most vehement criticism has its own history, now well-researched and better understood than during the 1980s, 1990s and 2000s. While it is an overused move in philosophy to claim to understand, *contra* previous interpreters, what a philosopher *really* argued, it has been thoroughly documented that much of the earlier criticism of Rorty was misguided, not reasonably evidenced, and unjustly personal rather than on point.[2] Fortunately, most of this kind of critique has dissipated. Yet, amongst those of us convinced that Rorty continues to offer a position of significant value, it is far from uncommon to enter a room and know that stating this conviction in current company will earn less than friendly comments, often straight out of the Theory Wars. Paradoxically, then, the supposed 'back in the day'-ness of these wars is also regularly invoked to dismiss—suggesting that Rorty *was* a controversial figure who very much belonged to the latter half of the twentieth century, a postmodernist, now passé.

---

2   Alan Malachowski advanced an early analysis of Rorty criticisms. See Alan Malachowski, *Richard Rorty* (New York: Routledge, 2002), https://doi.org/10.1017/UPO9781844653140. Rorty talked about the personal toll this took in Richard Rorty, 'Trotsky and the Wild Orchids', *Common Knowledge*, 1.3 (1992), 140–53, and in Jeffries, 'Richard Rorty'. See also the following examples of scholarship that meticulously works to consolidate Rorty's work and situate it within the philosophical tradition:, Richard Rorty, *On Philosophy and Philosophers: Unpublished Papers, 1960-2000*, ed. by W. P. Małecki and Christopher Voparil (Cambridge: Cambridge University Press, 2020), https://doi.org/10.1017/9781108763967; Christopher Voparil, *Reconstructing Pragmatism: Richard Rorty and the Classical Pragmatists* (New York, NY: Oxford University Press, 2021), https://doi.org/10.1093/oso/9780197605721.001.0001

1. Introduction: From Explication to Application

So, why Rorty, and why Rorty now? Why look back to a self-declared 'postmodern bourgeois liberal'[3] amidst postliberal challenges to democratic liberalism from left and right? Why, in a time of global democratic backsliding, look to someone who maintained a faith in aspirational democracy that to many now (at best) appears naïve? Why, at a moment when capitalist extraction and political polarisation is pushing us towards the brink of collapse, discuss Rorty, who did not propose policy changes or revolutionary system transformations? As a better future seems increasingly harder to imagine, why discuss whether a shift in our use of words or our epistemological stance makes a difference? Surely, we need new impulses, new thoughts, new tools, and most of all new practical and material strategies? We do. What this collection shows is that there are ideas and approaches in Rorty that can be, should be, shaped into novel tools for grappling with today's circumstances.

The papers in this collection emerge from the belief that *in times of radical uncertainty, we might learn from a philosopher who summed up his stance as working from radical acceptance of uncertainty*. Rorty recognised and embraced the 'contingency' of 'all starting points'.[4] From there, he inquired into what kind of intellectual and discursive practices we need[5] if our overarching aim is to lessen human cruelty. He saw the embrace of contingency as *productive* if our aim is a more just, equitable, free and caring society. Implicit is a belief that these practices matter to the shape of society at large—and that there is benefit in taking a mindfully humble approach to the question of how to forge intellectual and discursive practices that align with the aim of lessening human cruelty. It is the *combination* of Rorty's systematic, analytic case against essentialism and representationalism and his demonstration of these as drivers of our failure to properly engage with oppression and cruelty in the world that makes his work so compelling and important.

Reducing human cruelty was Rorty's lodestar. While he did not think we could dig down to firm and eternal foundations, Rorty instead proposed that we steer by those aims and purposes we understand as

---

3   Richard Rorty, 'Postmodernist Bourgeois Liberalism', *The Journal of Philosophy*, 80.10 (1983), 583, https://doi.org/10.2307/2026153
4   Richard Rorty, 'Pragmatism, Relativism, and Irrationalism', *Proceedings and Addresses of the American Philosophical Association*, 53.6 (1980), 719–38 (p. 726).
5   This includes epistemological, metaphysical, ontological practices, but also political, public, and philosophical practices understood more broadly.

helpful, even if 'only' comparatively and pragmatically justified. In fact, Rorty did not see a paradox between anti-foundationalism and standing unflinchingly for what one believes, on such grounds, to be good. The challenge he placed at our feet was to continually engage in *the work* of negotiating what 'good' entails, as an integral part of realising it. Rorty's work is thus as much an epistemological outlook as it is a moral approach and a deeply political philosophy. This complexity and capacity is reflected in the contributions herein.

This collection thus presents seven framings of Rortyan thought that articulate novel insights and approaches in light of today's challenges. Drawing lessons from Rorty's embrace of contingency and insistence that such an embrace should compel us to turn to each other in conversation and practical collaboration, the contributions in this volume assess these presumptions and difficulties within Rorty's reasoning, evaluate his suggestions, but also ask how these might better equip us for acting in line with an overall desire to reduce human cruelty. Attempting to, as was Rorty's Hegelian mantra, hold our time in thought, the chapters address feminism, epistemic and structural cruelty, radical politics, the current conditions of utopian thought, the possibility of more conciliatory politics in a post-truth reality, the generative potential of doubt and how to resist authoritarianism, the skills needed to secure a democratic future, how we might redescribe Rortyan 'ironism' as hope and how we might defend the humanities as fostering such hope.

Marianne Janack begins the conversation with a chapter on Rorty's contribution to feminist thought and his reorientation of philosophy towards literature as bolstering the possibility of social change. She illustrates how Rorty valued feminist perspectives as transformative forces, and explores how his pragmatic approach opens avenues for feminist reinterpretations. Janack argues that attending to how Rorty supports forms of discourse that seek radical change, while refusing to be 'tamed' by the forms that aim at Truth and accurate description, is a strategy for helping us understand how interpretation and reinterpretation are not simply intellectual endeavours, but are also potentially revolutionary.[6]

---

6   Throughout this collection, whenever notions such as 'Truth' or 'Goodness' are capitalised, it indicates an essentialising understanding of the relevant idea.

Paul Giladi then addresses an important question initially posed by Bjørn Ramberg:[7] Can we devise a strategy for 'Radical Rorty' that constitutes progress? Can we get to a point where 'tenderness is the norm'? Arguing that Rorty's most crucial observation in CIS is that human beings can be given a 'special kind of pain' through the 'forcible tearing down' of their language and beliefs,[8] Giladi demonstrates that Rorty provides resources for understanding moral-epistemic injuries and countering epistemic injustice and oppression. However, even if Rorty succeeds in showing how such harm and oppression is built into our current systems, he fails to provide the kind of structural critique that might tear those structures down. Thus, while Rorty provides crucial resources for diagnosis, it is necessary to articulate this missing critique and, to get us beyond the *status quo*, forge what Gialdi calls 'theories that move'.

While Richard Bernstein suggested, in 1982, that it would be a 'mistake' and even a 'slander' to suggest Rortyan thought displays an attachment to the *status quo* at all,[9] the evidence for such an attachment in Rorty's work is a key concern in Elin D. Huckerby's contribution, too. Huckerby examines Ruth Levitas's critique of Rorty as functionally upholding present hegemonies to the point where he is 'anti-utopian'. Huckerby contrasts this with Michael Bacon and Nat Rutherford's influential attempt to recover Ramberg's aforementioned 'Radical Rorty', which, on their view, is characterised by precisely utopianism in combination with practical-mindedness.[10] Presenting a novel take by distinguishing between 'ordinary' and 'strong' utopianism in his work,

---

7   Bjørn T. Ramberg, 'Strategies for Radical Rorty ("… but is it progress?")', *Canadian Journal of Philosophy*, 23, Supplementary Volume 19: New Essays on Metaphilosophy (1993), 223–46, https://doi.org/10.1080/00455091.1993.10717349

8   Richard Rorty, *Contingency, Irony and Solidarity* (Cambridge: Cambridge University Press, 1989), https://doi.org/10.1017/cbo9780511804397, p. 177.

9   Richard J. Bernstein, 'What Is the Difference That Makes a Difference? Gadamer, Habermas, and Rorty', *Proceedings of the Biennial Meeting of the Philosophy of Science Association*, 1982 (1983), 331–59, p. 351, https://doi.org/10.1086/psaprocbienmeetp.1982.2.192429

10 Ruth Levitas, 'Pragmatism, Utopia and Anti-Utopia', *Critical Horizons*, 9.1 (2008), 42–59, https://doi.org/10.1558/crit.v9i1.42; Michael Bacon and Nat Rutherford, 'Rorty, Habermas, and Radical Social Criticism', in *The Ethics, Epistemology, and Politics of Richard Rorty*, ed. by Giancarlo Marchetti, Routledge Studies in American Philosophy (Oxon, New York: Routledge, 2021), pp. 191–208, https://doi.org/10.4324/9780429324734-14

Huckerby argues that Rorty is indeed utopian if both of these aspects are accounted for. Moreover, the vital utopian imaginary Rorty offers, that of a fully 'poeticized' culture—presents a transformative possibility today. However, Huckerby suggests that Levitas is partially right: there is an intransigence in Rorty's work, which should be recognised and worked through to better realise the potential of this vision.

Michela Bella's chapter presents an original and novel reading of Rorty, arguing that we should attend to his idea of an 'eirenic' attitude. This is distinct from the ironic attitude most closely associated with Rorty. Eirenism, Bella shows, captures a capacity for seeing that differing vocabularies and theories might coexist peacefully in practice, for functional reasons, as different approaches to the same or similar issues, and, importantly, that the existence of (partly) incommensurable descriptions does *not* entail these being in combative opposition to each other. It is a practice of 'combining irony and curiosity'. While ironism fails to convey the active and democratic aspects of Rorty's cultural project, and might be perceived and experienced as a detaching move, eirenism preserves attachment. Moreover, it does not aim to 'win' by replacing other, partly incommensurable perspectives with one's own. In this way, Rorty's 'eirenic' approach can serve as 'an antidote to the dangers of the post-truth society and its tendency to hypostatise alternative viewpoints as poles in a contradiction'. It helps us to see that it is up to us to take action to facilitate conciliatory modes of engagement. Thus, Bella argues, recovering the notion of 'eirenism' in Rorty's sense can help us 'respond to the reductionism that characterises dogmatism, fanaticism, and extremism in our post-truth societies'.

Heidi Salaverría connects the Rortyan stance to reparative theories that valorise conflictual ambivalences, ambiguities, and creative doubts. In reparative aesthetics, Salaverría points out, 'creative and nurturing components are revealed precisely by working through relational tensions of self and other'. Salaverría finds a model for this in Rorty, in his discussion of the struggle between autonomy and self-doubt. The reparative position, as the Rortyan, 'acknowledges dependence on others'. This enables the establishment of 'a different, more permeable kind of autonomy', which is more responsive, less disposed to humiliation and egotism. Moreover, doubting as a practice of resisting inherited paradigms facilitates revaluation, also of oppressive structures and narratives. 'Welcoming doubts' might dislodge internalised authoritarian framings, such as racist, sexist or gender-oppressive beliefs, that make us feel shame or alienated. Ultimately, Salaverría argues, Rorty makes a case for the political importance and the reparative potential of non-humiliating, creative doubts. His philosophy offers a framework for challenging oppressive structures through creativity and self-reinvention, thereby fostering solidarity in democratic societies that value diversity and inclusivity.

In his contribution, Martin Müller argues that 'Rortyan irony, understood as a civic virtue that leads to openness and conversability, is an important resource for a renewal of democratic discourse' in our fraught era. We need openness, curiosity and 'conversability' across the bordered geographies of our political landscape: we cannot and should not restrict conversation to our own 'justification tribe'. Rortyan thought shows how we create selves and communities through communication with others. Irony, understood as a 'serene fallibilism', supports a pluralistic public sphere, capable of such communication, by fostering open-mindedness and an appreciation for diverse perspectives. Müller frames irony as a democratic virtue that enables citizens to engage in productive discourse without succumbing to absolutism, thus positioning it as a response to the polarised, post-truth era. It represents a vital and viable alternative to a 'nostalgic return to "Truth" and "Reality"', a solution Müller suggests is at best useless, and perhaps, dangerous.

Finally, Bryan Vescio closes this collection with a chapter that reconstrues Rortyan irony as hope. Vescio explores deficiencies in Rorty's construal of irony and suggests it can be rehabilitated through attending to Rorty's own understanding of it as hope—a longing to become better, create something better. Moreover, locating it in hope orients irony toward the future and toward possibility, making it more consistent with the values of both pragmatism and democracy. Vitally, this 'preserves its power' to defend the humanities today. Irony, Vescio proposes, enables the humanities to confront challenges of legitimacy by encouraging both intellectual flexibility and moral commitment. Arguing against defences of the humanities that place it in the role of 'public saviour', and against a disciplinary self-conception centred on a particular political orientation, Vescio suggests we defend the humanities for its capacity to turn individuals and public life towards new possibilities—a defence grounded in a recognition of the plurality of purposes within the humanities, as well as its pluralism and openness as a model for engagement. Referencing the ongoing political interference in US universities, Vescio makes it clear that the point is not to be apolitical, nor to suggest that individuals within the humanities should refrain from engaging in politics. The point is to establish the humanities as a discipline that embodies social hope, open, conversational engagement, and pluralistic ideals; a place where young people might find instruction in hopefulness and cultivate hopes of their own.

Overall, what emerges most clearly from this collection of perspectives on Rortyan philosophy today are two things. One is that Rorty's systematic anti-essentialism still stands as a uniquely radical and transformative proposal—unique because of its comprehensiveness and methodical force. The other is that we have yet to elucidate and realise the transformation it promises: what we here discuss as Rorty's constructive project. There is a push in each contribution in this volume to rethink established opinions on key Rortyan ideas, in particular 'ironism' and his engagement with politics. But this push comes from a desire to better apply Rorty's systematic anti-essentialism in a world that has evolved a great deal since his death in 2007. While most of us writing in this volume wish to retain a variant of Rorty's conception of irony, it might be that in a world where 'irony poisoning' is deliberately deployed as a destabilising political strategy, and liberalism is increasingly recognised as upholding precisely a *status quo* of market economies and individualism, there is a need—if we take seriously the suggestion that Rorty's systematic anti-essentialism indeed holds a transformative potential—to redescribe some of his takes on the consequences of this deconstructive part of his work. That is, to redescribe aspects of his 'positive', constructive project. Rorty explicitly construed being a 'liberal' as working to lessen cruelty, as inseparable from creating human solidarity, and not as entailing universalist positions or firm attachments to specific economic systems or versions of government. But how different his position was to what we usually mean by 'liberal' risks getting lost if we fail to critically examine how he talked about the cultural and political consequences of his anti-essentialism and work to redescribe it for our time. His transformative antiessentialist and anti-authoritarian project risks going with it.

What these contributions also work to get across, is that despite its analytic origins, Rorty's project was and remains a fundamentally *human* one. At its heart is a choice to face up to human finitude. His constructive project is an attempt to answer questions like: What do we do now—in the face of this choice? How do we create something better than we did when we thought we could be redeemed through manifesting the answers God, or Nature, would provide; when we thought we were immortal, or superior to the beasts through our access to Truth? How do we forge a public and political sphere that takes human finitude and diversity of life and desires and creative endeavours into proper account? How do we create solidarity and human agency in uncertainty and contingent material conditions? This volume attempts to challenge, deepen and advance some of Rorty's own answers, as an invitation to others to continue the project.

As the journey from conference to finished product has been a particularly long one, we first and foremost want to thank our contributors not only for stimulating discussions and their excellent work, but also for their patience and unfailing positivity. It has been a gift to learn from our conversations. We want to thank Michael Bacon and Nat Rutherford for their contribution to this project early on. Bacon presented a joint paper with Neil Gascoigne at the original conference, alongside papers and prepared responses by Susan Dieleman, Nicholas Gaskill, Gregory Currie, Yvonne Hütter-Almerigi, Wojciech Małecki, Tracy Llanera, Andrew Bowie, Rachel Malkin, as well as Giladi, Müller, Janack and Huckerby. Professor Bowie and Louis Thorne made the conference especially memorable by playing jazz for us during break times. Nicholas Devlin, Céline Henne, Erlend Owesen and Ross Wilson co-convened the conference and served as respondents and discussants. We owe them all our thanks. The practical and financial support received from CRASSH was invaluable, and we extend further thanks to Cambridge University Press, the Mind Association, the Society for the Advancement of American Philosophy, the University of Cambridge's Department of History and Philosophy of Science, the Faculty of English, and Cambridge's School of the Arts and Humanities for supporting this conference. We are especially grateful to Dr Tosi and Open Book Publishers, who believed in the project more than once, supported it throughout, and saw it through to the end.

2. Rorty's Interpretations and the Possibility of Social Change

Marianne Janack

§ 1 §

'You don't really think that Rorty was a *feminist*, do you?' That was the question a friend of mine raised when I was working on the collection I edited, *Feminist Interpretations of Richard Rorty*.[1] Was the actual, living and breathing person, Richard Rorty, a feminist? I have no doubt that he was. But I do not think that was the question that my friend was asking. She seemed to think it odd—or maybe troublesome—that I was encouraging a feminist reading of Rorty's writings.

The series Feminist Interpretations of the Canon (published by Penn State University Press) includes, among others, *Feminist Interpretations of Plato; of Aristotle; of Hegel; of Descartes; of Quine; and of Nietzsche* (in spite of his many statements about women that make him sound like a misogynist). There is also a volume titled *Feminist Interpretations of Simone de Beauvoir*—about whom a colleague of mine said, 'I don't think that she was really a feminist', citing Beauvoir's procurement of women for Sartre. Those of us who have read and tried to teach *The Second Sex* know that figuring out how and if Beauvoir was a feminist does not end with the details of her biography. Beauvoir's feminist legacy is 'complicated', as the kids say.

---

1   Marianne Janack (ed.), *Feminist Interpretations of Richard Rorty* (University Park, PA: Pennsylvania State University Press, 2010).

So, was my friend saying that feminist interpretations of Rorty were more troublesome than feminist interpretations of these other figures in the history of philosophy? Or maybe she thought that it was a project that should not be undertaken to begin with. But Rorty had already entered the discussion about feminist philosophy on his own in 1990 when he delivered his Tanner Lecture at the University of Michigan, which was about pragmatism and feminism. Unlike his many white male contemporaries, Rorty actually read and was interested in feminist philosophy, and using the Tanner Lecture as an opportunity to discuss the work of Adrienne Rich, Catherine MacKinnon and Marilyn Frye was, I am guessing, a first for white male philosophers who had delivered these lectures.[2] Do I think Rorty was a feminist? Yes. Do I think it's worth offering feminist interpretations of Rorty's work? The answer seems pretty obvious: yes, since I've been doing a lot of that.

Perhaps it does not matter whether or not Rorty was a feminist or whether he intended to offer a sympathetic reading of feminist authors. Rorty himself seemed to be suspicious of the distinction between what a text *really* means and what we use it for, and his tendency to use other thinkers as 'mouthpieces' for what seem to be his own positions is often thought to be irresponsible at best. In his obituary for Rorty in the *LA Times*, Crispin Sartwell put it this way:

> What absolutely killed philosophy professors was Rorty's interpretation of the great figures of the Western tradition. The average philosophy professor may spend a decade or a career trying to elucidate the works of [...] Heidegger or [...] Quine. Rorty lined up such figures in support of his own positions in a fundamentally careless way. He quoted them out of context and ignored everything he couldn't use [...] .
>
> Rorty almost pathologically attributed his every thought to other people. He wielded the names 'Heidegger' or 'Sellars' like talismans: shorthand for whole swathes of argumentation. It was important to Rorty to connect his radical conclusions to an existing tradition. Every time I turned to his writings, I wanted to grab him by the lapels and tell him that, next time out, he would have to speak merely on his own

---

2   I could not do a complete inventory, but the male lecturers who are listed as having given Tanner Lectures between 1976–77 and 1990–91 on the Wikipedia page (https://en.wikipedia.org/wiki/Tanner_Lectures_on_Human_Values) as of 14 July 2019 do not stand out as having any (positive) interest in feminist work, and with the exception of Rorty, no Tanner lecturer has given a lecture with a title that was explicitly about feminist thought.

behalf. Rorty had plenty to say, and why he needed to claim that Dewey had already said it—when, as 50 Dewey scholars had shown, he hadn't—was a mystery.[3]

§ 2 §

This is one of the most frustrating aspects of reading Rorty: he cites a lot of different writers—some philosophers, some not—and his readers generally must take his word that the writers he cites said what he says they said. So, for instance, Rorty will attribute positions to people like Willard Van Orman Quine, or Ludwig Wittgenstein, or Wilfrid Sellars, or Michel Foucault which seem to be more like 'strong readings' of those authors rather than nuanced and scholarly statements of their claims. Sometimes, in fact, the authors do not recognise the claims as theirs. (Quine's essay, 'Let Me Accentuate the Positive' in Alan Malachowski's volume *Reading Rorty* is one example.) This problem is less prickly with dead authors, of course, but even they sometimes wrote things that would lead one to doubt that they would have accepted Rorty's interpretations of their writings. And sometimes, as seems to have happened when Rorty took up the mantle of defending feminist philosophers by praising feminist writing as 'prophetic', the recipients of the approval are less than happy about the terms of the advocacy.

Umberto Eco's *Foucault's Pendulum* received Rorty's approval, though Eco does not seem to have been happy about the terms of Rorty's advocacy. The papers by Rorty and Eco that were presented as part of the Tanner Lectures at Cambridge in 1990 testify to a lively discussion about authorial intentions and the distinction, which Rorty rather insouciantly tried to pitch overboard, between a text's meaning and its use(s). Rorty's hedgehoginess in his attacks on philosophy and the Perennial Questions approach to the history of philosophy returns in these discussions of whether there is any reason to limit the number of possible interpretations of literary texts. As he does in his criticisms of philosophy and its disciplinary commitments, Rorty is suspicious of the idea that there is some secret meaning to which only the elect have

---

3   Crispin Sartwell, 'The Provocateur's Philosopher', *Los Angeles Times* (12 June 2007), https://www.latimes.com/archives/la-xpm-2007-jun-12-oe-sartwell12-story.html

access; that there is something like 'the meaning of a text'; that new and contested interpretations are anything more than reframings of inquiry and appeals to a different vocabulary or context.

When he cites the work of feminist philosophers and talks about that work as poetic and prophetic, he intends this as a compliment. 'Normal Philosophy' does not aim to change the world, Rorty thinks, but rather to work out puzzles that are 'of the time'; these puzzles are taken to be the Real Problems and generally to be the same problems that have animated and perplexed philosophers for millennia. 'Normal Philosophy' (like 'Normal Science', in Thomas Kuhn's sense of the term) does not create new meanings, problems or visions but instead works within the boundaries set by the dominant discourse. Those who resist the rules or try to create their own paradigms are often seen as crazy, but they may be the ones who bring about revolutions.

As Nancy Fraser says in her comments on Rorty's Tanner Lecture on pragmatism and feminism, Rorty wants to say that feminist philosophers are doing something more important than what ordinary philosophers are doing—that bringing about social change and speaking in a way that does not appeal to or try to court the approval of the dominant voices in academic philosophy is much more important than adding to the pile of philosophical argument about what is True (or just true).[4] But, of course, this puts the revolutionary feminist 'philosophers' in the same position as those scientists who pursued alternative paradigms in the sciences—and, of course, some of those alternative paradigms became the accepted paradigms of a later age; however, some did not. Some alternative paradigms and programs passed out of existence; their advocates sidelined as crackpots or 'non-scientists'—or, maybe worse in the eyes of scientists: relegated to the category of 'metaphysicians'.

Rorty's contribution to the discussions about Eco's book *Foucault's Pendulum* was to double down on the reader-response theory that he and Stanley Fish advocated, though he also acknowledged, in his comments, that Eco disapproves of that reading. And this brings us to the issue of the biographical person—the writer—as the source of a text's meaning. Rorty, in his discussion of Eco's novel, seems to think that the writer is

---

4   Nancy Fraser, 'From Irony to Prophecy to Politics: A Reply to Richard Rorty', in Janack, *Feminist Interpretations of Richard Rorty*, pp. 47–54.

just another reader who has no special claim to know the 'true' meaning of a text. He argues that there is no difference between a novel's meaning and its use—which seems to be a way of using Wittgensteinian scepticism about the meanings of linguistic acts and Quine's 'meaning holism' as ways of thinking about texts and novels, and not just about the verbal performance of speech acts.

§ 3 §

But going back in time, to Rorty's chapters on Vladimir Nabokov and George Orwell in *Contingency, Irony and Solidarity* (CIS)—which I did recently—was an odd experience.[5] As I was reading those chapters in CIS, I almost felt like I had stumbled on two chapters that were supposed to be part of Martha Nussbaum's *Love's Knowledge*, rather than chapters written by the iconoclastic Richard Rorty—the Richard Rorty who thought that a text has no single meaning; that an author's biography and intentions were not that important for thinking about how to read a text; who tried to show the value of the prophetic, poetic voice; who sought to up-end discursive expectations and 'colour outside the lines', so to speak.

In his discussions of Nabokov and Orwell, Rorty argues that *Lolita*, *Pale Fire*, *1984* and *Animal Farm*, though very different sorts of books with different narrative structures and aesthetic qualities, all teach us about the dangers of cruelty. In spite of Nabokov's claim that *Lolita* has 'no moral in tow' Rorty insists that it *does* have a moral in tow—and Rorty tries to make this case by rejecting Nabokov's explicit statements about the novel. He gives us a psychological profile of Nabokov that connects Nabokov's motivations to his ideas about the eternal, immortality and his father's political career. In some sense, this is consistent with his discussion of Eco's novel—he treats the author as just another reader and is not at all troubled by the prospect of rejecting the author's explicit claims about what the text is intended to be or do.

And yet, Rorty's reading of *Lolita* seems like *a different way of talking* about authorial intention, rather than a *rejection* of authorial intention,

---

5   Richard Rorty, *Contingency, Irony and Solidarity* (Cambridge: Cambridge University Press, 1989), https://doi.org/10.1017/cbo9780511804397

since it seems that Rorty is arguing that Nabokov's intentions are either not accurately reflected in his comments about *Lolita*, or that Nabokov himself did not realize what his intentions were. Rorty, it seems, thinks that he has a better way of getting at what Nabokov's text means (or was intended to do?) because he can look (objectively?) at Nabokov's biography and see *Lolita* as an effect of Nabokov's psychological history, his relationship with his father, and his struggles with the idea of artistic creation. Note that Rorty does not acknowledge that this is just his reading—this, he seems to be saying, is the *correct* reading. Anyone who reads the book correctly should come away with a sense of how cruelty might arise as a result of following one's own project of self-creation or artistic expression.

The chapters on Nabokov and Orwell in CIS read like old-fashioned discussions of novels, in which the novel teaches us—the careful readers—something about how to live. In this case, Rorty argues that these novels dramatise the liberal idea that cruelty is the worst thing humans can do, and that they portray the challenges of balancing the private pursuit of self-creation with the public pursuit of solidarity and justice. Claims about what one learns from these two disparate novelists would seem to have to assume that there is some relatively stable meaning of the books in question and that, furthermore, their different aesthetic properties and narrative structures are independent of their 'message'.

This is generally a line of argument we might find in Nussbaum: discussions about what we readers can learn from novels generally begin by assuming a particular interpretation as the best or only one, with no recognition of the possibility of different interpretations or readerly responses that deviate from those of the well-educated reader. And Nussbaum also thinks that the process of reading narratives itself (at least when it comes to canonical works of fiction) is what makes readers 'finely aware and richly responsible'.[6] However, unlike Rorty, Nussbaum does not appeal to the writer's biography in developing the didactic themes of the books about which she chooses to write. Rorty, on the other hand, since he knows that the writer, Nabokov, has said

---

6   Martha C. Nussbaum, '"Finely Aware and Richly Responsible": Moral Attention and the Moral Task of Literature', *The Journal of Philosophy*, 82.10 (1985), 516–29, https://doi.org/10.2307/2026358

that his novels are not didactic, seems compelled to account for this expression of authorial intent. Rorty offers biographical information about Nabokov to undermine the author's claims about what the books mean (or do not mean).

We might ask: is this just a rhetorical tactic? Is Rorty simply appealing to the kind of evidence he thinks philosophers or other readers of CIS will be persuaded by? If so, then it might not be an argument to which he is committed but rather simply one he uses to convince his readers. However, if this were the case, one would think it would be more above-board to say, 'this is one way to think about what Nabokov's and Orwell's works do for the liberal ironist, but I recognize that this is just one reading'. And yet he does not say this. Generally, I think Rorty will tell us if he is just making an argument that will appeal to a given audience, so I consider this absence to be significant.

In an earlier work (another comment on another Tanner Lecture: Clifford Geertz's 'The Uses of Diversity' at the University of Michigan in 1985), Rorty claimed that anthropological accounts provide the same sorts of benefits to readers and liberal democracy that novels provide. In 'On Ethnocentrism: A Comment on Clifford Geertz', Rorty argues that anthropologists and novelists are the 'connoisseurs of particularity' who try to get the dominant (Western liberal) culture to recognize the existence and humanness of 'others' whom we think of as closed off to us, and to extend the embrace of justice and care to them. Novelists and anthropologists help us to see marginalised others as 'possible conversation partners'.[7] The

> moral tasks of a liberal democracy are divided between agents of love and agents of justice. In other words, such a democracy employs and empowers both connoisseurs of diversity and guardians of universality. The former insist that there are people out there whom society has failed to notice. They make these candidates for admission visible by showing how to explain their odd behavior in terms of a coherent, if unfamiliar, set of beliefs and desires—as opposed to explaining this behavior with terms like stupidity, madness, baseness, or sin.[8]

---

7   Richard Rorty, 'On Ethnocentrism: A Reply to Clifford Geertz', in Richard Rorty, *Objectivity, Relativism, and Truth* (Cambridge: Cambridge University Press, 1990), https://doi.org/10.1017/cbo9781139173643.014, pp. 203–10 (p. 203).

8   Rorty, 'On Ethnocentrism', p. 206.

That fiction writers and anthropologists *actually* do the work that Rorty attributes to them seems to be either an assumption about authorial intentions or an empirical claim (and maybe both, of course): that is, it either depends on assuming that this is one of the goals of writing such narratives, or it depends on assuming that such narratives *actually do* lead to a greater awareness of, and extension of empathy to, these odd or invisible creatures. This, in turn, allows the 'we' of liberal democracy to expand.

Even if we assume that this is, in fact, what such authors—these 'connoisseurs of diversity'—try to do, the empirical claim seems to be suspect. In her work on narrative empathy, Suzanne Keen argues that there does not seem to be evidence for the claim that novel reading increases one's ability to empathise with others. Furthermore, she raises the issue of misplaced empathy—that readers who feel empathy for the wrong characters (Humbert Humbert? Dick Hickock in *In Cold Blood*? The pigs in *Animal Farm*?) are usually re-educated in classrooms or in other discussions about the appropriateness of their responses—that is, they learn that these are *not* the characters toward whom one should extend empathy. So, if we take Rorty's claims about the expansion of the 'we' via the narratives offered by the 'connoisseurs of diversity' to be an empirical claim— and even if we think that the empirical claim is true—then Rorty's claims depend for their truth on certain ways of reading and on a particular education in the norms of how to read narratives. We learn, as readers, with whom we should sympathise; whom to revile, and, above all, why one ought to respond in those ways to different characters. The narratives themselves carry no messages that cannot be ignored or interpreted in ways that extend empathy in ways that do not expand the circle of the 'we' of liberal democracy.

But notice that such norms of reading are not 'let a thousand flowers bloom', nor are they norms that would license the kinds of strong readings that Rorty offers, or that would license Rorty's later commitment (in the essay about Umberto Eco's *Foucault's Pendulum*) to the idea that reader-response is the whole story about our interactions with these narratives. Stanley Fish is quick to point out that the plausibility of a certain reading depends on an interpretive community that will license such a reading, and this, of course, is consistent with Rorty's emphasis on intersubjective agreement (solidarity) in place of coercive justification by 'the facts' or

2. Rorty's Interpretations and the Possibility of Social Change 19

'the world'. But what, then, ought we to think of Rorty's interpretations that reject, or even fly in the face of, the conventional wisdom about what these stories or texts mean, or try to communicate?

Rorty's readings of Orwell, Nabokov and anthropologists seem to be inconsistent with his commitment to reader-response theory, and do not seem to fit with his insistence that there is no difference between a text's interpretation and its use. Should this lead us to think that Rorty changed his mind later about the liberatory aspects of imaginative writing? Would he have separated anthropologists from fiction writers? Or is there some other Rortyan story about liberal democracy that makes this a merely apparent contradiction, that can be resolved by a yet more fundamental theory of democracy and social change that is latent in his work? Are these all the wrong questions?

Of course, as you expected (I know the format), I am going to say that these are the wrong questions to ask. But I do think, as I've suggested already, that there is something both potentially deep and as-yet undeveloped or underappreciated in Rorty's appeals to poetry, fiction, creative writing and his rejection of 'philosophical discourse' for the purposes of social change.

§ 4 §

I would like to return here to the idea of the prophetic and the poetic, and to Rorty's use of the poetry of Adrienne Rich to advocate for the role of the inexpressible and the non-descriptive as tools for social change. This, notice, is different from his uses of anthropologists and fiction writers as 'connoisseurs of diversity'. Rorty claims that feminist authors like Rich are doing something more important than philosophy— philosophy, in contrast with poetry, he says, is fairly boring. Philosophy involves 'normal' kinds of puzzle-solving. But people like Adrienne Rich, Rorty says, are using the tools of poetry to invoke and gesture toward another, different (revolutionary) paradigm (I'm using the Kuhn terminology here because it seems to be the best way of understanding Rorty's reframing of feminist work). Rorty seems to be thinking of some feminist writing as a species of something like nonfiction (which would put it in the category with anthropologists like Geertz), but also as a type of speech act whose conditions for intelligibility are not in place: a form of 'creative projection' which is meant not to describe and convince by way of appeal to what is, but as a form of bringing into being that which can be imagined.

While feminist discursive interventions are, he thinks, aimed at changing the world rather than describing it, the political force they exert seems to be undermined by the fact that they do not speak in the lingua franca, or appeal to what he might call the dominant paradigm. Rather than thinking of this as 'non-sense', Rorty tries to show how we can think of feminist writing as making sense, in a way. He wants to suggest that it is not aimed at truth or accurate description; rather these discursive interventions should be understood as artistic: as gestures toward creation—visionary acts, rather than descriptive (and thus truth-apt) acts. They are not simply redescriptions, but are, instead, aimed at creating new conditions of intelligibility.

§ 5 §

I am enrolled in an MFA program in creative writing, and I have to admit that when I talk to the poets in the program, I get very frustrated. When reading one poem that was essentially one long run-on sentence with no stanza or verse breaks, I asked, 'Why write this poem this way?'. The instructor—a very patient person, and a wonderful poet, said, 'well, she probably wants you to read it very fast, without stopping'.

'Duh', I wanted to say. But instead I asked, 'Yes, but why would she want us to read it this fast? What's significant about that?'. The teacher asked the other poets what they thought—why would one want to make the reader read this quickly (we had, by the way, just read another poem by the same author which was written in a way that required that you read it very slowly, with words scattered all over the page.) When I asked why one poem was supposed to be read slowly and one was meant to be read quickly, one poet in the class looked at me like I had four heads and said, 'it *reads* better that way'. A couple of other poets in the class nodded sagely. I gave up.

Of course, there was something about the musicality—the rhythm—of the writing that I was missing when I was looking at the text and not hearing it read aloud, and that, presumably, was part of the reason for the author's choice. But what I am trying to highlight here is not this aspect of poetry, but the fact that, as Plato said, the poets do not seem to be able to give reasons for what they do. And this, for Plato, is an objection to poetry and the creations of the poets. What they say is not false, it is simply unjustified and not a candidate for knowledge. The poets do not have reasons to offer for what they are moved to say or how they are moved to say it.

The program at the Rainier Writing Workshop in which I was a student also includes morning talks by the MFA faculty. One of the talks given by one of the nonfiction writers was a criticism of the idea of the ineffable. Poets, he said, often invoke the ineffable to explain poetic practice. This, he said, led to the idea of poets as being in touch with something beyond language. He objected to the idea of a select few—the mystics and poets— who had access to the secret trove of truth and wisdom, which only they could deliver to us mere mortals in the form of poetry. Visions that exceed the mundane cannot be translated into pedestrian prose; the poets, our speaker argued, wanted to be priests and priestesses.

The poets at the talk took up the gauntlet immediately. It was not that they were in touch with some higher realm or Truth, they said, it was that they were doing something visionary, that was not merely descriptive or analytic. My poetry instructor, whose subsequent talk responded to the nonfiction writer's challenge, invoked a line from Adrienne Rich's 'Twenty-One Love Poems', published in *A Dream of a Common Language*: 'no one has imagined us'. The 'form of life' that Rich projects is one where there is a new discursive space opened up—for things, experiences, ways of living, forms of love. 'This all sounds like bullshit', one of my fellow students said after the talk—she was another woman with a PhD in philosophy, like me. And like me, she was raised in an analytic department. I would once have agreed with her immediately. But this time I stopped to think. Maybe, I thought, this is what Rorty was trying to say. Maybe, however, he wanted to put the point in terms that those of us who know Wittgenstein and Kuhn, but not Rich, would understand.

I think Rorty would accept this formulation of his point: feminist discourse aims at the projection of new possibilities and may not 'play by the rules' of philosophical argumentation. The appeal to the imagination—to new ways of seeing—would have been, for Rorty, a refreshing break from the attempt to argue someone into submission, to give them an argument that would coerce acceptance of the claims of liberal tolerance and feminist demands.

However, the danger for many feminist writers is the danger of not being taken seriously, of not being heard, or of being taken to be appealing to 'women's ways of knowing'—non-rational intuitions, or feelings and emotions. Forms of discourse and ways of arguing (or not) are gendered, and professionalism in philosophy means that to be taken seriously is to play by the rules. But here, I think, Rorty would want to shrug: if it's professional recognition you want, go ahead. Play by the rules. You'll get tenure. You'll be promoted. The number of women in the profession will increase. The number of women will increase, however, only because we/they fail to really do anything different. If it is dramatic social change you want, not little reforms, then you need to risk being the prophet who is only recognized as such by later generations, and who dares to be obsessive and iconoclastic. 'I see the desire for ever-new, revisionary, extraordinary, paradoxical languages and problems as the manic eros which gave us the Platonic dialogues, *The Phenomenology of Spirit*, *Concluding Unscientific Postscript*, "Empiricism and the Philosophy of Mind", "A Nice Derangement of Epitaphs", and *The Postcard*', Rorty says in his reply to James Conant's criticism of his interpretation of Orwell's *1984*.[9]

In her essay, 'Anarchism: What It Really Stands For', Emma Goldman quotes Oscar Wilde in response to critics who say that anarchism is a beautiful idea but not practical:

> A practical scheme, [...], is either one already in existence, or a scheme that could be carried out under the existing conditions; but it is exactly the existing conditions that one objects to, and any scheme that could accept these conditions is wrong and foolish. The true criterion of the practical, therefore, is not whether the latter can keep intact the wrong or foolish; rather is it whether the scheme has vitality enough to leave the stagnant waters of the old, and build, as well as sustain, new life.[10]

Poetry (or perhaps we should say, more generally, 'the poetic') does not look to make itself understood in the going terms of discourse and argument. Insofar as it traffics in the prophetic and utopian, it traffics in

---

9 Robert Brandom (ed.), *Rorty and His Critics*, Philosophers and Their Critics 9 (Malden, MA, Oxford: Blackwell, 2000), p. 396.
10 Emma Goldman, 'Anarchism: What It Really Stands For' (1910), *Digital History*, http://www.digitalhistory.uh.edu/disp_textbook.cfm?smtID=3&psid=1339

a kind of 'abnormal discourse'. The key to understanding the poetic as a form of utopian vision, Rorty says, is understanding the ways in which it challenges the going paradigm of representation and legitimacy.

So what do we say, then, about Rorty's uses of Orwell, Nabokov and Geertz's ethnographies? These works, I think Rorty would say, are trying to expand the reach of liberal democratic institutions and so are trying to make marginalised others visible and understandable. They aim at a form of social change that draws on and accepts the rules of liberal democracy—they are, essentially, reformist. But the abnormal discourses of poetry aim not at piecemeal revision: they aim at revolutionary change. Poetry and the poetic call into question the very framework of intelligibility and discourse—they may even overturn it. For Rorty, a free society requires both the revisionary and the revolutionary.

Rorty's interpretations of poets, novelists, ethnographers and the philosophers he admires usually aim, it seems to me, at helping his readers see new possibilities, helping us create new visions. Paradigm-shattering changes in philosophy generally do not occur by means of arguments that silence the critics, Rorty says, but generally take the form: 'Look at it this way instead of the way you've been looking at it'. Paradigm-shattering changes do not refute opponents: they dramatically change the terms in which the issues or problems are framed. This, we might say, is a non-rational process; Rorty would respond by pointing out that claims about rationality are paradigm-dependent. If my views can be used to support feminist theorising, I think he would say, then they are as feminist as they need to be. They will be made, rather than discovered to be, feminist and liberatory.

§ 6 §

In Jorge Luis Borges's story 'Tlön, Uqbar, Orbis Tertius', we learn that the metaphysicians of Tlön think of metaphysics as a branch of fantastic literature, and countless sciences exist: 'the metaphysicians of Tlön are not looking for truth, nor even an approximation of it; they are after a kind of amazement'.[11] Rorty's essays in CIS are about

---

11 J. L. Borges, *Ficciones*, trans. by Anthony Kerrigan (New York: Grove Press, 1962), p. 25.

the pointlessness of appeals to truth in the struggles over ethics and politics: the contingency of the language we speak; the vocabularies that tradition hands down to us; the fact that we are each born into a tradition, a society, and into a form of life mean that truths are, in some ways, trivial. But the question of how we can change that tradition, how we can live lives that might not fit easily into the contingent form of life we are born into, are nonetheless with us. The liberal ironist recognises the contingency of vocabularies and yet still seeks after newer and better vocabularies. Though it is interpretation and vocabularies all the way down, nevertheless the liberal ironist has also inherited a vocabulary of authenticity and autonomy, which can be in tension with the forms of life she has inherited. In our present form of life—the one that valorises science over poetry—we have come to think of Truth as the proper goal of all discourse. We need, Rorty suggests, to be more like Tlön. In *Philosophy and the Mirror of Nature*, we see the ways that philosophy has, since the Enlightenment, served the interests of science.[12] In CIS, Rorty tries to show us how philosophy might, instead, show us new ways of living and thereby serve poetry and literature—and feminist social change.

---

12 Richard Rorty, *Philosophy and the Mirror of Nature* (Princeton, NJ: Princeton University Press, 1979).

3. Tenderness as the Norm: Rorty on 'Intense Mental Pain'

Paul Giladi

In some of my work to date, I have argued that testimonial injustice *qua* the primary harm of credibility deficit attribution,[1] causes affected speakers to become alienated from their own rationality and the intersubjective practices constituting discourse between peers in an epistemic community.[2] I put forward the view that moral-epistemic nonrecognition and summary exclusion from the logical space of reasons amounted to discursive abuse, the experience of which, to use an expression from Axel Honneth, 'carries with it the danger of an injury that can bring the identity of the person as a whole to the point of collapse'.[3] Discursive abuse threatens a person's rightful self-interpretation as an epistemic agent. As I have pointed out, the kind of epistemic injury testimonial injustice causes can be made sense of by considering what Richard Rorty calls 'intense mental pain'.[4] For him,

---

1 See Miranda Fricker, *Epistemic Injustice: Power and the Ethics of Knowing* (Oxford: Oxford University Press, 2007), https://doi.org/10.1093/acprof:oso/9780198237907.001.0001
2 See Paul Giladi, 'Epistemic Injustice: A Role for Recognition?', *Philosophy & Social Criticism*, 44 (2018), 141–58, https://doi.org/10.1177/0191453717707237 and 'The Agent in Pain: Alienation and Discursive Abuse', *International Journal of Philosophical Studies*, 28 (2020), 692–712, https://doi.org/10.1080/09672559.2020.1784534
3 Axel Honneth, *The Struggle for Recognition: The Moral Grammar of Social Conflicts*, trans. by J. Anderson (Cambridge, MA: MIT Press, 1995), pp. 130–31.
4 Richard Rorty, *Contingency, Irony and Solidarity* (Cambridge: Cambridge University Press, 1989), https://doi.org/10.1017/cbo9780511804397, p. 40.

this notion of agential pain and suffering—the type of painful suffering unique to agents—

> reminds us that human beings who have been socialized [...] can all be given a special kind of pain: they can all be humiliated by the forcible tearing down of the particular structures of language and belief in which they were socialised (or which they pride themselves on having formed for themselves).[5]

In this chapter, I elaborate Rorty's idea of agential pain by directly relating it to recent developments in critical social epistemology and Cora Diamond's framework for making sense of what it is to lose concepts.[6] My principal argument is that by treating his notion of intense mental pain in conjunction with discourses about epistemic injustice and epistemic oppression, and Diamond's MacIntyre-Cavell-Murdoch trialectic, the quoted passage above is perhaps the most significant critical observation of Rorty's monograph.

Focusing on Rorty's reflections on *1984*'s depiction of the moral-epistemic injuries O'Brien's cruelty inflicts on Winston Smith, I contend that if one takes Rorty's concerns about O'Brien's cruelty to its *logical* conclusion, doing so puts pressure on Rorty's own valorisation of social democracy. For, if cruelty towards agents, as exemplified by O'Brien's brutalisation of Winston, is evocative of modern institutional design, then, *contra* Rorty's own shallow dismissal of Marx-inspired political theory and the 'cultural left', radical change is required to not better cope with but overcome the *status quo*. To answer an important question posed by Bjørn Ramberg,[7] this is the strategy for 'Radical Rorty' that counts as progress. The presence of 'Radical Rorty' reveals a significant and serious internal conflict within Rorty's complex socio-political framework: between 'Shallow Rorty'—an anti-theory thinker guilty of an egregious 'historical myth of the given' valorising Western

---

5   Rorty, CIS, p. 177.
6   For an additional but different conversation between Rorty's thought and critical social epistemology, see Susan Dieleman, 'Realism, Pragmatism, and Critical Social Epistemology', in *Pragmatism and Justice*, ed. by S. Dieleman, D. Rondel and C. Voparil (Oxford: Oxford University Press, 2017), https://doi.org/10.1093/acpro f:oso/9780190459239.003.0008, pp. 130–43.
7   Bjørn Torgrim Ramberg, 'Strategies for Radical Rorty ("... but is it progress?")', *Canadian Journal of Philosophy*, 23, Supplementary Volume 19: New Essays on Metaphilosophy (1993), 223–46, https://doi.org/10.1080/00455091.1993.10717349

liberalism[8]—and a thinker who recognises 'the unbearable lightness of liberalism [as social democracy]'[9] and is more invested in producing a theory-rich *structural* critique of Western social democracy.

Joshing Rorty

Contingency, Irony and Solidarity (CIS) is, in many respects, the definitive Rorty work. Perhaps even more so than *Philosophy and the Mirror of Nature* (PMN), the book which launched a thousand (or thereabouts) Anglo-American tirades. For, CIS seems to embody most explicitly Rorty's proclivity for merrily switching between different discursive practices: from pointed anti-representationalist, anti-foundationalist and anti-Philosophical critiques of metaphysical argumentation to centring novels and metaphor as the most effective media through which one can address cruelty, the moral vice Rorty deemed, following Judith Shklar, to be 'the *summum malum*, the most evil of all the evil'.[10]

What makes Rorty's characteristically jocund mélange of intellectual interests so idiosyncratic, to the point where reading CIS can be vexing and fascinating in equal measure, is how Rorty's reflections—even on cruelty—are evocative of 'his odd cocktail of dandyism and social concern', as Sarin Marchetti notes.[11] Such a drink might not just taste strange. It may be *undrinkable* insofar as mixing measures of mythopoetic valorisations of European modernity and social democracy to Panglossian levels[12] with the substantive business of confronting cruelty cannot form a good blend. For that matter, if one were to think of 'Joshing Rorty' in CIS as a light-minded thinker standing in a playful relation with the Joker's infamous expression in *The Dark Knight*, 'Why so serious?!', then one can sympathise with Richard Bernstein's labelling of CIS as 'a disturbingly challenging book'.[13] Bernstein's remark here is instructive. It is a challenge to encounter 'Joshing Rorty', who proposes that we

---

8   Richard J. Bernstein, *The New Constellation: The Ethical-Political Horizons of Modernity/Postmodernity* (Cambridge: Polity Press, 1991), p. 244.
9   Jean B. Elshtain, 'Don't Be Cruel: Reflections on Rortyan Liberalism', in *Richard Rorty*, ed. by C. Guignon and D. R. Hiley (Cambridge: Cambridge University Press, 2003), pp. 139–57, https://doi.org/10.1017/cbo9780511613951.008 (p. 139).
10 Judith N. Shklar, 'Putting Cruelty First', *Daedalus*, 111 (1982), 17-27 (p. 17).
11 Sarin Marchetti, 'Irony and Redescription', *Iride*, 32 (2019), 631–43 (p. 640).
12 Cf. Bernstein, *The New Constellation*, p. 234.
13 Bernstein, *The New Constellation*, p. 261.

need ironist light-mindedness for moral education and the cultivation of solidaristic sensibilities in the liberal polity. The ironist's incredulity towards the alleged authoritarian metanarratives of 'grandeur' and 'profundity'[14] is engendered by a commitment to contingency and redescription that avoids any metaphysical and essentialising discourse about solidarity:

> In my utopia, human solidarity would be seen not as a fact to be recognised by clearing away 'prejudice' or burrowing down to previously hidden depths but, rather, as a goal to be achieved. It is to be achieved not by inquiry but by imagination, the imaginative ability to see strange people as fellow sufferers. Solidarity is not discovered by reflection but created.[15]

Ironist solidarity, so Rorty's story goes, is dialogical, intersubjective and post-Philosophical.[16]

Such solidarity is the only kind that can be practically achieved, as it sunders communication and empathy from the (allegedly) anti-democratic vocabularies and sense-making frameworks embedded in metaphysical thinking. For Rorty, the central aspect of the shift to 'post-Philosophical culture'[17] is the ironist's ability to josh—i.e. playfully redescribe normativity in a way that facilitates the withering away of representationalism and its array of ontotheological dualisms. These binary frameworks, in conjunction with modernity's representationalist semantics in terms of word-world descriptive relations, are totems to be toppled. They exhibit, as Rorty sees it, a pathological, sadomasochistic propensity for regarding normative constraints and the source of justification as necessarily lying beyond human cultural practices.[18]

---

14 Viz. Richard Rorty, *Philosophy as Cultural Politics* (Cambridge: Cambridge University Press, 2007), https://doi.org/10.1017/CBO9780511812835
15 Rorty, CIS, p. xvi.
16 As I will detail later in this chapter, Rorty holds that such solidarity can only be a moral-*aesthetic* achievement, rather than a moral-*theoretic* one.
17 Richard Rorty, *Consequences of Pragmatism* (Minneapolis, MN: University of Minnesota Press, 1982), p. xlii.
18 See Richard Rorty, 'Words or Worlds Apart? The Consequences of Philosophy for Literary Studies, *Philosophy and Literature*, 26 (2002), 369–96, https://doi.org/10.1353/phl.2003.0015 (p. 391). Cf. 'we can hear the mutterings of the desire for a return of terror' (Jean-François Lyotard, *The Postmodern Condition: A Report on Knowledge*, trans. by G. Bennington and B. Massumi (Manchester: Manchester University Press, 1984), p. 82).

In order to get over the effects of Philosophical culture's centuries-old predilection for seeking the 'golden nugget'[19] of justification in practice-transcending sites of sacral ontotheological authority, Rorty recommends adopting ironism. Under ironism, for example, the concept of value undergoes redescription precisely through the development of pragmatic naturalism *qua* anti-foundationalism and anti-representationalism. One moves from making sense of norms as *extra-human* dictates to making sense of norms as contingent 'social achievements'[20] without the justifications sought by representationalists that hook our beliefs to God, Reason, Experience or the World.

The pragmatic naturalist argument begins by recognising that since human beings are natural creatures, our moral and epistemic vocabulary are products of our evolutionary history as language-using agents. In this way, key moral and epistemic vocabulary components, such as *truth* and *objectivity*, do not point to any substantive metaphysical relations between what we say and how the world is. Rather, pragmatic naturalism redescribes truth and objectivity under a 'broadly anthropological' strategy.[21] Truth functions as a meta-norm that governs practices of human inquiry; objectivity is expressive of our collective epistemic efforts to be as intersubjectively inclusive as possible.[22] Norms are social achievements, the results of historically-mediated doxastic practices between language-using agents. Norms get their normative purchase by being assented to and acknowledged by a linguistic community. Normative content itself is the product of fallibilistic communal warranted assertibility, a set of epistemic practices exemplified by our best scientific endeavours and achievements that help keep conversation going. As Sharyn Clough comments,

---

19 See Elizabeth V. Spelman, *Inessential Woman: Problems of Exclusion in Feminist Thought* (Boston, MA: Beacon Press, 1988) for the original, postmodernist feminist use of 'golden nugget'.

20 Robert B. Brandom, *Tales of the Mighty Dead: Historical Essays in the Metaphysics of Intentionality* (Cambridge, MA: Harvard University Press, 2002), p. 216.

21 David Macarthur and Huw Price, 'Pragmatism, Quasi-realism, and the Global Challenge', in *New Pragmatists*, ed. by C. Misak (Oxford: Clarendon Press, 2007), pp. 91–121, https://doi.org/10.1093/oso/9780199279975.003.0006 (p. 101).

22 Viz. 'For pragmatists, the desire for objectivity is not to escape the limits of one's community, but simply the desire for as much intersubjective agreement as possible, the desire to extend the reference of 'us' as far as we can' (Richard Rorty, *Objectivity, Relativism, and Truth* (Cambridge: Cambridge University Press, 1990), https://doi.org/10.1017/CBO9781139173643, p. 23).

Rorty thinks that the success of science at its best comes from the commitment of scientific communities to the solidarity-building process of un-forced agreement, and he encourages all of us to model this commitment in our community-building more generally, especially when different communities clash over cultural commitments.[23]

Pragmatic naturalism's heralding of 'the anthropological turn', expressed by its commitment to articulating the various human linguistic practices that constitute normativity,[24] signifies, for Rorty, that humanity has not only broken free from the Enlightenment's philosophical conception of human mindedness as the mirror of nature. Humanity has also emerged from the 'shadows of God',[25] and now started to bathe in the life-affirming qualities of how modernity, as Jürgen Habermas puts it, 'has to create its normativity out of itself'.[26]

For Rorty, then, pragmatism centres the political virtues of the Enlightenment and Romanticism, which are epitomised by the ironist's historicist-cum-nominalist cultural '[...] substitution of fraternity for authority'.[27] This substitution, which, according to Rorty, is rendered possible by vocabularies in the business of imaginative and prophetic redescription, opens the necessary space for developing discourses and practices of solidarity. As Michael Bacon writes, 'ironic reflection and innovation can be useful for public purposes, leading to a greater awareness of the causes of humiliation experienced by one's fellow citizens'.[28] In recognising contingency, the ironist, according to Rorty, is inherently open to others. This quality, in turn, makes the ironist more pragmatic, more tolerant, and more liberal, so much so that 'post-Philosophical political culture is also identified with a profound

---

23 Sharyn Clough, 'Rorty as Liberal Ironist Peace Warrior', in *The Ethics, Epistemology, and Politics of Richard Rorty*, ed. by G. Marchetti (New York: Routledge, 2021), pp. 29–49, https://doi.org/10.4324/9780429324734-3 (p. 35).
24 Cf. Alexander Kremer, 'Rorty and Normativity', *Human Affairs*, 17 (2007), 71–77, https://doi.org/10.2478/v10023-007-0007-8 (p. 77).
25 Friedrich Nietzsche, *The Gay Science*, trans. by J. Nauckhoff (New York: Cambridge University Press, 2001), https://doi.org/10.1017/CBO9780511812088, p. 109.
26 Jürgen Habermas, *The Philosophical Discourse of Modernity: Twelve Lectures*, trans. by F. Lawrence (Cambridge: Polity Press, 1987), p. 7.
27 Richard Rorty, 'Pragmatism as Anti-authoritarianism', in *A Companion to Pragmatism*, ed. by J. R. Shook and J. Margolis (Oxford: Blackwell Publishing, 2006), pp. 257–66, https://doi.org/10.1002/9780470997079.ch26 (p. 262).
28 Michael Bacon, 'A Defence of Liberal Ironism', *Res Publica*, 11 (2005), 403–23, https://doi.org/10.1007/s11158-005-5761-0 (p. 418).

rejection of—or a visceral disgust with—all forms of cruelty', as José-Manuel Barreto remarks.[29]

Not only that, Rorty makes it clear that he thinks ironism in no way serves to block the possibility of moral conviction and integrity.[30] Light-mindedness is not incompatible with being prepared to die for one's beliefs.[31] For Rorty, then, the likes of Sir Thomas More do not have a monopoly on deeply serious normative commitments. It is sufficient for having unimpeachable moral integrity that S participates in 'open and honest dialogic engagement'[32] with others operating in the logical space of reasons and that their vocabulary survives the complex game of giving and asking for reasons.

Indeed, such *praxis* would be emblematic of an ironist's habits and ways of being with others, under Rorty's definition of ironism:

> I shall define an 'ironist' as someone who fulfils three conditions: (1) She has radical and continuing doubts about the final vocabulary she currently uses, because she has been impressed by other vocabularies, vocabularies taken as final by people or books she has encountered; (2) she realises that argument phrased in her present vocabulary can neither underwrite nor dissolve these doubts; (3) insofar as she philosophises about her situation, she does not think that her final vocabulary is closer to reality than others, that it is in touch with a power not herself.[33]

For Eric Gander (to name but one of Rorty's many critics), however, liberal ironism is incoherent. It fails because it is impossible to square Rorty's account of liberals as '[...] people who think that cruelty is the worst thing we do'[34] and Rorty's construal of ironists as agents who engage in practices of perennial redescription having 'face[d] up to the contingency of [their] own most central beliefs and desires':[35]

---

29 José-Manuel Barreto, 'Rorty and Human Rights: Contingency, Emotions and How to Defend Human Rights Telling Stories', *Utrecht Law Review*, 7 (2011), 93–112, https://doi.org/10.18352/ulr.164 (p. 104).

30 Cf. Elshtain, 'Don't Be Cruel', p. 143.

31 Viz. Rorty, CIS, p. 189. Rorty also appears to make a stronger and more positive claim, namely that light-minded playful joshing—what he calls 'kibitzing'—*enables* the development of a robust moral community.

32 David Owen, 'The Avoidance of Cruelty: Joshing Rorty on Liberal Irony', in *Richard Rorty: Critical Dialogues*, ed. by M. Festenstein and S. Thompson (Cambridge: Polity Press, 2001), pp. 93–110 (p. 99).

33 Rorty, CIS, p. 73.

34 Rorty, CIS, p. xv.

35 Rorty, CIS, p. xv.

> Rorty's vision of liberalism and his vision of irony are fundamentally incompatible [...] [T]he liberal wishes the desire to avoid acts of cruelty (in particular acts of humiliation) to be an invariant part of everyone's final vocabulary, while the ironist rebels against the suggestion that any part of anyone's final vocabulary should be seen as invariant.[36]

However, if there is any charge of incoherence to be levelled, it is not so much because the stark private/public split of liberal ironism[37] constitutes a contradiction. It is more so because I think there are 'deeper conflicting tendencies in [Rorty's] own thinking'[38] about cruelty as the *summum malum*. The deeper conflicting tendencies I have in mind here are between 'Shallow Rorty' and 'Radical Rorty'.

'Shallow Rorty'

Rorty's writings equally indicate strong praise for the underlying logic and political structure of social democracy, and strong opposition to more radical forms of social criticism (apart from feminism):[39]

> I think that contemporary liberal society already contains the institutions for its own improvement—an improvement which can mitigate the dangers Foucault sees.[40]

> I think of the European and American left as having tried to evade this fact by taking refuge in theoretical sophistication—acting as if practical scenarios were unnecessary, and as if the intellectuals could fulfil their political responsibilities simply by criticising obvious evils in terms of ever more 'radical' theoretical vocabularies.[41]

> [T]he American Declaration of Independence had been an Easter dawn.[42]

---

36 Eric M. Gander, *The Last Conceptual Revolution: A Critique of Richard Rorty's Political Philosophy* (Albany, NY: State University of New York Press, 1999), p. 114.

37 See Jeffrey Rivera, 'The Irony of Ironism: A Critique of Rorty's Postmetaphysical Utopia', *Macalester Journal of Philosophy*, 20 (2012), 61–76 (p. 67).

38 Rorty, CIS, p. 247.

39 Viz. Rorty's 1990 Tanner Lecture. See Susan Dieleman, 'Revisiting Rorty: Contributions to a Pragmatist Feminism', *Hypatia*, 25 (2010), 891–908, https://doi.org/10.1111/j.1527-2001.2010.01133.x, as well as Chapter 2 in this volume, for further on Rorty's relationship with feminism.

40 Rorty, CIS, p. 63.

41 Rorty, CIS, p. 182.

42 Richard Rorty, *Achieving Our Country: Leftist Thought in Twentieth Century America* (Cambridge, MA: Harvard University Press, 1998), p. 22.

> [W]e should not let speculation about a totally changed system, and a totally different way of thinking about human life and human affairs, replace step-by-step reform of the system we presently have.[43]

> Few of the people who wrote for leftist periodicals [...] had any doubt that America was a great, noble, progressive country in which justice would eventually triumph.[44]

> [T]he American Left could have gotten along perfectly well without Marxism.[45]

> They want the sublime and ineffable, not just the beautiful and novel—something incommensurable with the past, not simply the past recaptured through rearrangement and redescription. They want not just the effable and relative beauty of rearrangement but the ineffable and absolute sublimity of the Wholly Other; they want Total Revolution.[46]

> To my mind, this genre—unmasking bourgeois ideology—has long been overworked, and has by now turned into self-parody. Belief in the utility of this genre has persuaded a whole generation of idealistic young leftists in the First World that they are contributing to the cause of human freedom by, example, exposing the imperialistic presuppositions of Marvel Comics, or campaigning against the prevalence of 'binary oppositions'. This belief has helped produce the idiot jargon that Frederick Crews recently satirised as 'Leftspeak'—a dreadful, pompous, useless mash of Marx, Adorno, Derrida, Foucault, and Lacan. It has resulted in articles that offer unmaskings of the presuppositions of earlier unmaskings of still earlier unmaskings. It has created the contemporary equivalent of the self-involved Trotskyite discussion groups of the 1930s.[47]

> I just can't think of anything I learned from post-Mill writings that added much.[48]

While Jean-François Lyotard's postmodern contempt for all varieties of metaphysics chimes with Rorty's Oedipal conceptualisation of pragmatism as 'liberation from the Primal Father', Rorty's fondness for Lyotard is tempered by what he sees as a failing endemic to *Ideologiekritik*:

---

43 Rorty, CIS, p. 105.
44 Rorty, CIS, p. 59.
45 Rorty, CIS, p. 46.
46 Rorty, CIS, p. 101.
47 Richard Rorty, 'Thugs and Theorists: A Reply to Bernstein', *Political Theory*, 15 (1987), 564–80, https://doi.org/10.1177/0090591787015004004 (pp. 569–70).
48 Rorty, CIS, p. 64.

Lyotard unfortunately retains one of the left's silliest ideas—that escaping from institutions is automatically a good thing, because it insures that one will not be 'used' by the evil forces which have 'co-opted' these institutions. Leftism of this sort necessarily devalues consensus and communication, for insofar as the intellectual remains able to talk to people outside the avant-garde she 'compromises' herself.[49]

For Rorty, a constitutive feature of *Ideologiekritik* is the contention that existing social institutions (the products of modernity) are irredeemably pathological. To put this another way, Rorty individuates *Ideologiekritik* by its commitment that incremental piecemeal reform as a mechanism for social amelioration is, at best, normatively impotent.[50]

These passages are not examples of contextually contingent remarks made in the service of politics, but symptoms of a systematic issue. While Rorty's anti-representationalism should block him from privileging existing (or any) political arrangements, he continually affirms them as superior. Despite suggesting that all vocabularies are contingent tools, the vocabulary of bourgeois liberalism is to be exempt from radical scrutiny. It is as if Rorty fails to take his own fundamental presuppositions into account, no longer joshing, but reverting to a superficial kind of lightness that comes across as mere shallowness.

As an example, anticipating aspects of Karl Marx's 1844 analysis, G. W. F. Hegel details in his *Elements of the Philosophy of Right* (1820) that the exercise of market capitalism and the proliferation of exchange discourse result in the accumulation and hoarding of wealth by dominant social groups at the expense of a thoroughgoingly disenfranchised and impoverished 'rabble' (*Pöbel*). The harm of poverty consists in crippling capability deprivation, which produces *Pöbelhaftigkeit*, a fractured and broken subjectivity that hinders the development of a healthy practical relation-to-self. The rabble increasingly think, feel and act disconnectedly from modern social institutions, as well as from

---

49 Richard Rorty, 'Habermas and Lyotard on Postmodernity', in Richard Rorty, *Essays on Heidegger and Others* (Cambridge: Cambridge University Press, 1991), pp. 164–76, https://doi.org/10.1017/cbo9780511609039.011, p. 175.

50 Cf. Michael Bacon and Nat Rutherford, 'Rorty, Habermas, and Radical Social Criticism', in *The Ethics, Epistemology, and Politics of Richard Rorty*, ed. by Giancarlo Marchetti, Routledge Studies in American Philosophy (Oxon, New York: Routledge, 2021), pp. 191–208, https://doi.org/10.4324/9780429324734-14 (pp. 191–92).

those individuals who realise their self-interpretations through those institutions. Importantly, because both poverty and the rabble directly emerge out of the pathological logic and practices of capitalism, no proto-welfare provision can solve this modern problem. The veneer of 'benevolent' directives of market capitalism and 'auto-correcting' price signalling controls has now fallen away to reveal the insatiable and violent logic embedded in capital. Such structurally-embedded violence sets society on the road to anomie.

For critical social theorists, if one wishes to prevent the descent into anomie, then one must replace the current material and symbolic vocabulary (the mode of production + its concomitant hegemonic lifeworld norms) with a material and symbolic vocabulary (a mode of production + lifeworld norms) devoid of social pathological qualities. As Herbert Marcuse writes:

> But critical analysis must dissociate itself from that which it strives to comprehend; the philosophic terms must be other than the ordinary ones in order to elucidate the full meaning of the latter. For the established universe of discourse bears throughout the marks of the specific modes of domination, organisation, and manipulation to which the members of a society are subjected.[51]

Rorty correctly construes the radical social critic's position as claiming that, given the normative deficiencies of existing social reality, '[...] we are too far gone for reform to work—that a convulsion is needed, that our imagination and will are so limited by the socialisation we have received that we are unable even to propose an alternative to the society we have now'.[52] However, he thinks discourses about social (and conceptual) convulsions qua 'grandeur' and 'profundity' that favour radical change over incremental amelioration[53] are anti-democratic. This is because Rorty

---

51 Herbert Marcuse, *One-Dimensional Man* (London/New York: Routledge, 2002), p. 197.
52 Rorty, CIS, p. 64.
53 Prefigurative politics—the effort to build an imagined utopian future through mass-coordinating the transformative activities and practices of existing anarcho-syndicalist communities—falls under 'radical change', rather than 'piecemeal reformism'. Prefigurativism, unlike Jacobinism, is not hostile to *everything* about current social formations, insofar as prefigurativism maintains the new and better world can be built-up from the anti-hierarchical structures and practices of participatory democratic communities in the present. See Paul Raekstad and

i) deems ideology-disclosure as displaying elitist contempt for everyday consciousness; ii) thinks the belief that liberal reformism is normatively impotent reveals disdain for consensus and reconciliation; and iii) is part of that intellectual tradition, comprising figures such as Ralph Waldo Emerson, Anton Chekov, Henry David Thoreau and Stanley Cavell, which regards the banal as beautiful, and the quotidian as redemptive.[54]

Ideologiekritik and its proclivities towards 'grandeur' and 'profundity' are judged by Rorty to not only loathe democratic values but also to reproduce a representationalist and essentialist metaphysics that views 'social institutions [...] as attempts to embody a universal and ahistorical order'.[55] Under Rorty's account, as Clayton Chin puts it, the effort to disclose structural violence and overcome systemic oppression reveals 'the general weakness of radical thought: its failure to engage normatively with the present and its persistent attempt to escape, rather than transform, the practices of contemporary sociopolitical life'.[56]

From a critical theoretic perspective, however, Rorty's liberal ironist is more Last Man than *Übermensch*. The political vocabulary and praxis of the liberal ironist are, to quote Barry Allen, 'dull, banal, bourgeois— values Rorty tried to rehabilitate'.[57] It is, therefore, perhaps unsurprising that Gilles Deleuze and Félix Guattari are of the view that 'Western democratic conversation between friends [...] [only produces] pleasant or aggressive dinner conversations at Mr. Rorty's'.[58] More substantively, the critical theoretic worry is that liberal ironism's commitment to incremental, piecemeal reforms serves to preserve the *status quo*,[59] rather than make way for the principal engine of progressive social

---

Sofa Saio Gradin, *Prefigurative Politics: Building Tomorrow Today* (Cambridge: Polity Press, 2020).

54 Cf. Tracy Llanera, *Richard Rorty: Outgrowing Modern Nihilism* (New York: Palgrave, 2020), https://doi.org/10.1007/978-3-030-45058-8
55 Rorty, 'Pragmatism as Anti-authoritarianism', p. 270.
56 Clayton Chin, *The Practice of Political Theory: Rorty and Continental Thought* (New York: Columbia University Press, 2018, https://doi.org/10.7312/chin17398), p. 187. Cf. Ramberg, 'Strategies for Radical Rorty', p. 244.
57 Barry Allen, 'The Rorty-Deleuze *Pas de Deux*', in *Deleuze and Pragmatism*, ed. by S. Bowden, S. Bignalli and P. Patton (New York: Routledge, 2015), pp. 163–79 (p. 174).
58 Gilles Deleuze and Félix Guattari, *What is Philosophy?*, trans. by H. Tomlinson and G. Burchill (London: Verso, 1994), p. 6, p. 144.
59 Cf. Bacon and Rutherford, 'Rorty, Habermas, and Radical Social Criticism', pp. 191–92.

transformation: the discursive formations of oppressed folk (and their allies) which actively resist assimilation or integration into the ever expanding and legitimating 'we' of the utopian liberal.[60]

As is well-known, Rorty's response to critique—whether from analytic philosophers or continental philosophers—often involves a merry shrug of his shoulders. However, as Richard Bernstein comments, 'there is one line of criticism that Rorty has taken more seriously than most—that he is insensitive to the real pain, suffering, and humiliation of human beings, that the other side of his ironical light-minded joshing is a cruel streak'.[61] The problem of cruelty is the issue to which I now turn.

Rorty on Cruelty (Part 1)

Above, I drew attention to Shklar's basic notion of 'putting cruelty first'—that cruelty is 'the *summum malum*'. She defines cruelty in two (problematic) ways:[62]

> Cruelty, as the wilful inflicting of physical pain on a weaker being in order to cause anguish and fear, however, is a wrong done entirely to *another creature*.[63]

---

60   Viz. Michel Foucault, M. *The Foucault Reader*, ed. by P. Rabinow (New York: Pantheon, 1984), p. 385.
61   Bernstein, *The New Constellation*, pp. 260–61.
62   See John Kekes, 'Cruelty and Liberalism', *Ethics*, 106 (1996), 834–44, https://doi.org/10.1086/233675, and Volker M. Heins, '"More Modest and More Political": From the Frankfurt School to the Liberalism of Fear', in *Between Utopia and Realism: The Political Thought of Judith N. Shklar*, ed. by S. Ashenden and A. Hess (Philadelphia, PN: University of Pennsylvania Press, 2019), pp. 179–97, https://doi.org/10.9783/9780812296525-010 (p. 183) for critiques of Shklar's definitions. Heins notes that American slavery and modern racism are at the centre of Shklar's thinking about public cruelty. Kamila Stullerova observes that, for Shklar, '[...] it is the infliction of cruelty "here and now" that matters and that takes precedence over other considerations, such as historical injustices or structural violence' (Kamila Stullerova, 'Cruelty and International Relations', in *Between Utopia and Realism*, pp. 67–85, https://doi.org/10.9783/9780812296525-004 (p. 79)). What Heins and Stullerova write raises two legitimate questions: i) If American slavery and modern racism are indeed central to Shklar's worries about cruelty, then how can historical injustice or structural violence be deemed *secondary* concerns of liberal agents? ii) If American slavery and modern racism are indeed central to worries about cruelty, then are Shklar's definitions of cruelty fit for her own normative purposes?
63   Shklar, 'Putting Cruelty First', p. 17.

> What is meant by cruelty here? It is the deliberate infliction of physical, and secondarily emotional, pain upon a weaker person or group by stronger ones in order to achieve some end, tangible or intangible, of the latter.[64]

Shklar also maintains that liberalism—individuated by the modern principle of tolerance and maximal protection of personal freedom[65]—is the political ideology borne from disgust at cruelty, to the extent that liberals are the only political-moral agents deeply concerned about cruelty.[66] For that matter, Rorty's definition-without-being-a-definition[67] of cruelty as 'the worst thing we do' appears to largely follow Shklar without any significant qualification or critical amendment to either of Shklar's construals of cruelty.

The central utopian aspiration of Rorty's liberalism, much like that of Shklar's, is that 'suffering will be diminished, that the humiliation of human beings by other human beings may cease'.[68] In this respect, then, the Rortyan (and Shklarian) liberal, disparaging the impulse for the radical overhaul of existing social institutions and forms of production in favour of more empathetic coping with the social world, contends that 'the only way to avoid perpetuating cruelty within social institutions is by maximising the quality of education, freedom of the press, educational opportunity, opportunities to exert political influence, and the like'.[69]

What matters, then, for Rorty, is not the ability to successfully unravel and decipher the structure of reality and attain a God's-eye-view of things

---

64 Judith N. Shklar, 'Liberalism and Fear', in *Liberalism and the Moral Life*, ed. by N. L. Rosenblum (Cambridge, MA: Harvard University Press, 1989), pp. 21–38 (p. 29).
65 Viz. Shklar, 'Liberalism and Fear', p. 21.
66 Shklar's position strikes me as quite strange, not least because she is not anti-capitalist: there is every reason to think that social democracy, at best, limits one's conceptual resources for both diagnosing what is morally abject about cruelty and detailing what needs to be done to *end* institutionalised forms of cruelty. Additionally, the ameliorative vocabulary of the liberal paradigm appears restricted to *quantitative* expressions such as 'reducing cruelty', 'diminishing cruelty'. While, of course, accounting for the volume of cruelty is important and vital work, to focus predominantly on the *amount* at the expense of understanding the *dynamics* of cruelty seems to be counter-productive for someone who thinks cruelty is the *summum malum*.
67 To think of Rorty as formally defining cruelty would be counter-intuitive, as doing so would involve charging him with contradicting a central tenet of his own post-analytic metaphilosophical commitments.
68 Rorty, CIS, p. xv.
69 Rorty, 'Pragmatism as Anti-authoritarianism', p. 67.

but to engage in practices of ironist moral educative development that forge bonds of solidarity. In this way, Rorty's liberal utopia is not centred on the practices and achievements of the earnest Peircean, nor on those of the Barack Obama-esque politician, nor on those of the unbowed Deweyan secularist. Instead, 'an ideally liberal polity would be one whose culture hero is [Harold] Bloom's "strong poet" rather than the warrior, the priest, the sage, or the truth-seeking, "logical," "objective" scientist'.[70] From this perspective, the strong poet's sense of achievement in redescription and perennial fallibilist discursive experimentation is not the pride one feels having solved a philosophical problem or made a scientific discovery. It is in saying 'Thus I willed it'.[71]

Rorty, however, is alert to a problem with ironism here. As he writes,

> [i]ronism, as I have defined it, results from the awareness of the power of redescription. But most people do not want to be redescribed. They want to be taken on their own terms—taken seriously just as they are and just as they talk. The ironist tells them that the language they speak is up for grabs by her and her kind. There is something potentially very cruel about that claim.[72]

The 'power of redescription' consists in the ability to josh people out of multiple myths of the Given by shifting towards historicism and nominalism. However, a moral realist who is casually informed that their central values and vocabularies are merely the product of contingency can understandably feel deeply pained by such light-minded discourse. Ironism's irreverence-to-the-point-of-humiliation of the moral realist's (final) vocabulary sees that person lose either the specific constellation of concepts they require to be-in-the-world, or the background lifeworld context required for the intelligibility of the concepts they use. If ironism's joshing light-mindedness causes suffering, then it is in the business of cruelty *qua* humiliation. If so, a polity of strong poets is more akin to 'a new nightmare world'.[73] Such a world, of course, would be anything but utopian.

However, Rorty makes it clear that one key practice that counters creating dystopic cultures of cruelty is the ability to produce literature

---

70 Rorty, CIS, p. 53.
71 Rorty, CIS, p. 37. Cf. Rorty, CIS, p. 78.
72 Rorty, CIS, p. 89.
73 Shklar, 'Putting Cruelty First', p. 19.

(especially novels). This is because Rorty claims that literature, unlike deductive logic or intellectual theorising, is capable of 'increasing our sensitivity to the particular details of the pain and humiliation of other, unfamiliar sorts of people. Such increased sensitivity makes it more difficult to marginalise people different from ourselves'.[74] For, literature, as a medium for communication, is considerably less technical and more emotionally resonating than academic prose. The highly specialised and often daunting vocabularies emblematic of so much intellectual theorising also stultify the fostering of intersubjective emotional investment and cultures of empathy and care. Additionally, intellectual theorising *qua* Theory invariably ends up as authoritarian, even when thoroughly ironist, if it is pitched as the *last* word in the discourse on Theory (a problem Rorty identifies in Derridean postmodernism).

To use an example that illustrates the 'increasing our sensitivity'-use of literature, reading Toni Morrison's *The Bluest Eye*, under Rorty's account, would be far more effective than a Black feminist philosophical treatise for intersectional consciousness-raising efforts about whiteness and its deleteriousness. This is because Morrison as a novelist is able to use the aesthetic-communicative advantages of novels to richly detail the tragedy of Pecola Breedlove, a young African-American girl growing up in post-Great Depression Ohio who internalises anti-Black racism, develops a crippling inferiority complex,[75] and whose eventual insanity constitutes her only protection from the racist-misogynist world.

In response to Rorty's valorisation of the strong poet and his Tanner Lecture claim that '[p]hilosophy's function is rather to clear the road for prophets and poets', it strikes me that a stark divide between narrative and literature (novels) on the one side and theory and argument (Philosophy) on the other side not only reproduces the essentialising dualism he so famously loathes.[76] The strictness of such a distinction also forecloses the possibility of being emotionally moved by theory and creating *emotionally moving theories* themselves. Theory that emotionally moves, such as Frantz Fanon's postcolonialism and decolonial thought, operates in the logical space of reasons, not to provide the bourgeois thrill of good deontic scorekeeping in hyper-specialised technical

---

74 Rorty, CIS, p. xvi.
75 Viz. Toni Morrison, *The Bluest Eye* (New York: Vintage International, 2007), p. 46.
76 Bernstein, *The New Constellation*, p. 240.

academic debates. To paraphrase Gillian Rose, theory that moves is not interested in communicating how 'clever' one is. It is solely orientated towards 'feeding the soul', a decidedly concrete, inferential-narrative activity that is necessary for the very possibility of democracy, solidarity, and the (re)production of care. Theory that *moves* is precisely *moving* because it communicates to inquirers the normative scene of the theorist-as-'phenomenologically orientated sociologist'.[77] Such a theorist thinks very hard and very sensitively about cruelty *qua* i) agents who do cruel things, ii) victims' experiences of cruelty, and iii) institutions that are geared towards cruelty. The strictness of Rorty's distinction, by occluding theory that is not only emotionally resonating in and of itself but also nourishing for progressive activism, prevents inquirers from developing, as Rosa Calcattera rightly contends,

> an idea of solidarity that does not correspond to a mere feeling of closeness to other people, but rather calls up the vital blending of the affective with the logical-argumentative sphere, thanks to which solidarity can be directed onto the social path of values, aims and common practices.[78]

Ramberg, therefore, is correct to claim that Rorty's error here is his failure to see that 'the practical purpose of alleviating suffering requires not only the education of sensibility [through literature]'.[79] To put my point another way, theory without literature is empty; literature without theory is blind.[80]

While I think Richard Bernstein's characterisation of Rorty as someone who 'seems to be far more concerned with the cruelties that intellectual liberal ironists may inadvertently commit than with the forms of cruelty and humiliation that pervade our liberal societies' is not completely accurate,[81] the type of cruelty Rorty is keen on alerting his readers to in relation to ironism seems odd for someone who wishes to 'put cruelty first'. To see why, I would like to return to my previous comment that, according to Rorty, the 'power of redescription' consists in the ability

---

77 Max Horkheimer, 'Traditional and Critical Theory', in his *Critical Theory: Selected Writings*, trans. by M. O'Connell (New York: Continuum, 2002), p. 192.
78 Rosa Maria Calcaterra, *Contingency and Normativity: The Challenges of Richard Rorty* (Leiden and Boston: Brill, 2019), https://doi.org/10.1163/9789004393837, p. 97.
79 Ramberg, 'Strategies for Radical Rorty', p. 243.
80 Cf. Ramberg, 'Strategies for Radical Rorty', p. 244.
81 Bernstein, *The New Constellation*, p. 286. Bernstein, crucially, does not appear to countenance the presence of 'Radical Rorty'.

to josh people out of multiple myths of the Given by shifting towards historicism and nominalism.

Imagine now, however, that the agent whose vocabulary is subject to playful redescription by an intellectual liberal is a person with deep-seated racist beliefs grounded in white supremacism and white nationalism. This racist agent will staunchly resist having their central values and vocabularies for being-in-the-world translated in terms of inherent contingency and historical circumstance.[82] To then contend that the racist agent, who did not want to be redescribed, consequently has been treated cruelly by the intellectual liberal would be difficult to plausibly justify for at least two principal reasons. Firstly, instead of spending time and effort on the real issue—the victims of white supremacist and white nationalist abuse—time and effort would now be spent on caring for the racist's bruised ego and on ensuring more robust protections from intellectual interference. Secondly, it is far from clear how showing a racist that their beliefs in white supremacy and white nationalism rest on myths could ever count as *cruel* in the first place. To better understand what counts as cruel in the first place, I think it would be helpful to reflect on Michel de Montaigne's position on cruelty.

For Montaigne, cruelty is wholly repulsive:

> Among the vices, I have a cruel hatred of cruelty, as the ultimate vice of them all [...] I live in a season when unbelievable examples of this vice of cruelty flourish because of the licence of our civil wars; you can find nothing in ancient history more extreme than what we witness every day. But that has by no means broken me in. If I had not seen it I could hardly have made myself believe that you could find souls so monstrous that they would commit murder for the sheer fun of it; would hack at another man's limbs and lop them off and would cudgel their brains to invent unusual tortures and new forms of murder, not from hatred or for gain but for the one sole purpose of enjoying the pleasant spectacle of the pitiful gestures and twitchings of a man dying in agony, while hearing his screams and groans. For there you have the farthest point that cruelty can reach: '[That man should kill man should kill man not in anger or in fear but merely for the spectacle]'. As for me, I have not even been able to witness without displeasure an innocent defenceless beast which has done us no harm being hunted to the kill.[83]

---

82 Joshing people with racist commitments and views can also delegitimate their vicious views about people of colour.

83 Michel de Montaigne, *The Complete Essays*, trans. by M. A. Screech (London andNew York: Penguin, 1993), p. 481, p. 484.

To use an expression from Raymond Geuss, cruelty creates 'objectively horrifying conditions' designed to brutalise the targets of cruel acts.[84] The wrong of cruelty consists in hurting particularly vulnerable agents so that the symbolic and/or material pain inflicted on the hurt agents 'unmakes' them[85] by damaging and even breaking their practical relation-to-self.[86] As John Kekes writes,

> [c]ruelty requires the infliction of pain that harms the victim in a way that endangers the victim's functioning as a full-fledged agent [...] [I]n its primary sense, cruelty is the disposition of human agents to take delight in or be indifferent to the serious and unjustified suffering their actions cause to their victims.[87]

Cruel actions—such as acts of torture, sexual violence, and forms of epistemic violence[88]—often involve external and forcible control over S's own bodily and/or psychic integrity, such that injuring S's bodily and/or psychic integrity prevents S from trusting others and themselves. By breaking S's practical relation-to-self, to the distressing extent that S's practical relation-to-self ends up being 'devastated', in Jay Bernstein's technical sense of the term,[89] S loses the concept of the world as an environment facilitating and encouraging trust, a concept central to our developmental psychosocialisation process as human beings.[90]

The racist agent whose vocabulary was playfully redescribed cannot be said to have been 'unmade' here. To be sure, they would very likely insist that the ironist has awfully mistreated them. However, were the

---

84 Raymond Geuss, *The Idea of a Critical Theory* (Cambridge: Cambridge University Press, 1981), p. 50.
85 Viz. Elaine Scarry, *The Body in Pain: The Making and Unmaking of the World* (Oxford: Oxford University Press, 1985).
86 Cf. Heins 2019, p. 183.
87 Kekes, 'Cruelty and Liberalism', p. 837, p. 838.
88 Kristie Dotson, partly inspired by Gayatri Spivak's landmark 1988 article on subalternity, defines epistemic violence as 'a refusal, intentional or unintentional, of an audience to communicatively reciprocate a linguistic exchange owing to pernicious ignorance' (Kristie Dotson, 'Tracking Epistemic Violence, Tracking Practices of Silencing', *Hypatia*, 26 (2011), 236–57, https://doi.org/10.1111/j.1527-2001.2011.01177.x (p. 238)).
89 Viz. Jay M. Bernstein, *Torture and Dignity: An Essay on Moral Injury* (Chicago, IL: University of Chicago Press, 2015), https://doi.org/10.7208/chicago/9780226266466.001.0001, pp. 75–76.
90 Cf. Philip Spencer, '"Putting Cruelty First": The *Summum Malum*, Genocide, and Crimes Against Humanity', in *Between Utopia and Realism*, pp. 179–97, https://doi.org/10.9783/9780812296525-011 (p. 198).

racist agent to place such a judgement in the logical space of reasons in the hope of having others assent to their horrifying suffering, they would readily find their judgement does not survive rational scrutiny.

If someone wishes to 'put cruelty first', they need to prioritise confronting forms of cruelty and humiliation that do not simply pervade social domains but are also expressive of how those social domains are *structured*. The cruelty and humiliation that concern me range from individual credibility deficit attribution, contributory injustice,[91] epistemologies of ignorance,[92] epistemic exploitation[93] and gaslighting[94] to identity enforcement of trans folk.[95]

In what follows, I argue that one feature of Rorty's analysis of *1984* is evocative of 'Radical Rorty', a thinker who, contrary to 'Shallow Rorty' (and 'Joshing Rorty'), 'wants to make claims of the following kind: that our [...] society is structurally repressive; that its institutions serve the interest of privileged social groups in opaque ways; that social theory at one and the same time can reveal this to be so and lay the ground for new and better practices, and is therefore emancipatory',[96] as Ramberg contends. *Contra* Rorty, 'Radical Rorty's contention does not require any buy-in to ontotheological dualisms, not least because a structural critique of society begins by acknowledging the contingency of past and present social arrangements.

---

91 See Kristie Dotson, 'A Cautionary Tale: On Limiting Epistemic Oppression', *Frontiers: A Journal of Women Studies*, 33 (2012), 24–47, https://doi.org/10.1353/fro.2012.a472779

92 See Charles W. Mills, *The Racial Contract* (Ithaca, NY: Cornell University Press, 1997).

93 See Emmalon Davis, 'Typecasts, Tokens, and Spokespersons: A Case for Credibility Excess as Testimonial Injustice', *Hypatia*, 31 (2016), 485–501, https://doi.org/10.1111/hypa.12251; Nora Berenstain, 'Epistemic Exploitation', *Ergo*, 3 (2016), 569–90, https://doi.org/10.3998/ergo.12405314.0003.022; and Paul Giladi, 'Epistemic Exploitation and Ideological Recognition', in *Epistemic Injustice and the Philosophy of Recognition*, ed. by P. Giladi and N. McMillan (New York: Routledge, 2022), pp. 138–70, https://doi.org/10.4324/9780429435133-8

94 See Kate Abramson, 'Turning Up the Lights on Gaslighting', *Philosophical Perspectives*, 28 (2014), 1–30, https://doi.org/10.1111/phpe.12046; and Kelly Oliver, 'Gaslighting: Pathologies of Recognition and the Colonisation of Psychic Space', in *Epistemic Injustice and the Philosophy of Recognition*, pp. 138–70, https://doi.org/10.4324/9780429435133-7

95 See Talia M. Bettcher, 'Trans Women and the Meaning of "Woman"', in *Philosophy of Sex: Contemporary Readings (Sixth Edition)*, ed. by N. Power, R. Halwani and A. Soble (New York: Rowan and Littlefield, 2012), pp. 233–50.

96 Ramberg, 'Strategies for Radical Rorty', p. 224.

Whereas 'Shallow Rorty' claims that 'pain is nonlinguistic', that 'victims of cruelty, people who are suffering, do not have much in the way of a language', and that is there is no 'voice of the oppressed' or 'language of the victims',[97] 'Radical Rorty' gives an inquirer every reason to reject such contentions. For, radical social criticism makes it clear that oppressed folk are more than capable of speaking and communicating their pain, and that they often have no difficulty articulating the full range of their experiences. They have the hermeneutical resources required to make sense of their own experiences. They also have a wealth of knowledges and discursive formations of their own making and expressive of their interests and lives. So much so that if the pain of oppressed folk were nonlinguistic and if oppressed folk did not have voices, then it would be impossible for them to author a plurality of progressive social movements that, *contra* Rorty's Tanner Lecture claim, go further than 'just mak[ing] invidious comparisons between the actual present and a possible, if inchoate, future'.

Rorty on Cruelty (Part 2)

Two writers feature prominently in the literary criticism section of CIS: Vladimir Nabokov and George Orwell. According to Rorty,

> Nabokov wrote about cruelty from the inside, helping us see the way in which the private pursuit of aesthetic bliss produces cruelty. Orwell, for the most part, wrote about cruelty from the outside, from the point of view of the victims, thereby producing [...] the kind of book which helps reduce future suffering and serves human liberty.[98]

Orwell is the figure of particular interest to me with respect to Rorty's reflections on *1984*'s depiction of O'Brien's cruelty and the moral-epistemic injuries such cruelty inflicts on Winston.

Winston is methodically, brutally, and systematically tortured during his imprisonment in the Ministry of Love. O'Brien eventually breaks Winston by having Winston genuinely believe that '2+2=5' is true. What I take to be so horrifying about the torture scene is O'Brien's success in permanently shattering Winston's ability to cling to what is, in the novel,

---

97   Rorty, CIS, p. 94.
98   Rorty, CIS, p. 146.

held to be an anti-authoritarian concept of mind-independent truth.[99] In other words, the horror of what happens to Winston is how he ends up losing this crucial concept:

> 'Just now I held up the fingers of my hand to you. You saw five fingers. Do you remember that?'
> 'Yes.'
> O'Brien held up the fingers of his left hand, with the thumb concealed.
> 'There are five fingers there. Do you see five fingers?'
> 'Yes.'[100]
> [...]
> The pencil felt thick and awkward in his fingers. [Winston] began to write down the thoughts that came into his head. He wrote first in large clumsy capitals:
> FREEDOM IS SLAVERY
> Then almost without a pause he wrote beneath it:
> TWO AND TWO MAKE FIVE[101]

I think now is the apt time for Diamond's landmark article 'Losing Your Concepts' to enter the fray. In her 1988 paper, Diamond provides a rich analysis of how Alasdair MacIntyre, Stanley Cavell and Iris Murdoch understand what it is to lose concepts. For MacIntyre, conceptual loss involves the actual disappearance of the lifeworld required for central concepts of moral life to make sense, causing loss of meaning for the moral agents residing in that lifeworld.[102] Importantly, as Diamond explains,

> the argument is not directly that we have lost concepts; rather, it is an argument [...] that certain concepts require for their content or intelligibility background conditions which are no longer fulfilled [...] [W]e go on using the old words, but the words can no longer carry their old significance.[103]

---

99 Viz. 'you are clinging to your disease under the impression that it is a virtue' (George Orwell, *Nineteen Eighty-Four* (London: Plume, 2003), p. 171).
100 Orwell, *Nineteen Eighty-Four*, p. 181.
101 Orwell, *Nineteen Eighty-Four*, p. 195.
102 See Alasdair MacIntyre, *After Virtue* (Notre Dame, IN: Notre Dame University Press, 1981).
103 Cora Diamond, 'Losing Your Concepts', *Ethics*, 98 (1988), 255–77, https://doi.org/10.1086/292940 (p. 257).

For Cavell, losing concepts does not involve the irrecoverable vanishing of backdrops of intelligibility and the resulting scar on the social world itself. Instead, he contends that it comprises 'conceptual amnesia'—an objectionable habit of writing, thinking and speaking as if one really lives in an environment in which certain concepts genuinely no longer feature in existing human practices.[104] However, for Murdoch, conceptual loss involves neither MacIntyrean concerns about background conditions for concept-intelligibility nor Cavellian concerns about 'as if' habituations. According to her, losing concepts largely stems from what she judges as the deleterious effects of naturalistic tendencies to promote behaviourist philosophies. Their technical pictures of personhood and subjectivity have produced an extirpated philosophic and literary culture. Such a culture's practices cannot picture the thoroughgoingly complicated complexities of human personality in a way that satisfies the humanism of the Enlightenment and of Romanticism.[105]

A key question to ask and answer is 'what kind of loss it is to lose concepts'.[106] I am of the view that losing concepts involves a Hegelian genus of alienation *qua* discursive atrophy: capability deprivation and epistemic impoverishment. As such, I am more sympathetic to Murdoch's position than MacIntyre's or Cavell's. For, her position, more so than theirs is sensitive to how losing concepts results from 'a cold and ruthless *Entzauberung*',[107] one which is deeply injurious to human beings. I take Marx to argue the same Hegelian point in this passage:

> [o]ur objects in their relation to one another constitute the only intelligible language we use with one another. We would not understand a human language, and it would remain without effect. We are so much mutually alienated from human nature that the direct language of this nature is an injury to human dignity for us, while the alienated language of objective values appears as justified, self-confident, and self-accepted human dignity.[108]

---

104 See Stanley Cavell, *The Claim of Reason* (Oxford: Clarendon Press, 1979).
105 Viz. Iris Murdoch, 'Against Dryness: A Polemical Sketch', *Encounter*, 16 (1961), 16–20 (p. 18).
106 Diamond, 'Losing Your Concepts', p. 256.
107 Roger Scruton, *Sexual Desire: A Philosophical Investigation* (London: Phoenix Press, 2001), p. 182.
108 Karl Marx, 'Excerpt-Notes of 1844', in *Writings of the Young Marx on Philosophy and Society*, ed. by L. D. Easton and K. H. Guddat (Garden City, NY: Doubleday and

It is tempting, but mistaken, to read Marx here as articulating alienation in terms of a social geologic elegy, to construe his worry about concept-loss as mournful of what has happened to our pre-capitalist discursive architecture, language and habits of speech since the period-defining change to capitalist forms of life. To be sure, the capitalist form of life has led to an erosion of the concepts people used in pre-capitalist contexts, but Marx's point about alienation is stronger, as he understands concept loss as a painful *metaphysical* infliction: the capitalist language damages human *nature*.

With respect to the destruction of Winston's ability to cling to the concept of mind-independent truth, the Party's mutilation of Winston's body is meant to work hand-in-hand with a mutilation of Winston's nature as a rational thinker (as I understand the novel) by irreversibly disfiguring his web of beliefs. After all, as Orwell writes, '[t]he purpose of Newspeak was not only to provide a medium of expression for the world-view and mental habits proper to the devotees of Ingsoc, *but to make all other modes of thought impossible*'.[109] O'Brien, representing the totalising authority of the Party, aims to tear Winston's mind to pieces and put it together again in new shapes of the Party's choosing.[110]

According to Rorty, though,

> [t]he point of breaking Winston is not to bring Winston into line with the Party's ideas. The Inner Party is not torturing Winston because it is afraid of a revolution, or because it is offended by the thought that someone might not love Big Brother. It is torturing Winston for the sake of causing Winston pain, and thereby increasing the pleasure of its members, particularly O'Brien. The only object of O'Brien's intensive seven-year-long study of Winston was to make possible the rich, complicated, delicate, absorbing spectacle of mental pain which Winston would eventually provide.[111]

Contra Rorty, I think the entire point of breaking Winston is to ensure he is aligned with the Party's ideas. To repeat that chilling line from O'Brien before he sends Winston to Room 101: 'Whatever the Party holds to be

---

Co, 1967), p. 280.
109 Orwell, *Nineteen Eighty-Four*, p. 210—my emphasis. Viz. Orwell, *Nineteen Eighty-Four*, p. 216.
110 Viz. Orwell, *Nineteen Eighty-Four*, p. 174, p. 187, p. 192, p. 196, p. 199, p. 213. Cf. Orwell, *Nineteen Eighty-Four*, p. 204.
111 Rorty, CIS, p. 179.

the truth, *is* truth'. Getting Winston and anyone like him to see reality through the eyes of the Party and love Big Brother is accomplished by breaking Winston and anyone like him 'in a very particular way, namely in such a way that their minds can subsequently be enslaved'.[112] As Susana de Castro writes, this is 'institutionalised cruelty; the cruelty against a group or a person made in name of a credo, an ideology, or a state politics. This sort of cruelty involves a majority, a collectivity, society at large'.[113]

However, one feature of Rorty's analysis of *1984* and its phenomenological and metaphysical concern with the violation of agents' moral and epistemic integrity is not only particularly insightful but also evocative of 'Radical' as opposed to 'Shallow' Rorty: 'the worst thing you can do to somebody is not to make her scream in agony but to use that agony in such a way that even when the agony is over, she cannot reconstitute herself'.[114] As I understand Rorty here, his claim can help one draw an important distinction between 1) the kind of cruelty inflicted through violations of self-confidence, self-respect, and self-esteem[115] *qua* misrecognition, and 2) the kind of cruelty that functions to unmake the target's practical relation-to-self. Thinking in terms of 1) and 2) means that the following critique of Rorty by Jean Elshtain would only be effective against 'Shallow Rorty' (and 'Joshing Rorty'):

> The twentieth century was very cruel, probably the most cruel on a public-political scale. Rorty doesn't really offer an account of public cruelty of the fascist-Stalinist sort either, though he clearly stands in opposition to it. But how robust is his stance? With the don't-be-cruel rule in mind, he poses alternatives that, I fear, make us dumber than we may have any right to be at this late stage. It 'just happened' that liberal societies condemn torture because liberals want to be reasonable [...] Amnesty International doesn't talk about reasonableness; it talks about violation of fundamental human dignity taken as an ontological given, not a historic contingency.[116]

---

112 James Conant, 'Freedom, Cruelty, and Truth: Rorty versus Orwell', in *Rorty and His Critics*, ed. by R. B. Brandom (Oxford: Blackwell, 2000), pp. 268–342 (p. 290).
113 Susana de Castro, 'Can We Avoid Cruelty?', *Contemporary Pragmatism*, 11 (2014), 143–52, https://doi.org/10.1163/18758185-90000282 (p.143).
114 Rorty, CIS, pp. 177–78.
115 Viz. Honneth, *The Struggle for Recognition*.
116 Elshtain, 'Don't Be Cruel', p. 151, p. 152.

Regarding 1), the kind of cruelty involved in misrecognition causes intense hurt and pain in those who are misrecognised. By way of illustration, I would like to focus on Black Lives Matter (BLM) discourse. BLM, as a social movement, is borne out of distress at structural racism and its logical relation with state-sponsored and legally codified degradation of Black bodies, minds and lives. However, reactionaries viciously misrecognise the vocabulary of BLM discourse against racial oppression. As Robert Gooding-Williams observes, the reactionary view is 'a failure to regard the speech or actions of Black people as manifesting thoughtful judgements about issues that concern all members of the political community'.[117]

BLM demonstrations typically involve the declarative expression 'Hands Up, Don't Shoot!', where marchers raise their hands above their heads while chanting as part of the collective effort to explicitly challenge the longstanding right-wing socio-epistemic discursive formations that construe anti-racist protestors as clear and present dangers to society.[118] Furthermore, the BLM chants 'Whose streets? Our streets!' and 'No Justice, No Peace!' are deliberately misinterpreted by reactionary agents and institutions to imply that the core anti-racist and rehumanising view—'Black lives matter'—is equivalent to 'Black lives matter more than White lives'.

The protests against police brutality and the longstanding ideological racialisation of Blackness as a threat to social order and political stability detail how hegemonic vocabularies and institutions have failed to live up to binding moral principles. The morally-politically salient reactive attitudes at the core of BLM emerge from righteous rage at institutional and individual agents' failures to comply with a basic moral demand which is a deontic standard for intersubjective care and protection. As R. Jay Wallace writes on demanding compliance, '[i]t is to expect or demand compliance with those standards, where these expectations

---

117 Robert Gooding-Williams, *Look, a Negro!: Philosophical Essays on Race, Culture and Politics* (New York: Routledge, 2006), https://doi.org/10.4324/9781315870618, p. 14.
118 See José Medina, 'Misrecognition and Epistemic Injustice', *Feminist Philosophy Quarterly*, 4 (2018), 1–16, https://doi.org/10.5206/fpq/2018.4.6233 (p. 12).

lead to attitudes of reactive blame in case they are disappointed, such as resentment and indignation'.[119]

Certainly, expressing distress and anger—rather than disappointment—at the failure to comply with 'the relational standard of interpersonal morality'[120] is a key part of BLM discourse. When protesters chant 'Say Her Name!', the illocutionary content of such a declarative does not so much centre how the powerful are falling short of the promised egalitarian model and the expectation that the dominant social group needs to improve its practices, to 'actualise the untapped normative surplus' of a social order. Rather, demands for recognition communicatively prioritise and illuminate distress at the way the *status quo* is currently structured and reproduced, namely through relations of (unearned and harmful) privilege that cruelly silence and degrade.[121] What is asserted in a demand for recognition is not merely the expectation that the powerful should do their utmost to include minorities as their equals. That would constitute a slippery slope to a plea and to perhaps even a form of interpellation. The recognition struggle, crucially, demands radical system change—a progressive transformation in the moral grammar and concomitant institutional design of contemporary

---

119 R. Jay Wallace, 'Recognition and the Moral Nexus', *European Journal of Philosophy*, 29 (2021), 634–45, https://doi.org/10.1111/ejop.12677 (p. 637).
120 Wallace, 'Recognition and the Moral Nexus', p. 638.
121 On this point, I would like to draw attention to this claim by Christine Korsgaard: '[i]t is impossible to hear words of a language you know as mere noise. In hearing your words as words, I acknowledge that you are someone' (Christine M. Korsgaard, *The Sources of Normativity* (Cambridge: Cambridge University Press, 1996), p. 143). It is questionable to assert that familiarity with S's language *eo ipso* means that T cannot construe S's speech as just sonic content and thereby degrade S. For, focusing on conservative attitudes towards BLM representatives' speech here, the *status quo* often understands exactly what BLM demands—a progressive transformation of existing intersectional environments—but the *status quo* often produces misrecognising epistemologies of ignorance to delegitimise BLM's demands. However, in response, Korsgaard's claim is justified to have such strong modal content in the following qualified sense: it is possible to hear BLM representatives' words as noise only in those very rare cases when there is an absence of antecedent recognition (viz. Axel Honneth, *Reification: A New Look at an Old Idea—with Commentaries by Judith Butler, Raymond Geuss, and Jonathan Lear* (Oxford: Oxford University Press, 2008), https://doi.org/10.1093/acprof: oso/9780195320466.001.0001, p. 52).

social life. It is not sufficient to keep the base of the *status quo* intact while its superstructure engages in ameliorative projects.[122]

Concerning 2), however, violations of normative recognition relations that devastate and unmake one's practical relation-to-self cause even more hurt and pain than the hurt and pain of misrecognition. Such epistemic-moral injury is not just designed to agonise S but to use that agony in such a way that S cannot reconstitute themselves. By way of illustrating this Rortyan point, I would like to focus on gaslighting. For Kate Abramson, gaslighting is

> a form of emotional manipulation in which the gaslighter tries (consciously or not) to induce in someone the sense that her reactions, perceptions, memories and/or beliefs are not just mistaken, but utterly without grounds paradigmatically, so unfounded as to qualify as crazy.[123]

There is much to agree with in Abramson's definition of gaslighting. However, Kelly Oliver's conceptualisation of gaslighting as 'the colonisation of psychic space' is an improvement:

> [...] gaslighting works as a form of domination through colonising the psyche. In order for gaslighting to be successful, the target(s) must internalise the worldview, norms, and values of the perpetrator(s). This internalisation is not benign. The internalisation of norms that undermine one's self-interpretation as a reliable agent is essential to the operation of gaslighting—in this case, sexist norms enforced by misogynistic practices. Gaslighting turns its targets into unreliable narrators of their own experiences. Its tactics are decidedly psychological with distressing material affect [...] Gaslighting puts the victim in an affective double bind: damned if they do stand up to their abuser and damned if they do not stand up to their abuser. It is this affective double bind, the affective injustice inherent in gaslighting, that makes its unconscious and unintentional perpetuation so pernicious and harmful to its targets, whose very souls are penetrated [...][124]

Successful gaslighting as the colonisation of psychic space tears victims' minds to pieces and puts them together again in new shapes through losing i) the concept of the world as an environment facilitating and

---

122 Cf. Piergiorgio Donatelli, 'Rorty and Democracy', *Iride*, 32 (2019), 617–30, https://doi.org/10.1414/95827 (p. 627).
123 Abramson, 'Turning Up the Lights on Gaslighting', p. 2.
124 Oliver, 'Gaslighting', pp. 119–20, p. 127.

encouraging trust, and ii) the concept of oneself as sane. The result is as nightmarish as the Ingsoc hellscape.[125]

Importantly, if 'Radical Rorty' can help draw an important distinction between 1) and 2), then such a way of thinking about cruelty puts pressure on Rorty's valorisation of social democracy. For, if cruelty towards agents by reactionary forces, as exemplified by Winston's brutalisation at the hands of the Party, is evocative of, for example, institutionalised racism and institutionalised gaslighting in contemporary liberal societies, then, '[l]imiting one's political imagination to liberalism [as social democracy] runs counter to Rorty's anti-authoritarianism'.[126] The liberal ironism of 'Shallow Rorty' (and 'Joshing Rorty') is, at best, normatively toothless, insofar as its conceptual resources can only ask 'don't be cruel'.

The 'theoretical superficiality'[127] of liberal ironism also means that liberal ironism, as Rachel Haliburton writes, is 'unable to show what institutional arrangements follow'[128] from recognising that 'cruelty is the worst thing we do'. This is not to say that critical theories *simpliciter* do not have their infelicities. Nor is it to say that Rorty's warnings about the authoritarian potential of revolutionary movements and Theory should go unheeded. However, the intellectual habit and practice of 'subjecting the roots of our social institutions to systematic critical scrutiny',[129] unlike the insistence of 'Shallow Rorty' 'that the liberal project does not need to be revised, it only needs to be supplemented',[130] provides one with clearly more intellectually and affectively powerful tools for two key activities: 1) better diagnosing the present, and 2) articulating what *structural* changes are amelioratively needed.

'Shallow Rorty' often argues, as part of his post-Philosophical ethnocentric standpoint, that we should direct attention to identifying and celebrating historical and contemporary concrete examples of

---

125 Viz. Orwell, *Nineteen Eighty-Four*, p. 188.
126 Bacon and Rutherford, 'Rorty, Habermas, and Radical Social Criticism', p. 205.
127 Rorty, CIS, p. 182. Shklar writes that '[i]nequality mattered insofar as it encouraged cruelty' (Shklar, 'Putting Cruelty First', p. 23). In a sense, her remark is also evocative of theoretical superficiality in liberalism-as-social-democracy, since inequality does not merely encourage cruelty. Inequality is built on and sustains cruelty.
128 Rachel Haliburton, 'Richard Rorty and the Problem of Cruelty', *Philosophy & Social Criticism*, 23 (1997), 49–69, https://doi.org/10.1177/019145379702300104 (p. 65).
129 Ramberg, 'Strategies for Radical Rorty', p. 239.
130 Donatelli, 'Rorty and Democracy', p. 626.

political agents or institutional arrangements that 'we liberals' admire, rather than questing after universally-binding, abstract, ahistorical normative principles. Though, as Richard Bernstein cautions here,

> [o]ne can be sympathetic with the critique of the modern obsession with rules, principles, criteria, and standards [...] But we also should not forget the lesson that Socrates teaches us when Euthyphro thinks it is sufficient to answer the question 'what is piety?' by citing examples.[131]

Part of the lesson that Socrates teaches inquirers is that one should avoid superficiality. However, this does not mean that inquirers are encouraged to be representationalists and foundationalists. Rather, Socrates encourages inquirers to think very hard and sensitively in a way emblematic of theory that *moves*. Such a way of reflecting and engaging in conceptual activity is more illustrative of 'Radical Rorty' than 'Shallow Rorty' (and 'Joshing Rorty').

Conclusion

Rorty writes in CIS that he is interested in 'the creation of a world in which tenderness and kindness are the human norm'.[132] As I have previously noted, Rorty also consistently self-describes as an anti-authoritarian. However, only 'Radical Rorty'—who rarely explicitly features in Rorty's published work—plausibly counts as anti-authoritarian. 'Shallow Rorty' (and 'Joshing Rorty') lack the requisite anti-authoritarian discursive architecture to create a world in which tenderness and kindness are the human norm, since as Giorgio Baruchello writes, '[a]version to cruelty is not a distinctive character of Western liberal democracies'.[133]

I previously drew attention to Richard Bernstein's claim that Rorty's defence of liberalism-as-social-democracy is an *apologia* for the *status quo*. Bernstein, however, does not countenance the presence of 'Radical Rorty'—a thinker interested in structural defects of existing social reality, defects that *theory-with-the-power-to-move* can detect and illuminate. One salient question that consequently arises can be expressed as follows:

---

131 Bernstein, *The New Constellation*, p. 242.
132 Rorty, CIS, p. 160.
133 Giorgio Baruchello, 'Rorty's Painful Liberalism', *Bijdragen*, 63 (2002), 22–45, https://doi.org/10.2143/BIJ.63.1.795 (p. 29).

'So, just who is Rorty?'. Hauke Brunkhorst gives a good answer, one with which I sympathise:

> [...] Rorty is not a full-time liberal, only a part-time liberal and—due to his strong utopian perspective—a full-time progressive, meaning that he is primarily progressive and only then liberal [...] Political liberalism is implied as a communicative mindset, but without democratic progressivism, liberalism is ideology.[134]

'Radical Rorty', unlike both 'Shallow Rorty' and 'Joshing Rorty', understands that a capitalist base with a democratic superstructure is incoherent: capitalism with a human face is still capitalism. John Dewey, who is Rorty's classical pragmatist hero, himself recognised that social democracy was incapable of enabling democratic sensibilities and forms of association:[135]

> Liberalism must now become radical, meaning by 'radical' perception of the necessity of thorough-going changes in the set-up of institutions and corresponding activity to bring the changes to pass. For the gulf between what the actual situation makes possible and the actual state itself is so great that it cannot be bridged by piecemeal policies undertaken ad hoc. The process of producing the changes will be, in any case, a gradual one. But 'reforms' that deal now with this abuse and now with that without having a social goal based on an inclusive plan, differ entirely from effort at re-forming, in its literal sense, the institutional scheme of things. The liberals of more than a century ago were denounced in their time as subversive radicals, and only when the new economic order was established did they become apologists for the status quo, or else content with social patchwork. If radicalism be defined as perception of the need for radical change, then today any liberalism which is not also radicalism is irrelevant and doomed.[136]

The presence of 'Radical Rorty' means that, to quote Bacon and Nat Rutherford, 'Rorty has much more in common with radicals than he is often credited with [...] Even though Rorty's commitment to liberalism

---

134 Hauke Brunkhorst, 'Not Just A Liberal–Social Philosophy as Antiauthoritarian and Utopian Social Criticism: Richard Rorty's *Achieving Our Country Today*', *Philosophy & Social Criticism*, 48 (2022), 1353–68, https://doi.org/10.1177/01914537221122270 (p. 1361).

135 This passage also goes some way to undermining Rorty's contention that Dewey is a hero of social democrats. Viz. Rorty, *Objectivity, Relativism, and Truth*, p. 21.

136 John Dewey, *Liberalism and Social Action* (New York: Capricorn Books, 1939), p. 130.

is clear, there are resources in his philosophy that point beyond the liberal reformism he espoused'.[137]

In this chapter, I hope I have identified those very resources in CIS that contribute to the accurate diagnosis of social pathology and, therefore, to the progressive transformation of political society, so much so that we are not limited to, at best, finding better ways of coping with the world but can overcome the *status quo*. If my arguments have been convincing, then Rorty's distinction between 'radicals' and 'utopians'[138] and his own 'hunch [...] that Western social and political thought may have had the last conceptual revolution it needs'[139] may well be mistaken.

---

137 Bacon and Rutherford, 'Rorty, Habermas, and Radical Social Criticism', p. 192.
138 Viz. Rorty, ORT, pp. 18–19.
139 Rorty, CIS, p. 63.

4. Actually (Anti-)Utopian? Levitas, Rorty and the Conditions of Utopianism

Elin Danielsen Huckerby

We identify two features of Rorty's radical criticism: utopianism and practicality.

Michael Bacon and Nat Rutherford[1]

[The] end-point of Rorty's project of endorsing social hope and utopian envisioning is in fact deeply anti-utopian... To equate acceptable utopianism with a particular vision and a particular mode of social change is not an exercise in the education of hope, but, rather, an exercise in social and ideological control.

Ruth Levitas[2]

[Anti-representationalism offers] not just a new stage in the history of philosophy, but a new self-image for humanity... a culture unlike anything that has existed in the past.

Richard Rorty[3]

---

[1] Michael Bacon and Nat Rutherford, 'Rorty, Habermas, and Radical Social Criticism', in *The Ethics, Epistemology, and Politics of Richard Rorty*, ed. by Giancarlo Marchetti, Routledge Studies in American philosophy (Oxon, New York: Routledge, 2021), pp. 191–208, https://doi.org/10.4324/9780429324734-14

[2] Ruth Levitas, 'Pragmatism, Utopia and Anti-Utopia', *Critical Horizons*, 9.1 (2008), 42–59, https://doi.org/10.1558/crit.v9i1.42 (p. 52).

[3] Richard Rorty, 'Philosophy as a Transitional Genre', in *Pragmatism, Critique, Judgment: Essays for Richard J. Bernstein*, ed. by Richard J. Bernstein, Seyla Benhabib and Nancy Fraser (Cambridge, MA: MIT Press, 2004), pp. 3–28 (p. 4).

Co-opting utopianism in the service of reform?

We often think, Ruth Levitas observes, that there is a 'direct conflict between pragmatism and utopia'.[4] Instead, she argues, genuine utopianism hinges on being sufficiently pragmatic. Nevertheless, when she looks at Richard Rorty—perhaps the most well-known pragmatist philosopher of the twentieth century and widely regarded as defined by his utopianism—Levitas sees an *anti*-utopian intellectual. To her, Rorty's attachment to existing institutions creates a form of closure that limits radical alterity. His affirmation of democratic liberalism and market economy precludes visions of otherness or altered possibilities more apt to bring about the social justice he aspires to. Rorty, Levitas concludes, co-opts utopian terminology to solidify the *status quo* in ways that reinforce existing structures and norms. He is thus, in practice, 'deeply anti-utopian'.[5] Rorty might avow utopianism, but cannot legitimately lay claim to it.

In stark contrast to Levitas's seminal assessment (but without taking it into account), Michael Bacon and Nat Rutherford recently reasserted the view that utopianism defines Rortyan thought.[6] In their assessment, anti-essentialism and practical-mindedness combine with a persistent utopian orientation to shape Rortyan pragmatism *qua* political philosophy. So, how do we read Rorty on utopia? Is Rorty co-opting genuine utopianism in the service of pragmatic, piecemeal change, thereby diluting its potential and power, or, worse, does his rhetoric serve to sustain the *status quo*? Could Levitas be missing something—or are perhaps Rorty, Bacon and Rutherford alike missing a vital dimension of what it takes to be utopian?

---

4 Levitas, 'Pragmatism', p. 45; Ruth Levitas, *Utopia as Method: The Imaginary Reconstitution of Society* (Basingstoke: Palgrave Macmillan, 2013), https://doi.org/10.1057/9781137314253

5 Levitas, 'Pragmatism', p. 52. Chantal Mouffe expresses similar concerns when she characterises Rorty's political vision as 'piecemeal type of social engineering' and worries about whether he is not 'missing an important dimension of the democratic vision?'. Rorty, Mouffe is suggesting, might be too stuck in the *status quo* to get beyond it. See Chantal Mouffe (ed.), *Deconstruction and Pragmatism: Simon Critchley, Jacques Derrida, Ernesto Laclau and Richard Rorty* (London, New York: Routledge, 1996), p. 3.

6 Bacon and Rutherford, 'Rorty, Habermas, and Radical Social Criticism', p. 203.

In the following, I explore what is at stake in these opposing readings of Rorty to clarify the relationship between Rortyan pragmatism and utopianism, and what his approach might teach us today. I come to agree with Levitas that Rorty exhibits a degree of intransigence—and, *pace* Bacon and Rutherford, I find that an attachment to the *status quo* is also on display in his philosophy. Despite this, I see Rorty as utopian, and as offering a valuable framing for the pragmatic utility—pragmatic primacy, even—of encouraging and supporting radical social reimagination. Levitas worries that utopianism is becoming impossible, at a juncture where it is most needed. Most importantly, then, Rortyan philosophy offers a philosophical framework that reconfigures, and reasserts, the conditions of possibility for utopianism in post-postmodernism.

Imagination in the service of politics

Bacon and Rutherford admit they cast Rorty as more radical than he might have permitted.[7] Rorty stressed political reform, rooted in a steady conviction that 'the vast inequalities within American society' could be corrected by 'using the institutions of constitutional democracy'.[8] However, they also assert that Rorty stood firmly left of centre: his conventional-sounding outlook was advanced to help revitalise an electorally viable left in the US,[9] his political remarks were a product of his time. What Bacon and Rutherford are keen to add to this familiar defence is that Rorty's *philosophy* commits him to a more radical political position than expressed in his political remarks.[10] There is, then, a tension between Rorty's affirmation of existing institutions and his uncompromising, philosophically radical and sweeping, anti-essentialism.

To get a handle on this, Bacon and Rutherford take up a character, 'Radical Rorty', invented by Bjørn Ramberg three decades ago. Ramberg argued for the independence of metaphilosophical and political commitments, thus setting up the possibility of a politically radical

---

7   Bacon and Rutherford, 'Rorty, Habermas, and Radical Social Criticism', p. 203.
8   Richard Rorty, *Achieving Our Country: Leftist Thought in Twentieth-Century America* (Cambridge, MA: Harvard University Press, 1998), p. 54, cited in Bacon and Rutherford, 'Rorty, Habermas, and Radical Social Criticism', p. 191.
9   Bacon and Rutherford, 'Rorty, Habermas, and Radical Social Criticism', p. 192.
10 Bacon and Rutherford, 'Rorty, Habermas, and Radical Social Criticism', p. 202.

Rortyan pragmatist.[11] One can be a thoroughgoing anti-essentialist and committed to liberal democracy and progress. The former—abandoning foundationalist, metaphysical defences in favour of contingent and comparatively justified, materially orientated reason-giving—*also* permits one to be much more radical in politics. In Bacon and Rutherford, 'Radical Rorty' is the anti-essentialist who also departs from the universalist ethos of liberalism to embrace a thoroughgoing ant-iauthoritarianism aligned with 'the emancipatory ambitions of critical theory'.[12]

While Rorty explicitly did reject universalism of any kind, his failure to embrace these ambitions is what Bacon and Rutherford take issue with. Rorty's philosophy 'commit[s] him to a political radicalism that goes beyond what he proposed'.[13] Rortyan pragmatism says we must start from where we are, but Rorty consistently refused to accept that where we are is where it ends.[14] Moreover, Rorty's explicitly reconstrued pragmatism as anti-authoritarianism.[15] As Bacon and Rutherford demonstrate, Rorty's vision of aspirational democracy resembles the radical version envisaged by William Connolly; Rorty's emphasis on embeddedness, practice and action resonates deeply with Marx's materialism.[16] 'Radical Rorty', we might say, is Rorty when his occasional declarations not to be radical are taken as less definitory than the assertions and aspirations that characterise his work overall.

Still, Rortyanism precludes revolution in one specific sense. As Bacon and Rutherford observe, '[r]eformism as a political strategy [...] comports with Rorty's philosophical pragmatism'.[17] Thinking holistically but also materially and ameliorative results from the view

---

11 Bjørn T. Ramberg, 'Strategies for Radical Rorty ("... but is it progress?")', *Canadian Journal of Philosophy*, 23.19 (1993), 223–46, https://doi.org/10.1080/00455091.1993.10717349

12 Bacon and Rutherford, 'Rorty, Habermas, and Radical Social Criticism', p. 192. See also William Curtis, *Defending Rorty: Pragmatism and Liberal Virtue* (Cambridge: Cambridge University Press, 2015), https://doi.org/10.1017/cbo9781316272145

13 Bacon and Rutherford, 'Rorty, Habermas, and Radical Social Criticism', p. 202.

14 Cf. p. 194.

15 See for instance Richard Rorty, *Pragmatism as Anti-Authoritarianism*, ed. by Eduardo Mendieta, Robert Brandom (Cambridge, MA: Harvard University Press, 2021), https://doi.org/10.2307/j.ctv33mgbns

16 Bacon and Rutherford, 'Rorty, Habermas, and Radical Social Criticism', p. 192. Levitas, too, recognises Rorty's philosophy as aligned with Marxism on key issues.

17 Bacon and Rutherford, 'Rorty, Habermas, and Radical Social Criticism', p. 191.

that we can never *ground* practice on something outside our practices.[18] We are continually operating from within. We cannot take a God's-eye view or possess final truths or ideal systems (of ideas or government or anything else). Ramberg, Bacon, and Rutherford are keen to convey that nothing in Rortyan thought prohibits major, transformative changes in ideas, vocabularies or practices. But because humans, embedded and embodied, are the makers of change, what we make might be novel, different even to a radical extent, but never wholly *de novo*. The Rortyan approach is to do what we can, with what we have, from where we happen to stand. Given this, a revolution in the sense of starting anew through throwing out the old is not possible.

Rorty's *in medias res* narrative *also* means his commitment to democratic liberalism (and every other idea) is 'tentative', as Bacon and Rutherford point out.[19] 'Tentativeness' is indeed key to the Rortyan attitude. Rorty advanced a stance he dubbed 'ironism', a Socratic state of remaining open to the possibility that even those concepts and narratives you hold most firmly could become superseded as you learn, grow and adapt.[20] Bacon and Rutherford rightly argue that such tentativeness is key to developing a Rortyan radical critique.[21] It not only affirms that change is inescapable. It contains a mindful refusal to reify, the flipside of which is a defence of continual change as necessary. Rorty's 'tentativeness' is thus a productive feature that holds space for *imagining and practicing differently*.

Additionally, Rorty debunks any belief in 'respect' being 'owed to traditional forms of authority, such as that of revealed religion'.[22] By extension, we do not owe respect to traditional or hegemonic systems and dominant institutions. It is up to us to establish best practices, discursively and pragmatically, and continually amend these in response

---

18 Bacon and Rutherford, 'Rorty, Habermas, and Radical Social Criticism', p. 191, citing Rorty, 'Idealizations, Foundations, and Social Practices', in *Democracy and Difference*, ed. by S. Benhabib (Princeton, NJ: Princeton University Press, 1996).
19 Bacon and Rutherford, 'Rorty, Habermas, and Radical Social Criticism', p. 195, citing a description by Robert Talisse.
20 Richard Rorty, *Contingency, Irony and Solidarity* (Cambridge: Cambridge University Press, 1989), https://doi.org/10.1017/cbo9780511804397, pp. 73–74.
21 It 'grants Rorty a route to radical criticism which is foreclosed by a writer such as Habermas', i.e. those less thoroughly anti-essentialist. See Bacon and Rutherford, 'Rorty, Habermas, and Radical Social Criticism', p. 195.
22 Bacon and Rutherford, 'Rorty, Habermas, and Radical Social Criticism', p. 196.

to changing circumstances, needs and comprehension (as opposed to having what is right revealed by God, Nature, or any authority external to human conversation). '[S]ocial criticism', on this view, becomes 'a matter of comparing and contrasting different social practices'.[23] Past and contemporary imaginaries all become resources for pragmatic comparison of what is 'possible and important'.[24] Working out what needs to change becomes an evaluative exercise in relation to specific aims or observed outcomes. *We* become the authorities, which lays the burden of responsibility for our doings (with words included) squarely on our shoulders (as a species).[25]

Ultimately and interestingly, despite advancing Rorty as a progressive, radical and transformational thinker in many ways, Bacon and Rutherford land on a reading that resonates with Levitas's. Rorty's utopianism rests on never abandoning hope for change. Simultaneously, his pragmatism insists that we look to concrete political and economic realities when articulating critique and imagining necessary transformations (as I take up below, in a manner similar to Levitas). Yet, even as Rorty '[cut] liberalism adrift of its foundational moorings',[26] and thus *was* philosophically at liberty to be explicitly radical in his political views, he chose not to be. Moreover, he made this choice fully aware of concrete realities in his own time that he, too, saw as demanding radical, systematic, and structural change. As 'existing liberalism moved further and further away from the utopia of "inspirational liberalism" that Rorty envisaged', Rorty ought to 'have come to believe, with Marx, "that human emancipation must proceed not by repudiating the liberal tradition but by transcending its limitations"'.[27] Bacon and Rutherford

---

23 Bacon and Rutherford, 'Rorty, Habermas, and Radical Social Criticism', p. 197.
24 The phrase 'possible and important' is repeatedly used in CIS: see pp. 17, 23, 39, 48 and 82.
25 Individually responsible too, but the extent to which will wholly be a moral matter to examine in each case. What is important here, is that we no longer outsource the responsibility for human actions to non-human *metaphysical* forces or dictums. See also Christopher Voparil, 'Rorty and James on Irony, Moral Commitment, and the Ethics of Belief', *William James Studies*, 12.2 (2016), 1–30; Bjørn T. Ramberg, 'Irony's Commitment: Rorty's Contingency, Irony and Solidarity', *The European Legacy*, 19 (2014), https://doi.org/10.1080/10848770.2014.876197, 144–62.
26 Bacon and Rutherford, 'Rorty, Habermas, and Radical Social Criticism', p. 201
27 Bacon and Rutherford, 'Rorty, Habermas, and Radical Social Criticism', p. 201, citing James Oakes, 'What's Wrong with "Negative Liberty": Commentary', *Law & Social Inquiry* 21.1 (1996), 79–82, p. 82.

are keen to stress that there are important 'radical resources' in Rortyan thought, but also that Rorty's 'philosophy *should* commit him to a political radicalism that goes beyond what he proposed'.[28]

Lack of imagination in service of the *status quo*

Bacon and Rutherford soften their critique by once again stressing that Rorty's reformist liberalism was a 'political creed' and 'not a philosophical one',[29] adding that Rorty *did* suggest political revolution might become necessary:

> rich North Atlantic democracies, including the United States, are presently under the control of an increasingly greedy and selfish middle class—a class which continually elects cynical demagogues willing to deprive the weak of hope in order to promise tax cuts to their constituents. If this process goes on for another generation, the countries in which it happens will be barbarized. Then it may become silly to hope for reform, and sensible to hope for revolution.[30]

Rorty, they remind us, recognised that 'both liberalism and capitalism in practice have shown themselves to be incapable of achieving the democratic utopia he sought'.[31]

I suspect, though, that Levitas might respond that this admission simply affirms what she was saying all along: Rorty's claim to a radical position, his *avowal* of utopianism, clearly does not square with his actual approach to politics, especially given how apparent it has been for decades that we need transformational economic and institutional change—plain enough that Rorty himself saw it. I suspect she might say that while Bacon and Rutherford correctly characterise Rortyan political thought as combining pragmatism and what *Rorty* holds to be utopian thinking, what he prescribes **is** not really utopianism at all.

---

28 Bacon and Rutherford, 'Rorty, Habermas, and Radical Social Criticism', p. 202.
29 Bacon and Rutherford, 'Rorty, Habermas, and Radical Social Criticism', pp. 201–02, again citing Oakes.
30 Bacon and Rutherford, 'Rorty, Habermas, and Radical Social Criticism', p. 203, citing 'Anti-Representationalism, Ethnocentrism, and Liberalism', in Richard Rorty, *Objectivity, Relativism, and Truth* (Cambridge: Cambridge University Press), pp. 1–20 (p. 15).
31 Bacon and Rutherford, 'Rorty, Habermas, and Radical Social Criticism', p. 203.

An overarching worry for Levitas is indeed that the conditions of late modernity pose 'fundamental challenges to the project and projection of utopia' for *anyone*. Greater 'provisionality and reflexivity' of the utopian mode, combined with a shift from 'representation or content to an emphasis on process', weakens, in her estimation, 'the transformative potential of utopia'.[32]

According to Levitas, utopia has three key functions: 'compensation, critique and change'.[33] The first denotes expressions of what is lacking. Utopia as critique 'foregrounds' what is lacking and 'makes it explicit'. The third function is most vital: 'catalysing change'. Utopia's 'strongest function', Levitas asserts, 'its claim to being important', is 'its capacity to inspire the pursuit of a world transformed, to embody hope rather than simply desire'.[34] Hope goes beyond desire. It is 'educated' and concerned with the realities of realising what is desired. Utopian hope is for 'transformation and redemption'.[35] Utopianism proper should cultivate such hopes and motivate pursuits of concrete societal goals.

If so, it becomes a serious problem that the postmodernist response invites 'pathological pluralism', in which 'the acknowledgement of the positions and standpoints of others effectively undermines the capacity to occupy, even critically and provisionally, a ground of one's own', thus making commitment towards action, and specific and limiting choices or visions, impossible. In such a case, utopia cannot move 'beyond the function of critique', for actuating *change* requires 'imagin[ing] both what this might mean and how it might be possible, in order that we may be able to hope' *and* commitment to this vision.[36]

'Anti-utopianism', however, her charge against Rorty, goes further than falling short of appropriately engaging in the utopian mode. It entails '*active denial* of the merits of imagining alternative ways of living, particularly if they constitute serious attempts to argue that the world might or should be otherwise'.[37] Such denial is 'a constant feature of the

---

[32] Ruth Levitas, '3 For Utopia: The (Limits of the) Utopian Function in Late Capitalist Society', in *The Philosophy of Utopia*, ed. by Barbara Goodwin (London, Portland, OR: Frank Cass, 2001), https://doi.org/10.4324/9780203045565, pp. 25–43 (p. 25).
[33] Levitas, 'For Utopia', p. 28.
[34] Levitas, 'For Utopia', p. 28.
[35] Levitas, 'For Utopia', p. 30.
[36] Levitas, 'For Utopia', p. 40.
[37] Levitas, 'For Utopia', p. 30. My emphasis.

dominant ideology'.[38] Hegemonic worldviews *can* incorporate variants of (or more precisely, perhaps, pretensions to) utopianism, but in forms that suppress, rather than open for 'radical and transformative potential'.[39] To combat the inevitable anti-utopianism built into hegemonic discourses, 'the act of imagination itself, a process which disrupts the closure of the present' is key.[40] The crux is to disrupt and transgress 'the normative and conceptual frameworks of everyday experience', thus allowing a wanting of 'something other', desiring 'in a different way'.[41] This opens the possibility of hoping for and pursuing transformative change.

Overall, I take Levitas's core requirement for genuine utopianism to be that it strikes a productive balance between utopianism and realism, idealism and pragmatism. If one is not sufficiently attentive to realism, one's utopianism veers into wishful thinking. If you are too stuck on realism and political bargaining—not sufficiently willing to look beyond the current conditions of possibility—your utopianism deflates into 'mere pragmatism'.[42] In sum, Levitas stresses that the 'effective synthesis of provisionality and responsibility may be the condition of keeping utopia open as a space [to] reach out to the real possibility of a transformed future'.[43]

While this might sound highly reminiscent of Rorty's position, Levitas sharply disagrees. Rorty serves as a focal point of critique in an analysis of the idea of 'realistic utopia'. Such a construct, Levitas observes, is usually seen as 'oxymoronic'.[44] Being a 'utopian' is to be seen as enthralled by fantasy or to side with a variant of totalitarianism: 'utopianism that is

---

38 Levitas, 'For Utopia', p. 31.
39 Levitas, 'For Utopia', p. 31.
40 Levitas, 'For Utopia', p. 39.
41 Levitas, 'For Utopia', p. 39.
42 In the sense 'pragmatism' is often used in politics or everyday language: dealing with problems to resolve an issue here and now, making strategic compromises, sometimes detrimental to long-term goals, which in effect compromises values or what is actually good. I suspect that Levitas and Rorty might define 'pragmatism' in distinctly different ways. It is possible that this might be a root cause of there appearing to be significant differences in their outlooks, when close scrutiny seems to reveal substantial overlap in their views.
43 Levitas, 'For Utopia', p. 40.
44 Levitas, 'Pragmatism', p. 45. Rorty's CIS is arguably a defence of the possibility of combining pragmatism with utopianism, fallibilism with commitment. Rorty notes this has often been seen as paradoxical, and he is keen to disprove that it is. See especially the chapter on 'Solidarity'.

perfectionist, holistic, radically other, revolutionary in its methods of implementation' is judged as 'incipiently totalitarian' on the basis of being 'impossible'.[45] As a reaction, 'pragmatic, gradual, piecemeal and essentially minor change' is considered 'good'.[46] Yet *genuine* transformation hinges, as touched on above, on us being *both* utopian and realistic. Only when 'concrete utopias' come to the fore will there be an 'education of hope', the expression of will, and acting on hope.[47] Thus, for utopia to have a political function, it demands 'the consideration of *what is really possible*, not simply what it is possible for us to imagine as possible, or what it is possible for us to imagine'.[48] Rorty—in his refusal to engage with proposals that transcend the limits of the liberal tradition (to borrow Bacon and Rutherford's (Marx's) words)—fails to be open to what is possible, to 'radical alterity', and thus falls short of genuine utopianism.[49]

In fact, most proponents of this kind of reformist thinking are, Levitas suggests, actually 'anti-utopian'. Rorty constitutes a particularly egregious example, she argues, as 'in his case the anti-utopian effect is *disguised* by his explicit commitment to social hope, leading commentators to read him as utopian'.[50] Avoiding this trap hinges on noticing that the tension between realism and utopia can 'be resolved in either anti-utopian or utopian direction' depending on 'its closure of or openness to the future'. Rorty is not open to a future different from (a perfected) version of the present and is, in practice, anti-utopian.[51]

In Levitas's estimation, three strands come together to make Rortyan thought closed off in this way. His 'celebration of a utopian view of America', his hostility to the Foucauldian Marxist Left (overt exclusion of alternative visions),[52] and his attachment to market economy. Rorty might be

> utopian in promoting an image of the good society; he is perhaps also utopian in the derogatory sense of being unrealistic as to the means, if not the possibility, of achieving it. But it is an anti-utopian utopianism, in

---

45 Levitas, 'Pragmatism', p. 45.
46 Levitas, 'Pragmatism', p. 45.
47 Levitas, 'Pragmatism', p. 43.
48 Levitas, 'Pragmatism', p. 44.
49 Levitas, 'Pragmatism', p. 45.
50 She enumerates 'John Rawls, Anthony Giddens and Jeffrey Alexander, as well as [more] recognizably Leftish thinkers, Leo Panitch, Immanuel Wallerstein and Erik Olin Wright'. Levitas, 'Pragmatism', p. 45. My emphasis.
51 Levitas, 'Pragmatism', p. 42.
52 Levitas, 'Pragmatism', p. 56.

that its effects are to close down both explorations of radical alterity and avenues of social change.[53]

Levitas can see 'no room for non-capitalist envisioning', no 'alternative', no 'room for questioning whether non-gradual change may be either necessary, or indeed forced on us by the contradictions between capitalist accumulation and environmental sustainability'.[54] Ultimately, Rorty 'substitute[s] a continuing present for a future of possibilities', which is 'an exercise in social and ideological control'.[55]

Significantly, Levitas's final objection is that Rorty's unwillingness to forego liberalism and market economies goes against his general 'pragmatic refusal to posit an external Platonic ideal to which reality must tend'.[56] In practice, Rorty's political remarks and dismissal of radical and revolutionary alternatives serve to hypostasise, as an ideal, a US version of liberal democracy and its concomitant economic structures. Her charge here is, somewhat contrary to the above, that he is not being *pragmatic* enough; his politics do not align with his philosophy. While Bacon and Rutherford might take exception to the suggestion that Rorty engages in '*active* denial' of the possibility of a different future, what Levitas here observes is, in essence, what they argue too. They would dismiss that Rorty posits a Platonic ideal (reverts to essentialism) and counter that his commitments to existing ideals, institutions and practices were (in theory) productively 'tentative'. Yet they conclude that Rorty appears unwilling to be as radical in politics as his radically anti-essentialist, materially inflected philosophy commits him to.[57] There *is* an intransigence at work.

Rorty's utopian vision

The generative response to this observation is neither to dismiss Rorty's philosophical work as a whole on the back of it, nor to set his remarks on politics aside as an anomaly. The observation has, I want to suggest,

---

53   Levitas, 'Pragmatism', p. 56.
54   Levitas, 'Pragmatism', p. 52.
55   Levitas, 'Pragmatism', p. 52. The fact that Rorty rejected the 'Foucauldian Marxist Left' for reasons Levitas omits, which had everything to do with avoiding totalitarianism and closure of the kind Levitas worries about, is here rendered beside the point: the point is that the pragmatic *effect* is closure.
56   Levitas, 'Pragmatism', p. 52.
57   Bacon and Rutherford, 'Rorty, Habermas, and Radical Social Criticism', p. 202.

deeper roots in Rorty's writing. And if that is the case, a redescription of Rortyanism for our time, not just of his political vocabulary but aspects of his philosophy, is warranted. I take Ramberg, Bacon and Rutherford to be contributing to such an effort. I suspect it should be extended to other aspects of Rortyan philosophy than his political thought. Before exploring this suggestion, I want to establish that I hold Rorty to offer a novel and useful framing of utopianism and its societal necessity, and one which helps overcome some of Levitas's worries about the conditions of utopianism in postmodernism.

Rortyan pragmatism as heuristic 'grappling'

To lay some groundwork for my case, I want to take a cue from Levitas and attend to the word 'heuristic'. Levitas explains that in response to postmodernism, utopia morphs into 'a heuristic device', used to explore 'what might be possible or impossible' or as a 'regulative ideal'.[58] No longer 'systematic', utopias become 'exploratory projections' merely 'sketched as an alternative'.[59] The result is that postmodern utopias fall short in terms of 'content'—they fail to pin down an approach or endpoint; they are not instrumental enough. While they might contain *critique*, they do not motivate or produce *change*.

Rorty, on the other hand, *embraces* a heuristic mode of operation. He construes it as an effective response *to* the postmodern relativism that Levitas worries about.[60] It is regularly overlooked that working heuristically is a central methodological proposal in Rortyan thought. 'My holistic strategy', Rorty says, an approach 'characteristic of pragmatism',

---

58 Levitas, 'For Utopia', p. 26.
59 Levitas, 'For Utopia', pp. 35, 38. Levitas is here discussing Miguel Abensour and Thomas Osborne's conceptions of utopia. Abensour, as Levitas points out elsewhere, actually argues that this is the mode utopianism took on from around 1850. See Ruth Levitas, *The Concept of Utopia: Reissue with New Preface by the Author*, Ralahine Utopian Studies 3 (Oxford: Peter Lang AG, Internationaler Verlag der Wissenschaften, 2011), https://doi.org/10.3726/978-3-0353-0010-9, p. 140.
60 For more on this distinction, and how Rorty's project is one that reacts as much to postmodernism's response to anti-essentialism as to essentialism *per se*, see Tracy Llanera, *Richard Rorty: Outgrowing Modern Nihilism* (Basingstoke: Palgrave Macmillan, 2020), https://doi.org/10.1007/978-3-030-45058-8

is to reinterpret every [...] dualism as a momentarily convenient blocking-out of regions on a spectrum, rather than as recognition of an ontological, methodological, or epistemological divide. So I shall construct such a spectrum and use it as a heuristic device. [...][61]

Rorty suggests that while we must avoid constructing essentialising dichotomies held to properly map the structure of (an underlying) reality, we *can* still set up conceptual pairs as *devices t*hat help bring out *differences that make a difference in practice.*[62] We can use 'tentative' constructs or ideas to structure and experiment with various approaches.

Such devices need not be dichotomous. Humans consistently work heuristically, whether we are aware of it or not. A heuristic device is a model, tool, concept or idea that enables a better understanding of a phenomenon without being a direct representation of the object or phenomenon in question. It nevertheless aids analysis because a theory (model) built on what we already know can be used to approach or approximate something unknown; we can simplify complex problem-solving by navigating a proposed or previously successful trajectory. Moving along a known arc can facilitate the discovery of new paths. Trying something that does not quite fit might still generate modifications or prompt novel ideas. Vitally in the context of Rortyan pragmatism, heuristics facilitate learning and problem-solving without requiring a *final* answer. They provide a framework while acknowledging that the framework itself is tentative and 'merely' an exploratory device constructed for a specific context, situation, task, or for experimentation or play. We work heuristically when we approach by trial and error, work from a rule of thumb, use an analogy, or create a metaphor. Working heuristically parallels pragmatism's mode of thought, as it posits models but exempts us from viewing them as foundational or representational.

Significantly, then, when Rorty deploys dichotomies, such as the public and the private, say, the contrasted phenomena are *not* to be seen as discrete (ontological) entities. Moreover, the contrasted concepts lie at opposite ends of an *equally heuristic* 'spectrum'. These pairs are best

---

61   Richard Rorty, 'Texts and Lumps', *New Literary History*, 17.1 (1985), 1–16, https://doi.org/10.2307/468973 (p. 8).
62   Cf., also, Richard Rorty, 'Pragmatism, Relativism, and Irrationalism', in Richard Rorty, *Consequences of Pragmatism: (Essays: 1972-1980)* (Minneapolis, MN: University of Minnesota Press, 1982), pp. 160–75.

understood as devices for grasping salient functional differences that are dynamically interlinked. This matters because it renders all Rortyan pairings in a specific light. The 'public' versus the 'private' no longer looks like a problematic quasi-essentialising distinction but as 'blockings out' on a sliding 'spectrum' of practices. In this case, it is a spectrum of practices that are more or less useful in our shared discursive and political sphere when the aim is lessening human cruelty.[63] More broadly, what I want to establish is that whenever Rorty deploys constructs or interpretations, he is placing a 'tentative', interpretive, 'grid'[64] on a relational phenomenon in flux to enable us to converse about differences that might make a difference. On my reading, then, Rortyan constructs are rhetorical or narrative devices made to permit a specific story to be told, a given weighing to be allocated, or a specific effect to come into play (e.g. persuasive, experimental or playful). I would suggest it as a legitimate reading of Rorty to consider his pragmatist approach as centred on inventing heuristics to 'grapple' as he often puts it, with what to do, how to live, and what is, as he repeatedly puts it in CIS, 'possible and important'. It represents an active, creative response to life in conditions of uncertainty.

Rorty's utopia: A fully 'poeticized culture'

The above hopefully sounds at least largely reasonable, as well as practically minded and rooted in the 'realistic'. I detail it as a novel approach to clarifying Rorty's specific utopian vision of a fully 'poeticized culture'.[65] Philosophy has a long history of rejecting poets and poetry. Working heuristically, however, is a highly valued practice

---

63 See CIS. Fair interpretations of such dualisms in Rorty's writings ought to proceed by asking 'what spectrum do these sit on?', 'what difference is this pair construed to bring out in this conversation and for what reasons?'. I am aware that Rorty in one instance suggested there be a 'firm' division between the public and the private (CIS, p. 83). I take this up below.

64 Cf. Richard Rorty, 'The Pragmatist's Progress', in *Interpretation and Overinterpretation*, ed. by Stefan Collini (Cambridge: Cambridge University Press, 1992), pp. 89–108, https://doi.org/10.1017/CBO9780511627408.005. Rorty here explains interpretations as 'grids' the reader/interpreter lays down to arrive at an understanding. These are amendable or replaceable in response to changing contexts/information/experience.

65 Rorty, CIS, pp. 53–54.

at the core of the scientific method. The profoundly pragmatic nature of Rorty's talk of 'poetry' stays foregrounded when we see that in this talk, heuristics are poetic artefacts of human imagination and creativity, and vice versa. Appreciating the equivalence can help us avoid falling into the trap of thinking that Rorty's vision of a 'poeticized' or literary culture aestheticises or moves away from the 'realistic'.

What distinguishes Rortyan philosophy is precisely that *every* idea, model, theory, concept or vocabulary is a heuristic invention—or, in his later idiom, an artefact, a poem: a creation of the human imagination. We forge these to make our way forward from our contingent starting points—they help us figure things out, get by, communicate, experiment with effects,[66] or create sustaining narratives. Even our self-conception becomes a 'poem', a self-made moral locus we 'tinker' with as we grow in experience and respond to changing circumstances.[67] On this view, it no longer makes sense to suggest, as Levitas does, that heuristics are not capacious enough for 'systematic' thought; are less capable of motivating change, by virtue of their tentative and 'exploratory' nature. On the Rortyan view, even the most detailed, methodical, realistic yet inspirational programme for change *will be* 'tentative', beheld as 'poetry', an artefact of the human imagination, one that can be received in many ways and also taken very seriously as material for (re)making by some. Heuristics need not lack in 'content' merely because they are held lightly.

Rorty's utopian imaginary is a culture that has embraced such an outlook. It is an anti-essentialist, anti-representationalist culture, defined by its commonsensical acceptance of ideas, models, theories, vocabularies, selves and institutions *as* made—artefacts we might take up or put down, remould, reuse, for purpose or play, for a myriad of effects.[68] It does not provide, as Levitas indeed points out, a vision of a different social or economic system. *How* we would organise or create good

---

66 Including joy, laughter, satisfaction, or wonder. Rorty talks about effects of metaphors being like kisses or slaps in the face (CIS, p. 18).
67 'Practical identity': Richard Rorty, *Philosophy as Cultural Politics* (Cambridge: Cambridge University Press, 2007), https://doi.org/10.1017/cbo9780511812835, p. 198. 'Tinker': Richard Rorty, 'Freud and Moral Reflection', in Richard Rorty, *Essays on Heidegger and Others* (Cambridge: Cambridge University Press, 2010 [1991]), pp. 143–63, https://doi.org/10.1017/cbo9780511609039.010
68 Cf. CIS, p. 53, 87.

lives in this culture is deliberately left open-ended—but never ignored. What Rorty does provide is material 'content' on a transformation of mindset that better permits cultural and institutional change to happen. Radical embrace of human finitude and the 'contingency' of all 'starting points'[69] renders human minds more capable of resisting the kind of closure of horizons Levitas worries about.[70] Rorty's utopian imaginary is a culture that has undergone a radical change in *attitude*, and this is his 'systematic', specific utopian proposal. Levitas looks, at least in part, for 'content' in Rorty that sets out systematic and transformative proposals in the realm of politics. But Rorty is setting out a systematic, transformative, realistic and concrete, proposal (thus legitimately utopian also on Levitas's terms), for material change in the human family's approach to words and ideas, including and especially within philosophy as a practice embedded in society and deeply enmeshed with the practices of politics.

The pivotal attitude shift Rorty advances is, interestingly, not primarily a shift in how we view ideas, but rather in how we perceive ourselves. We are no longer seen as a privileged species somehow able to access something transcendent and essential. We are not in contact with divine beings or eternal Truths but are contingent products of material circumstances (linguistic imprinting included), merely and amazingly capable of creating and impressive range of artefacts. The key move is a complete de-divinisation of human beings: an unafraid acceptance of *not* having an essence (a soul, Rationality). In turn, what we say about the world becomes mere products of our very human, brilliant and limited brains.[71] Consequently and powerfully, it is a shift

---

69 Rorty, 'Pragmatism, Relativism, and Irrationalism', p. 726.

70 See Part III of Richard Rorty, *Philosophy and the Mirror of Nature* (Princeton, NJ: Princeton University Press, 1979). As Ramberg puts it, it leaves us better 'inoculated against the temptation to let theoretical vision override the lessons of practical experience' (Ramberg, 'Irony's Commitment', p. 145).

71 Rorty is not hostile to science. We can forge helpful practices (including linguistic practices) for prediction and control. He reconstrues objectivity as *solidarity*: the more of us willing to stand for a way to model and talk, the 'harder' the fact. See Yvonne Huetter-Almerigi, 'Two Forms of Realism', *ejpap*, 12.1 (2020), https://doi.org/10.4000/ejpap.1868; Richard Rorty, 'Solidarity or Objectivity?', *Nanzan Review of American Studies*, 6 (1984), 1–18; Richard Rorty, 'Science as Solidarity', in Richard Rorty, *Objectivity, Relativism, and Truth* (Cambridge: Cambridge University Press, 1990), pp. 35–45; Richard Rorty, 'Is Natural Science a Natural Kind?', in ORT, pp. 46–62, https://doi.org/10.1017/cbo9781139173643.004

to seeing human beings as the *makers* (the 'poets') of all ideas, theories, vocabularies, values and judgements (of any and all heuristics we invent to 'grapple' with existence, from sonnets to string theory).[72]

This attitude-transformation has the potential, Rorty proposes, to cause sweeping change: he believes it could result in nothing less than a 'new dawn'—not simply represent a 'new stage in the history of philosophy' but a 'new self-image for humanity', potentially ushering in 'a culture unlike anything that has existed in the past'.[73] If we accept our ideas and vocabularies, even our most firmly held convictions, as limited, material, intersubjectively negotiated products of the human imagination, he believes we will be less attached to 'final vocabularies' and current worldviews. The radically new lies in rejecting the impulse to look beyond human conversation for answers, and instead purposefully turn towards each other in conversation and collaboration. This is, to Rorty, the final emancipatory move that completes the secularisation Enlightenment thinkers began: a de-divinisation of our selves initiated and completed by ourselves.[74] Ceasing to outsource responsibility for what we say and do to the non-human (God, Nature) we might take on more responsibility but also grow in power, and especially in power to change.[75] Herein lies the significant potential for radical critique Ramberg, Bacon and Rutherford work to bring out.[76]

Importantly, Rorty paired such full acceptance of the 'contingency' of all 'starting points',[77] including the contingency of 'language', 'selfhood' and 'community', with the moral choice to work to lessen human cruelty.[78] He did not think it was given that everyone, not even all anti-essentialist pragmatists, would take this to be their purpose, but in his utopia, making that choice to accept contingency, would be followed

---

72 An attitude that, Rorty points out, would 'scandalize' C. P. Snow, and still is likely to scandalise anyone subscribing to a scientistic outlook. See Richard Rorty, 'Professionalized Philosophy and Transcendentalist Culture', *The Georgia Review*, 30.4 (1976), 757–69: the view that 'quantum mechanics' is a 'great... poem' (p. 765).
73 Rorty, 'Philosophy as a Transitional Genre', p. 4.
74 See also Robert B. Brandom, 'Achieving the Enlightenment', in *Pragmatism as Anti-Authoritarianism*, ed. by Eduardo Mendieta (Cambridge, MA: Harvard University Press, 2021), pp. vii–xxvi, https://doi.org/10.4159/9780674270077-001
75 Cf. CIS, p. 89.
76 See also Chapter 3 above, for a novel construal of 'Radical Rorty'.
77 Richard Rorty, 'Pragmatism, Relativism, and Irrationalism', p. 726.
78 CIS.

by a turn towards each other in conversation, and that by a desire to care for increasingly large circles of people different than ourselves, to include them in the conversation.[79]

In Levitas's terminology, what Rorty envisages is, then, a large-scale reorientation or education of desire, from a desire for final, metaphysical inquiry-closing answers and Truths, to a desire for open conversation and collaboration, and working *with*, rather than against, uncertainty. Levitas worried that postmodernist utopian thought lacks 'content' or is all about 'process', and while the Rortyan stance indeed can be deemed processual in its recognition of the constancy of change (its refusal to hypostasise and posit ultimate endpoints), it is also deeply attentive to the 'artefacts' we make along the way: ideas, vocabularies, selves, epistemic and societal structures and forms of government included. The Rortyan response to postmodernism is the same as the one to contingency: (shared) making, *poiesis*. It amounts to a transformation of intellectual process and a *centring* of form *and* content, the how, what and why of human making, rather than a decentring of it.

However, Levitas could grant all this and still contend that in politics, what actually happens is that Rorty insists we work on refining an outdated artefact: liberal democratic culture. His 'tinkering' with it obstructs from view both the urgent need for new visions and practices, and the actual work of realising these. This assessment might shift somewhat if we read Rorty as offering two modes of utopian engagement.

Ordinary utopianism

By ordinary utopianism, I mean the everyday future-orientation and future-making that suffuses pragmatism as a philosophical attitude: its basic ameliorative stance directed towards transforming our practices through figuring out 'plausible' next steps that take us towards the kind of lifeworld world or life we desire.[80] Precisely because the Rortyan

---

79 Rortyanism thus departs significantly from central strands of postmodernism in its concern with agency, responsibility and moral and political practices. See also Voparil, 'Rorty and James'; Ramberg, 'Irony's Commitment'.
80 'Plausible', CIS, p. 86. I could have said 'everyday utopianism', but I do not quite mean what Davina Cooper means by this in her 2014 book, *Everyday Utopias: The Conceptual Life of Promising Spaces* (Durham, NC: Duke University Press), https://doi.org/10.1515/9780822377153. 'Ordinary' conjures up ordinary language

bearing is set by unreserved acceptance of the contingency of all starting points, combined with the (then necessarily forward-looking) choice to do what we can, with what we have, from where we happen to stand, this attitude is future-orientated to a greater extent than less thoroughly anti-essentialist pragmatisms (an insight at the root of Bacon and Rutherford's claim that utopianism is a particular characteristic of *Rortyan* pragmatism). Rorty's stance encourages us to take stock, identify what we want more of (more flourishing, less cruelty, in his project), and align our practices with these aims and hopes.

This kind of everyday, materially 'grappling', habitual utopianism is the mode that shapes Rortyan political reformism and 'cultural politics', as practices of negotiating values, norms and ways today for a better tomorrow. Rorty's pervasive practical-mindedness, which Bacon and Rutherford confirm defines his philosophical and political orientation as much as utopianism, leads him to worry about how we *sustain* 'social hope'. It hinges, he believes, on 'members of [...] a society [being] able to tell themselves a story about how things might get better, and to see no insuperable obstacles to this story coming true'. Social hope depends 'on the existence of reasonably concrete, optimistic, and plausible political scenarios'.[81] That is, a large number of people in such a society must be able to realistically imagine a goal, the path there, and the steps to take. Creating the necessary solidarity to generate collective action in desired directions depends on being able to narrate, in terms familiar to a wide range of people, a credible story about how to move from a to b.

In ordinary, everyday politics and life-making, all kinds of human imaginaries are deployed as devices that can prompt, direct or shape open-ended conversation and pragmatic, ameliorative experimentation. Whether they take the form of scenes in novels, poems in the narrower sense, theories, or fully-fledged political programmes, they serve as 'touchstones' for reflection and conversation and shared points of reference that enable a sustained collective conversation that might

---

philosophy, which is not my intention, but also not necessarily unproductive. 'Normal' and 'familiar' are constructs from Rorty's work that chime in the background here, but drawing on these would require further elaboration. 'Ordinary' has the everyday, pragmatic, 'getting on with the work of change' connotations I want to bring to the fore.

81 Rorty, CIS, p. 86.

reconfigure what seems 'possible and important'.[82] Importantly, radical imaginaries are *not* precluded. Likewise we can make use of overtly essentialising imaginaries, as long as we hold them 'lightly', in a historicist light, as 'artefacts', material for comparison and cultivation of discernment.

Ordinary utopianism, as I construe it, contains the work of articulating 'narratives which connect the present with the past, on the one hand, and with Utopian futures, on the other'.[83] It thus entails both what Levitas calls an education of hope and desires, as well the work of sustaining hope and action. It must be a forging of hopeful *practices*, the bearing out of 'social hope' in the present. 'Utopian politics' of this kind might '[dream] of creating a hitherto unknown form of society', as Rorty puts it,[84] but it acts progressively.

Rorty remained sceptical towards the possibility of systematic (programmatic) social change. What I am trying to capture is that, in this ordinary mode, there is, if not a systematic, then a pervasive, pragmatic recognition of inertial forces and how to navigate these to achieve broad social change—change that might be both comprehensively imagined and sweeping in aims. If you are the captain of a large ship, even if what is beneath you is water, a substance of little resistance to a human hand, you must reckon with its cumulative counterforce when you want to turn your vessel around. You can do a one-eighty. You cannot do so instantaneously. There is nothing inherently anti-radical about this everyday kind of grappling with how to achieve social change.[85]

---

82 'Touchstones': cf. Rorty, CIS, pp. 53–54, Rorty, AOC, p. 136. See also Elin D. Huckerby, 'The Takeover by a Literary Culture: Richard Rorty's Philosophy of Literature' (Doctoral Thesis, University of Cambridge, 2021, https://doi.org/10.17863/CAM.76906), pp. 69–72.
83 Rorty, CIS, p. xvi.
84 Rorty, CIS, p. 3.
85 Rorty did suggest groups of people can undergo 'gestalt switches', most often, he thought, in response to literary works. But he sees these as events we can make sense of, works we can reconfigure our shared vocabularies and sensibilities around: '...we know that it's happened in the past. We know of the effect that Dickens, Harriet Beecher Stowe, Orwell, and others, have had on the way we think about politics and contemporary social issues. I think that the fact you need intersubjective agreement is perfectly compatible with the fact that a whole lot of people can suddenly undergo a gestalt switch as a result of reading a novel'. E. P. Ragg and Richard Rorty, 'Worlds or Words Apart? The Consequences of Pragmatism for Literary Studies: An Interview with Richard Rorty', *Philosophy and*

Levitas contrasts Rorty with Roberto Unger, whom she regards as a genuinely utopian pragmatist, properly combining realism with utopianism.[86] Rorty, too, praised the political 'romance' of Unger, the use of imaginative resources to get out from the 'bleakness' resulting from liberalism's inability to envisage alternatives to itself.[87] In CIS, Rorty's own Romanticism comes to the fore more strongly.[88] He still insists, however, that the political imagination operates through engagement with particular communities and specific (national) historical trajectories; that transformative change will come from examples of social improvement rather than changes in theoretical foundations.

If this is the case, it requires that anyone seeking to offer the kind of pragmatic narratives that can sustain 'social hope' must engage with these particularities. Ordinary utopianism is thus a risky business because it requires you to stand up for something that exists, today, in your time. In this mode, you lay claims and claims are laid on you, to borrow concepts from Stanley Cavell. You further a cause, commit to an approach, support or reject systems and institutions. And as soon as you do, you risk the charge of what Levitas calls 'closure'. Even if these commitments are understood by you (and even by others) as 'tentative', you risk being mistaken, missing the bigger picture, or being too firm in your convictions. But to be an agent, to accept 'responsibility' in the way both Levitas and Rorty ask us to, requires standing up for what you hold

---

Literature, 26.2 (2002), 369–96, https://doi.org/10.1353/phl.2003.0015. I address the works we cannot immediately make sense of below.

86   Levitas, 'Pragmatism'.
87   Richard Rorty, 'Unger, Castoriadis, and the Romance of a National Future', in EHO pp. 177–92, https://doi.org/10.1017/cbo9780511609039.012. In this essay, Rorty casually deflates his own utopianism and Romanticism in order to create a narrative that pitches 'we liberals' as lacking the Romanticism of Unger and Castoriadis, and these as exemplars to be held up against the 'School of Resentment' who reject Romanticism of this kind. Rorty's bluff style in this essay makes it easy to fall into the trap of not recognising the extent to which his position is in alignment with, and usefully supplements, that of Unger and Castoriadis.
88   See also Richard Rorty, 'Pragmatism as Romantic Polytheism', in *The Revival of Pragmatism: New Essays on Social Thought, Law, and Culture*, ed. by Morris Dickstein (Durham, NC: Duke University Press, 1998), pp. 21–36, https://doi.org/10.1215/9780822382522-002; Richard Rorty, 'Pragmatism and Romanticism', in *Philosophy as Cultural Politics* (Cambridge: Cambridge University Press, 2007), pp. 105–19, https://doi.org/10.1017/cbo9780511812835.008

to be good (possibly 'unflinchingly' as Rorty suggests)[89]—it requires, in Levitas's' idiom, rejection of 'pathological pluralism'. A cornerstone of Rortyan thought is to mindfully cultivate openness to being wrong *alongside* a willingness to commit to and act on what one thinks is right, materially and comparatively justified,[90] precisely to avoid the pathologies of relativism or even nihilism.[91] Ordinary utopianism bears this out.

Rorty's thoughts thus resonate deeply with Levitas's urging us to 'tak[e] responsibility' and work out a 'synthesis of provisionality and responsibility'.[92] Still, the key to genuine utopianism, in her view, is the aforementioned *balance* between (political) utopianism and realism, and in her assessment, Rorty lacks in the former. If we zoom out to encompass what I am calling Rorty's strong utopianism, the balance shifts significantly towards utopianism.

Strong utopianism

There are imaginaries we *cannot*—not yet—get a grip on by placing them in a connective, narrative about how the past might hang together with *this* kind of (imagined, utopian) future. The difference is too radical. To use Rorty's Kuhnian vocabulary from PMN, they are too 'abnormal' to make sense of from 'the point of view of some normal discourse'.[93] Rorty assigns the creation of such imaginaries at least as great a value as visions that are more readily assimilable into the ordinary, if not more.

By Rortyan strong utopianism, I mean the practice of encouraging, articulating and critiquing imaginaries capable of revolutionising individual and shared imaginative spaces and capabilities. The scope for what might be imagined in this practice, or how, is boundless because no 'realistic' constraints need to limit expression. Rorty does not use the term strong *utopianism* but talks of the crucial need for 'strong poetry'

---

89 Rorty, CIS, p. 60.
90 Rorty, CIS, p. 80.
91 For an extended exploration of how the Rortyan position helps us 'outgrow' the pathologies that lead to nihilism, see Tracy Llanera, *Richard Rorty: Outgrowing Modern Nihilism* (New York: Palgrave, 2020), https://doi.org/10.1007/978-3-030-45058-8
92 Levitas, 'For Utopia', p. 40.
93 PMN, p. 320. Rorty is there talking about radically new ways of talking relative to what is familiar, broadly established.

and 'strong poets'. 'Poetry' is here meant in that expansive sense of human imaginative artefacts. 'Strong poetry' pushes boundaries, aims to (Rorty borrows words from Ezra Pound here) 'make it new' in more radical ways.[94] Rorty also emphasises the importance of stimulating', or 'inspirational' works: those (and it might be different for different people or cultures) that instil a felt need to change and make us cast about for new narratives about how things hang together.[95] The concept of strong utopianism in this context refers to a subset of strong, stimulating imaginaries oriented towards exhibiting, and motivating action towards, a powerfully different kind of future.[96] These parallel the kinds of imaginaries Levitas talks about as capable of rupturing hegemonies.

Not all poets or poems are 'strong'. Rorty holds us all to be the poets of our lives in a down-to-earth, "ordinary"' sense: 'every human life not so racked by pain as to be unable to learn a language nor so immersed in toil as to have no leisure in which to generate a self-description' contains an 'attempt to clothe itself in its own metaphors'.[97] Additionally, individual self-understanding and meaning is fashioned from all sorts of material circumstances and curations, of 'spouses and children', 'fellow-workers', 'tools of their trade', 'cash accounts', 'businesses', 'possessions' or 'music', 'sports', or the 'trees [passed on the] way to work' because anything 'from the sound of a word to the colour of a leaf to the feel of a piece of skin can... serve to dramatise and crystallise a human being's sense of self-identity'.[98] *Strong* poets and poems are, however, different.

While he adapts the construct from Harold Bloom, Rorty understands 'strong' in an idiosyncratic way. Strong poets are strong in proportion to the extent they are ironist. 'Ironism' is, to Rorty, the capacity for facing up to the contingency of one's 'most central beliefs and desires'.[99] It

---

94 The 'poet' in the 'wide sense of the term—the sense of "one who makes things new"': CIS, pp. 12-13. As reference to Pound, see Richard Rorty, 'Philosophy as a Kind of Writing: An Essay on Derrida', *New Literary History*, 10.1 (1978), 141–60, https://doi.org/10.2307/468309, p. 153.
95 Rorty, CIS, pp. 143–44.; Richard Rorty, 'The Inspirational Value of Great Works of Literature', in AOC, 125–40.
96 Rorty's framework has a close parallel in Levitas urging the need for imaginative practices that rupture hegemony *and* inspire action.
97 Rorty, CIS, pp. 35–36.
98 Richard Rorty, 'The Contingency of Selfhood', *London Review of Books*, 8.8 (1986).
99 Rorty, CIS, p. xv.

results from 'awareness of the power of redescription',[100] arising in those who become 'sufficiently historicist and nominalist to have abandoned the idea that those central beliefs and desires refer back to something beyond the reach of time and chance'.[101] Rorty considers ironists to be more capable of autonomy and of 'making it new' because embracing identities, systems and ideas as *made* by humans is a more capacious starting point for re-making these. A fully-fledged *ironist* thus accepts all concepts, including her idea of who she is—and the culture and systems she happens to live within—as historically and culturally contingent products of the human imagination. A *strong poet* is a fully-fledged ironist who *also* actively seeks to mould what is, to (re)make—be it a self, a community, vocabularies, interpretations, systems, models, practices (science included), norms, institutions, nations, or futures.

Rorty considers strong poets to be 'the vanguard of our species'.[102] This position used to be reserved for those spearheading our search for (metaphysical) Truth. He gives it to those who further the expansion of human imaginative capabilities and, thus, in turn, practical capabilities. Strong poets help us in our efforts to be responsible by enriching our capacity for being responsive: they help us invent new ways of being in the world.

Not all strong imaginaries will have impact—it is partly a matter of skill[103] and partly a matter of 'luck'.[104] Nevertheless, Rorty's talk of 'stimulating' works offers a helpful anti-representational vocabulary for discussing imaginaries that rupture and prompt a need for self-reflection and new understandings. He suggests we can functionally separate works that grip our imaginations more strongly and 'supply novel stimuli to action' and transformation, from those that 'simply offer relaxation'.[105] There are 'inspirational' works that fill us with eagerness and impatience for change, and others that leave us undisturbed in our 'knowingness'.[106] Again, what is at stake are distinct attitudes. 'Knowingness' is 'a state of

---

100 Rorty, CIS, p. 89.
101 Rorty, CIS, p. xv.
102 Rorty, CIS, p. 20.
103 For instance, certain people have 'brains' wired for creating 'iridescent patterns', as he calls it when discussing Nabokov: Rorty, CIS, pp. 154–55.
104 Rorty, CIS, p. 29.
105 CIS, pp. 143–44.
106 Rorty, 'Inspirational Value'.

soul which prevents shudders of awe. It makes one immune to romantic enthusiasm'.[107] We attribute 'inspirational value' to works we experience as pushing us out of knowingness; when they succeed in making us 'think there is more to this life than [we] ever imagined'. However, for this to happen, the reader must allow the encounter (and Rorty talks about encounters with people this way, too,) to 'recontexualize much of what you previously thought you knew'.[108]

Another way of putting this is to say that works one experiences as stimulating or inspirational are those that succeed in bringing us out of our settled selves, for sometimes idiosyncratic and always contingently conditioned reasons. Such unsettling sets up a *potential* that might lead us to reweave our bundle of beliefs, change our (final) vocabulary, and thus transform our self as the moral locus from which we act.[109] 'Great' works of literature, Rorty suggests, are great because they have that kind of effect on many readers.[110]

Rortyan philosophy thus decidedly accommodates and highly values bold, transformative proposals that push us out of our comfort zone, rupture the comfort of 'knowingness', and shift what we see as 'possible and important'. Rorty indeed argues that our species' moral and political progress *depends* on cultivating such 'strong' *and* stimulating poetry (meaning artefacts: heuristics, models, systems, theories, vocabularies, artistic and literary works, et cetera). At first, we will not have what it takes to place such radically different artefacts into a narrative that smoothly connects the familiar or normal with the 'abnormal' (outside our current 'knowing').[111] Still, we can and often will 'grapple' with what is startling and unfamiliar. As we do, it might cause changes in how we think, talk, discern, and behave.[112] In this way, imaginaries that envisage the radically new can pull 'ordinary' dealings in their direction.

The significance of 'strong' exemplars, imaginaries, vocabularies that push and pull on the 'normal' in Rortyan thought is what I want to convey.

---

107 Rorty, 'Inspirational Value', p. 126.
108 Rorty, 'Inspirational Value', pp. 133–34.
109 See Huckerby, 'The Takeover', Chapter 6, and E. D. Huckerby, 'Finely Aware and Ironically Responsible: Rorty and the Functions of Literature', *Studium Ricerca*, 120.2 (2024), 22–37, https://www.edizionistudium.it/riviste/studium-ricerca-n-2-2024
110 Rorty, 'Inspirational Value', p. 136.
111 See PMN, Part III, in particular.
112 I elaborate this in Huckerby, 'Finely Aware and Ironically Responsible'.

Rorty is not simply stressing the importance of (personal) exposure to artefacts that knock us out of 'knowingness'. Using P. B. Shelley's words, he insists that public reason will always 'follow paths that the imagination has first broken. No words, no reasoning. No imagination, no new words. No such words, no moral or intellectual progress'.[113] The giving and taking of reasons we can articulate in a currently familiar language is a practice that is pragmatically *subsequent* to the creation of strong, stimulating, trailblazing visions and metaphors. Strong poetry is a necessary condition of an everyday language that is responsive to the human condition and avoids calcifying into oppressive cant.[114]

Proper utopianism versus pragmatism about utopian practices

When we zoom out, then, to see Rortyan philosophy as a whole, Rorty is not failing to stress the importance of imagining hegemony-rupturing radical difference or otherness. It looks unjust to say that Rorty is '*actively denying*' the 'merits of imagining alternative ways of living' or 'attempts to argue that the world might or should be otherwise'.[115] He *actively advocates* for such practices, defends imagining difference or novelty as a core skill and practice of any democratic society. He agrees with Levitas's assertion that 'the act of imagination itself, a process which disrupts the closure of the present' is vital.[116] Levitas is not convinced that postmodernist utopian thinking is capable of such re-education of desire,[117] and Rorty would likely agree on this as well: his case is that the pragmatism he advances—a combination of acceptance of contingency and concomitant centring of practices and (collaborative) making—constitutes a positive, constructive response *to* postmodern relativism.

Zoomed out, the pivotal difference between Levitas and Rorty appears to be that Rorty lets go of a constraint. Levitas holds that to be *appropriately* utopian is to articulate or intend a 'realistic' dimension.

---

113 Richard Rorty, 'The Fire of Life', *Poetry*, 191.2 (2007), 129–31 (p. 129).
114 On 'cant', see Richard Rorty, 'Redemption from Egotism: James and Proust as Spiritual Exercises', in *The Rorty Reader*, ed. by Christopher Voparil and Richard J. Bernstein (Malden, MA: Wiley-Blackwell, 2010), pp. 389–406.
115 Levitas, 'For Utopia', p. 30. My emphasis.
116 Levitas, 'For Utopia', p. 39.
117 Levitas, 'For Utopia', p. 38.

To Rorty, talk of anything 'proper' veers into quasi-essentialising and is best avoided. In line with his argument that moral problems do not have algorithmic solutions,[118] his stance on this would presumably be that we cannot know in advance when to spend time and effort on creating radically different, not *yet* directly socially useful, 'strong' imaginaries (without any thought for 'realism') and when to engage in ordinary, pragmatic, political, reformist utopianism. We cannot know in advance when and how to prioritise distinct efforts towards realising what we want more of (our values, aims). Thus, while Rorty never expressed it in these terms, his work supports being pluralistic about utopian imaginaries and practices alike to encourage a range of potentially incommensurable visions and approaches that manifest varying degrees of 'realism'.[119]

It is not, then, that Rorty is against imagining profound difference or working towards radically different social scenarios. When he occasionally objects to 'radicals', it is *not* an objection to those who propose novelty or work towards significant transformation. Pragmatists, Rorty says, 'cannot be radicals' in the singular sense of being someone who believes that

> there is a basic mistake being made, a mistake deep down at the roots. [...] that deep thinking is required to get down to this deep level, and that only there, when all the superstructural appearances have been undercut, can things be seen as they really are.

Pragmatists can, he offers as an alternative, be 'utopians', who 'do not think in terms of mistakes or of depth. They abandon the contrast between superficial appearance and deep reality in favor of the contrast between a painful present and a possibly less painful, dimly seen future'.[120] Being a 'radical' in the sense here defined runs entirely counter to being a pragmatist (it, here, entails a universalising, hypostasising, reifying thinking). He rejects, however, as Levitas does, too, that to be a pragmatist and a utopian is a paradox.

---

118 Rorty, CIS, p. xv.
119 See Rorty, CIS, pp. 89–90.
120 Richard Rorty, 'Feminism and Pragmatism', in *Truth and Progress* (Cambridge: Cambridge University Press, 1998), pp. 202–27, https://doi.org/10.1017/cbo9780511625404.012 (p. 214).

The worries Rorty has about 'radical' revolutionary (all) approaches that spring out from a worldview in which we can get to how things 'really are'—or should be—are moral and pragmatic. Ideologies built on the premise that it is possible to arrive at final solutions, even if they are supposedly in the service of freedom, can and have been used to legitimate the harms they cause with reference to ultimate concerns. Additionally, Rorty holds that universalising prescripts can cause 'humiliation', as a form of brutality that deprives individuals of their tools for sense-making. 'Humiliation' is, Rorty insists, a specific kind of cruelty particular to human animals as enlanguaged beings. 'Ironist intellectuals', Rorty points out, acquire distinctive powers of humiliation:

> Ironism, as I have defined it, results from awareness of the power of redescription. But most people do not want to be redescribed. They want to be taken on their own terms—taken seriously just as they are and just as they talk. The ironist tells them that the language they speak is up for grabs by her and her kind. There is something potentially very cruel about that claim. For the best way to cause people long-lasting pain is to humiliate them by making the things that seemed most important to them look futile, obsolete, and powerless... The redescribing ironist, by threatening one's final vocabulary, and thus one's ability to make sense of oneself in one's own terms rather than hers, suggests that one's self and one's world are futile, obsolete, powerless. Redescription often humiliates.

But replace the 'redescribing ironist' above with (totalitarian/absolutist/universalist) the ideological political revolutionary, and the humiliation resulting from forceful deprivation of one's preferred concepts for self- and sense-making is the same.

Implied here is that strong, radically different imaginaries should not be used to *impose* a blueprint for collective identity-making and action, *if* we want less cruelty and more solidarity in the world. While a subset of the population might find a radically different vision desirable, it will be so alien to the many that imposing it would serve to humiliate. Moreover, privileging revolutionary leaps over more modest, 'ordinary' steps that broader swathes of people can take together risks sacrificing 'social hope' and solidarity. Rorty's response is to pragmatically place democracy before philosophy,[121] to engage in 'continued trial and error'.[122]

It would be a mistake, however, as, for instance, Festenstein and Ramberg argue, an argument Bacon and Rutherford bolster, to say this amounts to 'acquiescence' or 'quietism'.[123] Rortyan anti-representationalism and consequent 'tentativeness' sustains an openness to radical critique that metaphysically grounded framings cannot accommodate. Moreover, the high valorisation of strong poetry in Rortyan philosophy is a push to move beyond the problem of pragmatists being reticent to formulate powerful new visions—a restraint Festenstein observes in Deweyan pragmatism. Rorty is simply insisting that while these strong visions are crucial to human progress and social transformation, we must hold them lightly and proceed with caution.

Rorty offers, then, a novel and distinctly helpful approach to emphasising the social and political necessity of utopianism as a response to postmodernist fragmentation, because it lets us defend utopian practices without essentialising 'utopia' or 'utopianism', or evaluate (apriori, rather than comparatively and experimentally) what the 'proper' functions of utopia are.[124]

Re-forming our way to utopia

Circling back to the start, Levitas's primary objection nevertheless appears to stand: the functional outcome of Rorty's insistence on consolidating our efforts around refining liberal democracy is a closure of political and social horizons. While Rorty might not be 'actively denying' the merits of '*imagining* otherwise', he fails to do so in politics. We should grant that Levitas fails to account for Rorty's rejection of the 'Foucauldian Marxist Left'[125] as rooted in the conviction that it manifests radicalism of that kind

---

121 Richard Rorty, 'The Priority of Democracy to Philosophy', in Richard Rorty, ORT, pp. 175–96.
122 See for instance Richard Rorty, 'Habermas, Derrida, and the Functions of Philosophy', in TP, pp. 307–26 (p. 320, 326).
123 Matthew Festenstein, 'Politics and Acquiescence in Rorty's Pragmatism', *Theoria: A Journal of Social and Political Theory*, 101 (2003), 1–24. Hanne Andrea Kraugerud and Bjørn Torgrim Ramberg., 'The New Loud: Richard Rorty, Quietist?', *Common Knowledge*, 16.1 (2010), 46–85, https://doi.org/10.1215/0961754X-2009-060
124 Cf. Levitas three functions, 'For Utopia', p. 28.
125 Levitas, 'Pragmatism', p. 56.

that is antithetical to pragmatism: a radicalism based on belief in True foundations, final solutions, or totalising 'grids' that leads to dangerous, oppressive kinds of 'closure' (Rorty, too, uses the term 'closure' repeatedly, and is deeply committed to 'openness', 'open conversation' and so on). Still, Levitas's omission does not change the fact that it does seem incongruent that Rorty is so reluctant to engage with more radical political proposals (in the sense of profoundly different from what is, on the ground, unfolding), as is indeed in Bacon and Rutherford's case. It likely seems even *more* incongruent against the backdrop I have just drawn up.[126]

There might be a defence in saying that Rorty did advocate for strong utopian imaginaries as socially and politically necessary, but we cannot chide him for *personally* failing to be a 'strong' poet of political genre (he was, as explicated above, a 'strong poet' within the philosophical one). There is value in arguing, as Bacon and Rutherford do, that Rortyan philosophy commits one to seek more radical alternatives in politics than Rorty did: his philosophy not only invites constant reassessments of what we take as given but also asks us to evaluate these against whether they contribute to increasing human flourishing. It would thus be a failure to live up to the moral decision Rorty placed at the heart of his constructive project if we refuse to engage with alternatives when faced with the blatant failures of the liberal tradition to adequately alleviate the human suffering it presides over. However, even if Rorty did not *refuse* engagement to the extent Levitas describes, or for the reasons she attributes to him, it appears that when it comes to political imaginaries, Rorty will not *allow* proposals to 'inspire', 'recontextualize' what he thought he knew.[127] He argued persuasively against 'taking refuge in self-protecting knowingness about the present' instead of being a 'romantic [utopian] trying to imagine a better future'.[128] Yet it appears to be what he himself does in politics, on behalf of our collective self.

---

126 Levitas's selection of writings by Rorty is specifically limited to texts where he appears to insist on liberalism, democracy and market economy as our only options. This choice serves to shear off Rorty's larger argument and concerns. What remains is 'Conservative Rorty', the inverse of 'Radical Rorty', who emerges, in Bacon and Rutherford, when the remarks she homes in on are sidelined.
127 Rorty, 'Inspirational Value', p. 133.
128 Rorty, 'Inspirational Value', p. 140.

Richard Bernstein suggested it would be a 'mistake' and even a 'slander' to suggest that Rorty's 'meditation on human finitude entails or leads to an acceptance of the *status quo*'.[129] I think that is right, and it is the basic point that Ramberg, as well as Bacon and Rutherford, make. However, it might be that Rorty's *meditations on postmetaphysical philosophy and public reasoning* manifest an intransigence. That is, it might be that an attachment to the *status quo* manifests in Rorty's elaboration of the social and political consequences of embracing human finitude—his imaginary of what follows from accepting the 'contingency' of all 'starting points'.[130] While it would require a separate paper to detail how this plays out in Rortyan thought,[131] I want to make some observations here that point to the conclusion that Rorty's affirmation-and-refinement stance on liberalism is not an anomaly, but a result of an underlying model of thought that shapes his political outlook.

Against the backdrop of Rorty's uncompromising anti-representationalism, it is not only his attachment to liberalism that seems incongruous, but his broader commitment to a public culture that sustains a fairly stable, 'commonsensical' 'final vocabulary'.[132] Rorty tells us that irony (a practice that destabilises the commonsensical and taken as given), should remain an 'inherently private matter', for two reasons. One is that ironists 'have to have' a vocabulary to serve as the basis against which they can be 'reactive', 'alienated'. The other is that he 'cannot imagine' a culture which socialises its 'youth' to be 'continually dubious about their own process of socialization'.[133] There is a 'final vocabulary' that is 'inherited', and which most people perceive as common sense. To be 'commonsensical is to take for granted that statements formulated in that final vocabulary suffice to describe and judge the beliefs, actions and lives of those who employ alternative

---

129   Richard J. Bernstein, 'What Is the Difference That Makes a Difference? Gadamer, Habermas, and Rorty', *Proceedings of the Biennial Meeting of the Philosophy of Science Association*, 1982 (1983), 331–59, https://doi.org/10.1086/psaprocbienmeetp.1982.2.192429, p. 35.
130   'Starting points': see 'Pragmatism, Relativism, and Irrationalism', p. 726.
131   This paper is now forthcoming as 'False Starts and Poetic Ends: Edifying Philosophy, Literary Culture, and Rortyan Pragmatism as Poeticism', in *Philosophy and the Mirror of Nature at 45*, ed. by David Rondel (Cambridge: Cambridge University Press, 2026).
132   CIS, pp. 73–74.
133   CIS, pp. 87–88.

final vocabularies'.[134] Rorty does hope for a culture in which common sense would include being unreflectively historicist and nominalist,[135] subscribe to a kind of "ironism light", and this does entail that such a culture would be less firmly attached to its hegemonic vocabularies than the metaphysical culture that preceded it. But Rorty still maintains that 'public rhetoric' must not undermine what counts as commonsensical lest the 'youth' should fail to be properly 'socialized'.[136]

Thus, when Rorty conceptualises public deliberation, he is not only observing that children inherit a vocabulary and for a while, a developmental stage, take it for granted. He posits a need to preserve, or at least not continually or too radically undermine this vocabulary. In CIS, ironism is pitched as the opposite of common sense, and the ironist as someone who not only reacts against this calcified vocabulary but *needs* it in order to emerge as an ironist.[137] The kind of open, 'novelistic', embrace of descriptive plurality, ways of talking and living, that Rorty on the whole uplifts as exemplary,[138] is here deliberately constrained.

The model Rorty builds on here seems, ironically enough (in the non-Rortyan sense), to be Western philosophy. Ironic because he wrote PMN to topple the hierarchies and self-perceptions of this tradition. Rorty's view of public common sense as opposed to private doubting can, I think, be traced back to the above-mentioned distinction between the 'normal' and 'abnormal' that Rorty takes up already in PMN. And this is intrinsic to his first attempt to forge a vision of the consequences of his own sweeping anti-essentialism: a postmetaphysical, 'hermeneutic' and 'edifying' culture. While this vision lauds the 'abnormal' and non-consensus seeking discourse as generative, Rorty still here makes it clear that while we should pragmatise epistemology and 'objectivity', these 'normal' practices are primary to human education and self-formation, as well as to the shared, and thus largely normalised 'Conversation of Mankind'.[139]

---

134 CIS, pp. 73–74.
135 CIS, p. 87.
136 CIS, pp. 87–88.
137 CIS, p. 88
138 See, for instance, Richard Rorty, 'Heidegger, Kundera, and Dickens', in Richard Rorty, *Essays on Heidegger and Others* (Cambridge: Cambridge University Press, 2010 [1991]), pp. 66–82, https://doi.org/10.1017/cbo9780511609039.005
139 See PMN, Part III.

Rorty might be right: it might be that in practice, for, for instance, psychological or sociological reasons, we must be cautious about destabilising public discourse if we aim to sustain 'social hope'. The point I am trying to make is that *his attachment to liberal democracy and market economy might have deep enough roots that we cannot dismiss them as anomalous remarks*.[140] We might need to examine if Rorty inability to 'imagine' more radical political alternatives is a manifestation of an inability to imagine more novel modes of intellectual discourse or 'socialization', an inability, perhaps, to move beyond the realm of philosophy and properly into that of poetry. But Rorty might also be wrong. I understand that part of Rorty's concern is that, as a community (not just as individuals) we need a shared vocabulary and a story about who we are in order to forge collective agency. Stringing together a story about how the past and present might hang together with a utopian future is about collective self-making and creating the moral locus from which we act. I appreciate that he believed liberalism represented our best bet for providing the necessary unifying narrative to (national) communities that harbour a vast range of beliefs and desires. Still, actively sidelining ironist advocacy as a helpful public intervention seems at best a missed opportunity. At worst it comes across as capricious. For the society he cannot imagine might very well be easily envisioned by others and might better serve the alleviation of suffering.

I would argue that becoming 'dubious about [one's] own process of socialization' is proving helpful to many. Segments of the 'youth' today are deeply engaged in publicly working out a thoroughly anti-essentialist conception of gender and gender roles, for instance. At the heart of the ongoing fight for trans rights and a fully gender equal and inclusive society, is a profound 'grappling' with essentialism. The problem blocking our path to less cruelty here is *not* the radical ironism of the young, but the lack of broad acceptance of ironism as a point of view, and a public understanding of how essentialism/anti-essentialism

---

140 It might also go beyond Rorty's explicit (Hegelian) wish to 'hold his time in thought', as he repeatedly stated. If the only model Rorty can imagine is based on the educational and discursive model philosophy as a discipline is constructed upon, what is being held in thought is the Western philosophical tradition—or at least it is being foregrounded at the expense of the demands, challenges and intellectual and political shifts of the latter decades of the twentieth century.

(the postmodern inheritance) shapes this discourse.[141] That we might need to talk more about anti-essentialism, be forthright about our 'ironist doubts' about commonsensical public vocabularies, is further testified to by the observation that vehement opposition to anti-essentialism ('postmodernism') is a hallmark of the rhetoric of autocrats and kleptocrats like Donald Trump and Vladimir Putin.

It is no coincidence that Trump's social platform is called 'Truth Social'. Extolling the virtues of Objective Truth in the most reactionary essentialising sense is the bread and butter of far/alt-right crusaders such as James A. Lindsey, who critiques what he calls 'critical social justice ideology', postmodernism, and critical theory, while lauding Enlightenment Rationalism and scientism. I do not think the best strategic response to reactionaries' expropriation of Truth is to proclaim 'you don't own the truth, *we* do' (we might feel justified to say so, but it will only backfire; politicisation leaves no room for politics, only partisanship). I think the better strategy is to say, with Rorty, that there is no truth. There is no such thing as a 'real man', or a 'real woman', or a 'genuine American' or a 'proper family'. We could start saying this aloud about all populist, sloganistic ideas that cannot be put forth *sans* an essentialising worldview to undergird them. We need to put forth 'possible and important' alternatives, narratives that sustain 'social hope', and utopian imaginaries to show that working towards these is not dependent of first digging down to Truths that compel everyone to agree—to arrive at the same, and foundational starting point. We can start from where we are.

Thus, in the end, while I do not agree with how Levitas makes her case against Rorty, she does identify a problem. And Rortyans wanting to partake in the pursuit of a more 'Radical Rorty', as advanced by Ramberg, Bacon and Rutherford, would be well-served by exploring it further.[142] Starting from where we are does not entail 'tinkering' with what we have. While Bacon and Rutherford argue that Rorty's 'philosophy should commit him to a political radicalism that goes beyond what he proposed',[143]

---

141 I am fully aware that people defending trans rights can also hold entrenched and essentialising ideas about gender. I am observing that the emergence of overtly anti-essentialist views on gender was a shift that facilitated this cause.
142 See also Chapter 3 in this collection.
143 Bacon and Rutherford, 'Rorty, Habermas, and Radical Social Criticism', p. 202.

I am suggesting that Rorty's embrace of contingency should commit him to a more radical philosophy than he articulated—one he gets closest to in his talk of a fully 'poeticized culture'.

There is another way of construing the word 'reform'. It does not have to mean incremental enhancements made to improve a system, institution, practice or policy, or improving one's own behaviour and character in a moral sense. Re-forming might be pictured as a practice of *forming again,* as opposed to merely 'tinkering' with what is. But *to form again requires first coming apart.* You must be sufficiently un-settled to re-settle in a recognisably different configuration. Rorty saw this, and rightly advocated for the need for regular encounters with 'strong' poetry, 'stimulating works', capable of unsettling settled selves. Not for the sake of it, but to set up a potential for change to follow.[144] Even if Rorty did not explain 'reform' in this manner, it is an understanding of it he likely would have recognised.

Today, still, the most unsettling proposal in Rortyan philosophy is radical embrace of the contingency of all starting points.[145] If it is, then this proposal also has the greatest potential to cause change. Thus one key lesson to take from the exploration in this chapter, is that Rorty's specific and material utopian vision of a fully 'poeticized' culture, which responds to the embrace of contingency by shifting attention to human conversation and (inter)actions, to what we make and how and why, is a worthwhile vision to pursue. Not because it is attached to liberalism or market economy, but, on the contrary, because a culture in which this vision was more fully realised would better facilitate radical critique and open-ended political experimentation. As Bacon and Rutherford demonstrate, this move 'grants Rorty a route to radical criticism which is foreclosed' to those less aware of maintaining anti-essentialist sensibilities.[146] Another takeaway to consider is that we might have to take the risk of moving 'ironism' (anti-essentialist advocacy or even activism) into public discourse. 'Risk' because further destabilising the idea of Truth in an already epistemically fragmented political landscape

---

144 See Huckerby, 'The Takeover', Chapter 6 ('Unsettling Iridescence'), and 'Finely Aware and Ironically Responsible'.
145 Cf. Rorty, 'Pragmatism, Relativism, and Irrationalism', p. 726.
146 Bacon and Rutherford, 'Rorty, Habermas, and Radical Social Criticism', p. 195. Their specific example is Habermas.

certainly is one. Nevertheless, doing so might be one strand of how we work to counter the authoritarian rhetoric enclosing us. It is an unsettling proposition in its own right: rather than being 'private' about our ironist convictions, using them to forge interventions against authoritarian narratives emerges as a crucial project for our time.

5. Pragmatist Eirenism in Post-Truth Society

Michela Bella

In a 1986 paper on 'Freud and Moral Reflection', Rorty suggested that the difference Freud scholars recognise between the 'energetic' and 'hermeneutic' aspects of psychoanalysis can be seen—if one adopts an 'eirenic attitude'—not as opposite poles in tension but as two compatible, alternative descriptions.[1] Taking Rorty's suggestion seriously, I want to broaden Rorty's statement and read eirenism as one of the attitudes he developed in *Contingency, Irony and Solidarity* (1989). What I want to propose is that Rorty's 'pragmatist eirenism' can be posited as an antidote to the dangers of the post-truth society and its tendency to hypostatise alternative viewpoints as poles in a contradiction. While Rorty rarely uses the term eirenism, he takes it up in significant passages, for example, when he explains that mere philosophical discussions can create tensions that do not necessarily exist in real-life scenarios. For Rorty, as in the cases of Eddington's paradox of the macroscopic/microscopic descriptions of a table, and different aspects of Freudian psychoanalysis, these debates pit

---

1 Richard Rorty, 'Freud and Moral Reflection', in *Pragmatism's Freud: The Moral Disposition of Psychoanalysis*, ed. by Joseph H. Smith and William Kerrigan (Baltimore, MD: Johns Hopkins University Press, 1986), pp. 1–27. Later published in *Richard Rorty, Essay on Heidegger and Others* (Cambridge: Cambridge University Press, 1991), pp. 143–63, https://doi.org/10.1017/cbo9780511609039.010 (p. 151). I would like to express my gratitude to Elin Danielsen Huckerby and Marianne Janack, the editors of this volume. I am grateful to Elin for her careful, passionate and always supportive editorial work on earlier versions of this chapter.

conflicting vocabularies against each other. Yet in practice, these prove able to coexist peacefully.²

Eirenism captures a significant aspect of Rorty's constructive project and one that warrants systematic investigation. It highlights the importance of not only distancing oneself from any univocal worldview, but also taking (or not taking) actions to promote peaceful coexistence. On the one hand, eirenism involves using an ironic approach; on the other, eirenism helps ironism reach its full pragmatist potential in fostering social change.³ In particular, recovering the notion of 'eirenism' in a pragmatist sense can help us respond to the reductionism that characterises dogmatism, fanaticism, and extremism in our post-truth societies. This focus moreover helps enhance Rorty's pragmatist inheritance and adds important nuances to his ironism that are useful today.

In this chapter, I therefore explore Rorty's eirenic attitude from two angles. First, I look to the past to strengthen Rorty's pragmatist-Jamesian inheritance. This move helps me strengthen my view of Rorty as a philosopher who shares pragmatism's conception of the social role of philosophy as a discipline that investigates issues of today and works to make a better future. I then envision how Rorty's understanding of contingency and solidarity as deeply intertwined can be relevant in contemporary debates on a post-truth society, all the more so when viewed from an eirenic perspective.

Eirenism as pragmatist inheritance

The relationship between Rorty and scholars of classical pragmatism remains one of contention. However, as Christopher Voparil asserts,

---

2   Cf. Richard Rorty, *Contingency, Irony and Solidarity* (Cambridge: Cambridge University Press, 1989), https://doi.org/10.1017/cbo9780511804397, p. 12.

3   My emphasis on the pragmatist eirenism of Rorty's project probably goes in the direction of Sharyn Clough's reading of Rorty's ironic liberalism as a form of pacifist activism, in Sharyn Clough, 'Rorty as Liberal Ironist Peace Warrior', in *The Ethics, Epistemology, and Politics of Richard Rorty*, ed. by Giancarlo Marchetti, Routledge Studies in American Philosophy (Oxon, New York: Routledge, 2021), pp. 29–49, https://doi.org/10.4324/9780429324734-3 Moreover, this reading also helps frame Rorty's questioning of the extent to which philosophy could produce social change. As Marianne Janack recalls, his critical stance represents a tension (also experienced by feminist philosophers) between his appreciation of philosophy and his view of philosophy as a problematic discipline: see Marianne Janack, 'Introduction', in *Feminist Interpretations of Richard Rorty*, ed. by Marianne Janack (University Park, PA: Pennsylvania State University Press, 2010), pp. 1–17 (p. 2ff). See also Chapter 2 of this collection.

'the path forward [for pragmatism] runs through, rather than around or against, Rorty'.[4] Without minimising points of contention, Voparil's recent *Reconstructing Pragmatism: Richard Rorty and the Classical Pragmatists* puts to rest parodies of Rorty as lacking understanding of classical pragmatism, and firmly establishes that Rorty belongs as a canonical figure to this tradition, alongside Charles Sanders Peirce, William James, John Dewey and Jane Addams.

I want to home in on the roots of eirenism in Jamesian pragmatism to show that Rorty's articulation of this attitude emerges against an established and useful pragmatist backdrop. Moreover, as I move to the usefulness of Rorty to post-truth societies in the second part, this allows me to draw on resources from others, too. Rortyan insights for understanding the risks connected to post-truth society and gleaning a way out are made clearer in light of James's view of contingency as the locus where solidaristic attitudes and peaceful relations may flourish. Rorty reinterpreted these in a different historical-cultural framework, but illuminating their origins lends force to both Rorty's argument and mine.[5] Moreover, while I focus on the James-Rorty relationship, I am convinced that the rediscovery of the pragmatist origins of eirenism can also be applied to other classical pragmatists, particularly Dewey, Addams and Mary Parker Follett. Exploring these connections could provide further insights into the ways Rorty's ideas could contribute to current social and political debates. Thus, while Rorty's view of eirenism provides a good starting point, what I am working towards is a comprehensive definition of eirenism that can encompass various pragmatist tools designed (whether implicitly or explicitly) to address conflicts such as James's ethics of beliefs, Peirce's notion of vagueness, Addams' sympathetic knowledge, Follett's integration of interests, and Dewey's perspective on problematic situations. Therefore, this chapter also serves as a foundational step toward further exploring what I call 'pragmatist eirenism'.

Rorty's specific eirenic strategy can benefit us today in preventing radicalisation within a post-truth society as a call for expanding our

---

4   Christopher Voparil, *Reconstructing Pragmatism: Richard Rorty and the Classical Pragmatists* (Oxford: Oxford University Press, 2021), https://doi.org/10.1093/oso/9780197605721.001.0001, p. 5.
5   Rorty and James seem to hold analogous attitudes toward philosophical activism. On the distance between Rorty's and Addams's dispositions see Voparil, *Reconstructing Pragmatism*, pp. 226–57.

moral vocabulary by engaging with others' lived or imaginary stories. In my interpretation of Rorty's concept of 'eirenism', this involves using irony and curiosity to challenge absolutist mindsets and the authoritarian tendency to see things in increasingly extreme, sometimes violent, oppositions. Rorty's blurring of the division between reason and emotion remains relevant today, as it can encourage the redefinition of emotional habits into more flexible, corrigible attitudes. Re-examining Rorty's cultural project through an eirenic lens underscores his effort to reconcile and integrate different perspectives in support of a vision of social progress that considers resorting to violence as a last option.

Linguistic contingency and pragmatist eirenism

Rorty makes several references to James in CIS, notably in the chapters devoted to the contingency of language (Ch. 1), self (Ch. 2) and community (Ch. 3). In each of these chapters, Rorty's characterisation of contingency is formulated in a more Jamesian vein than Rorty acknowledges. Rorty's first use of James appears as he articulates his break with the traditional notion of language, with the help of Davidson and Wittgenstein.

The role James plays in this case for the contingency of language is that of having contributed to sinking the idea of an 'intrinsic nature of reality' and dismissing the copy theory of truth, in accordance with the pragmatist belief that facts and values are deeply intertwined.[6] Rorty makes his Jamesian point by endorsing Davidson's attempt to break entirely with 'the notion that language is a medium—a medium either of representation or of expression'.[7] According to Rorty/Davidson, taking

---

6   C.f. Richard Rorty, *Philosophy and Social Hope* (London and New York: Penguin, 1999), pp. 237–38. On Rorty's dismissal of truth via Davidson and James see, among others, Robert Brandom, 'Introduction', in *Rorty and His Critics*, ed. by Robert Brandom (Malden, Oxford: Blackwell Publishers, 2000), pp. ix–xx; Mike Sandbothe, 'Davidson and Rorty on Truth', in *A House Divided: Comparing Analytic and Continental Philosophers*, ed. by Carlos Prado (Amherst: Humanities Press, 2003), pp. 235–58; Giancarlo Marchetti, 'The Philosophy of Richard Rorty', in *The Ethics, Epistemology, and Politics of Richard Rorty*, ed. by Giancarlo Marchetti (New York and London: Routledge, 2021), pp. 1–26, https://doi.org/10.4324/9780429324734-1

7   Rorty, CIS, p. 10. Rorty's reading here echoes his interpretation of Davidson's identification of persons with 'sufficiently coherent sets of beliefs and desires' (Rorty, 'Freud and Moral Reflection', p. 147). Davidson argues that

language as a medium is a way to reintroduce a metaphysical conception of consciousness within a naturalistic framework. Such a conception of language does not alter the traditional dualistic subject-object view wherein language/consciousness is the locus of human beliefs and desires. In this traditional view, beliefs and desires are accidental entities that express and represent the self in relation to the world, and their value depends on their capacity to copy internal or external reality. As Rorty puts it, on this view, '[b]eliefs are [...] criticizable because they fail to correspond to reality. Desires are criticizable because they fail to correspond to the essential nature of the human self—because they are "irrational" or "unnatural"'.[8] Rorty does not see beliefs and desires as lacking unique and independent characteristics within human experience/conduct. But he rejects the representationalist view that their primary purpose is to reflect fundamental entities, such as external 'reality' or the internal 'nature of the human self'. In this way, Rorty's anti-representationalist approach aligns with James's arguments against what he called copy theories of truth in *Pragmatism* and *The Meaning of Truth*, as well as all the implications that such a conception carries with it.[9]

Davidson's instrumental conception of language also reminds Rorty of Wittgenstein's notion of games as developed in his more pragmatist phase.[10] Neither philosopher tries to reduce language to any analytic definition nor to turn language into a metaphysical entity. According to Rorty, they 'treat alternative vocabularies as more like alternative

---

    communication processes presuppose attributing a broadly shared set of beliefs and desires to others, and against intellectualistic views of irrationality, he finds reasons for rational and irrational behaviours. Freud's 'partitioning of the mind' comes in to support an explanation of 'common form of irrationality' (Donald Davidson, 'Paradoxes of Irrationality', in *Problems of Rationality* (Oxford: Oxford University Press, 2004), pp. 169–88, https://doi.org/10.1093/0198237545.003.0011. In this view, we cannot deduce rational choices logically, as common irrational habits have rational motifs as well.

8   Rorty, CIS, p. 10.

9   William James, *Pragmatism* (Cambridge, MA, and London: Harvard University Press, 1975); *The Meaning of Truth* (Cambridge, MA, and London: Harvard University Press, 1975).

10 In Rorty's vocabulary, they walk the fine line between reductionist (analytical) and expansionist (continental) outcomes. For connections between Wittgenstein and pragmatism see Anna Boncompagni, *Wittgenstein and Pragmatism* (London: Palgrave Macmillan, 2016), https://doi.org/10.1057/978-1-137-58847-0; Rosa Calcaterra, *Contingency and Normativity. The Challenges of Richard Rorty* (Leiden and Boston, MA: Brill Rodopi, 2019), https://doi.org/10.1163/9789004393837

tools than like bits of a jigsaw puzzle'.[11] Rorty encourages us to give up thinking of vocabularies in terms of pieces of a puzzle because this view implies they are commensurable, interchangeable, and compatible parts of a 'grand unified super vocabulary'.[12] His pragmatist use of Davidson's philosophy of language and the late Wittgenstein's notion of games points instead toward 'a picture of intellectual and moral progress as a history of increasingly useful metaphors rather than of increasing understanding of how things really are'.[13] Significantly, Rorty here hints at what I called his pragmatist eirenism when he argues that '[m]erely philosophical' questions, like Arthur Eddington's two tables paradox, create 'factitious theoretical quarrel[s]' that do not exist on the practical level. Such quarrels seem to have as their primary and intentional goal pitting against each other vocabularies that 'have proved capable of peaceful coexistence'[14] The Eddington paradox is an excellent example of what Wittgenstein called 'mental cramps', that is to say, 'merely philosophical' quarrels that have no effects on everyday life except for creating 'factitious theoretical quarrels'.[15]

This observation sheds light on both the pragmatist-Jamesian background I want to emphasise in Rorty's view of the contingency of language and on the idea of eirenism I wish to establish. Eirenism is a concept that emphasises the significance of not adhering to a singular viewpoint *and* actively promoting the peaceful coexistence of many. It involves an ironic approach *and* also enables ironism to achieve its full potential in driving social progress. When closely examined, every situation may be problematic in the sense that conflicting vocabularies can address it. For Rorty, however, the point is moving from the abstract level of analysis to the practical one. If language is contingent, different vocabularies may conflict on specific issues but coexist in practice.

Not unlike James, moreover, Rorty suggests we instead view the ways we address conflicting situations as saying something about

---

11   Rorty, CIS, p. 11.
12   Rorty, CIS, p. 11. C.f. Richard Rorty, *Philosophy and the Mirror of Nature* (Princeton, NJ: Princeton University Press, 1979), p. 347.
13   CIS, p. 9.
14   CIS, p. 12.
15   CIS, p. 12. For Wittgenstein's description of 'mental cramp', see Ludwig Wittgenstein, *The Blue and Brown Books: Preliminary Studies for the 'Philosophical Investigations'* (Oxford: Blackwell, 1958), p. 1 ff.

our mentality. Rorty distinguishes between revolutionary and non-revolutionary thinkers and methods of reasoning. Revolutionary thinkers like Galileo, Hegel and Yeats aspire to solve linguistic conflicts by creating something new to replace what they had before. As to the method, they favour a 'gradual trial-and-error creation of a new, third, vocabulary'.[16] Non-revolutionary philosophers, instead, share a sort of antagonistic attitude resulting from the dichotomising assumption that only one vocabulary can survive by prevailing over the other. Their logic is inferential and it fails to give birth to new vocabularies. Rorty finds this view to be short-sighted because, first, it takes one part for the whole—as mentioned, conflicting vocabularies *de facto* coexist in practice. Second, it cannot look beyond existing vocabularies and imagine new ones, as revolutionary philosophers do. Non-revolutionary philosophers' partial and non-future-oriented vision forces them to struggle to assert the truth of one vocabulary over the other, or assert how one vocabulary can comprehend and explain the other. This antagonistic mentality offers no other solution but to reduce one of the two conflicting vocabularies to an accessory entity of the other. Such a narrow mentality is precisely what Rorty's pragmatist eirenism avoids:

> The proper analogy is with the invention of new tools to take the place of old tools. To come up with such a vocabulary is more like discarding the lever and the chock because one has envisaged the pully, or like discarding gesso and tempera because one has now figured out how to size canvas properly.[17]

That is, from a contingent perspective, which echoes the classical pragmatists' philosophical reception of Darwin's theory of evolution, new creations come up to cope with changing conditions.[18]

Thinking of social practices as 'creations' instead of 'discoveries' renders us open to future changes, and also advances Rorty's 'nonteleological view of intellectual history'. To revisit his categories of

---

16   CIS, p. 12.
17   CIS, p. 12.
18   Classical pragmatists believe that novelty is a genuine and significant aspect of reality. It is not a predictable factor emerging from the old, although it is continuous with existing reality. See Michela Bella, 'Novelty and Causality in William James's Pluralistic Universe', *European Journal of Pragmatism and American Philosophy*, 11.2 (2019), https://doi.org/10.4000/ejpap.1668; Maria Regina Brioschi, *Creativity Between Experience and Cosmos: C.S. Peirce and A.N. Whitehead on Novelty* (München: Verlag Karl Alber, 2020, https://doi.org/10.5771/9783495823958).

thinkers, this view of intellectual history can be considered revolutionary for its distance from dualistic and teleological perspectives. For Rorty, the classical dualistic view of language goes hand in hand with teleologism. Therefore, renouncing representationalist conceptions of language helps abandon the idea that the history of language follows a purposeful design.[19] In his philosophy of language, Davidson learned the Darwinian lesson of thinking about living organisms and their history in terms of 'constellations' of purposeless contingencies.[20] Rorty's narrative about intellectual history thus conceives new vocabularies as 'metaphoric redescriptions' of nature rather than insights into the 'intrinsic nature of nature'.[21] Against this backdrop, looking for eternal relations or goals in a world where things and relations result from continuous changes makes no sense. Instead, we must, with Rorty, think in terms of 'causal questions, as opposed to questions about adequacy of representation or expression'.[22]

Pragmatist eirenism and the contingency of selfhood

Rorty's most extended reference to James in CIS occurs in the chapter on the contingency of selfhood. Davidson and Wittgenstein are Rorty's more significant allies for displaying the contingency of language; Freud and Nietzsche for demonstrating the contingency of selfhood and the worth of such a description.[23] However, James's continued presence testifies to his substantial role in shaping Rorty's contingent view of both language and selfhood.

Rorty includes a lengthy quotation from James's essay 'On a Certain Blindness in Human Beings' (1899) and connects it with Freud's description of the contingency of self-identity.[24] James portrays the

---

19 That it has 'a *telos*– such as the discovery of truth, or the emancipation of humanity' (CIS, p. 17).
20 CIS, p. 16.
21 CIS, p. 16.
22 CIS, p. 15.
23 Rorty's idea of the history of culture is explicitly in line with Nietzsche's idea of truth as a 'mobile army of metaphors' (CIS, p. 17). Moreover, his description of non-revolutionary thinkers reminds of Nietzsche's *On the Genealogy of Morality*.
24 William James, 'On a Certain Blindness in Human Beings', in *Talks to Teachers on Psychology. And to Students on Some of Life's Ideals* (Cambridge, MA, and London: Harvard University Press, 1983), pp. 132–49.

epiphany of his blindness toward others' beliefs and desires. He recalls his spontaneous disappointment with the clearings of 'coves' characterising the landscape, during a journey in the mountains of North Carolina. Only after a small talk with a local mountaineer could he grasp the 'inward significance of the situation' and blame his blindness. Rorty cites James saying:

> The forest had been destroyed; and what had 'improved' it out of existence was hideous, a sort of ulcer, without a single element of artificial grace to make up for the loss of Nature's beauty.' But, James continues, when a farmer comes out of the cabin and tells him that 'we ain't happy here unless we're getting one of those coves under cultivation', he realizes that 'I had been losing the whole inward significance of the situation. Because to me the clearings spoke of naught but denudation, I thought that to those whose sturdy arms and obedient axes had made them they could tell no other story. But when they looked on the hideous stumps, what they thought of was personal victory [...]. In short, the clearing which to me was a mere ugly picture on the retina, was to them a symbol redolent with moral memories and sang a very paean of duty, struggle, and success. I had been as blind to the peculiar ideality of their conditions as they certainly would also have been to the ideality of mine, had they had a peep at my strange indoor academic ways of life at Cambridge'.[25]

James's invitation is to increase our sensitivity by expanding the margins of our experience. Connecting with embodied beliefs and desires helps us grow in awareness and responsiveness. It is only through concrete, living encounters that we can start recognising more and more distant fellows, as Rorty says, as 'one of us' and thus feel responsible for them.[26]

Voparil sees this well-known passage as an important moment of Rorty's assimilation of James's ethics of beliefs. It foresees Rorty's reception of the idea that we are morally responsible for the concrete claims of other human fellows,[27] as Rorty developed later in *Philosophy*

---

25 CIS, p. 38.
26 CIS, p. xv; p. 191. Of course, this is not a sufficient condition for James and Rorty (Voparil, *Reconstructing Pragmatism*, p. 121). Rorty stresses the importance of reading novels to get in touch with different human stories: 'I shall define an "ironist" as someone who fulfills three conditions: (I) She has radical and continuing doubts about the final vocabulary she currently uses, because she has been impressed by other vocabularies, vocabularies taken as final by people or books she has encountered' (CIS, p. 73).
27 Voparil, *Reconstructing Pragmatism*, p. 10.

and Social Hope and *Philosophy as Cultural Politics*. The experience of grasping the 'peculiar ideality' of concrete situations reveals to James and Rorty how human experience is variegated and irreducible to one 'single vision' perspective.[28] A 'richer universe' and a 'more inclusive whole' are the cardinal points guiding the moral philosopher's choices, together with an attentive and sympathetic ear for those who are suffering.[29]

This Jamesian shift in perspective on how conflicting vocabularies can address the same situation turns out, for Rorty, to be a fundamental step towards appreciating the cultural significance of Freud's lesson. In Rorty's reading, Freud is 'as much a pragmatist as James and as much a perspectivalist as Nietzsche'.[30] He confronted cultural blindness and moral judgement of human urges, showing that these cases do not constitute a break from humankind. They cannot be dismissed based on a univocal and morally ideal self-image, according to which they are classified as 'extreme, inhuman, and unnatural'.[31] The variety of human experiences is more multifaceted and profound than expected.

Freud's investigation radicalises James's anti-deterministic conviction of the lack of proportionality between stimuli and responses. In Rorty's words, for different persons, our (sense of) self can depend on '[a]nything from the sound of a word through the color of a leaf to the feel of a piece of skin [...] Any seemingly random constellation of such things can set the tone of a life'. Even the most peculiar idealities, as shown by James and Freud, are 'a commandment no less unconditional because it may be intelligible to, at most, only one person'.[32] An orientation towards contingency inevitably calls for increased attentiveness toward others' peculiar beliefs and desires, even those felt to be unfamiliar or incoherent.

However, even though Freud's new vocabulary is of the revolutionary kind, it is not necessarily competitive in a detrimental sense. 'He just wants to give us one more redescription of things to be filed alongside all the others, one more vocabulary, one more set of metaphors which

---

28 CIS, p. xiv.
29 James, 'On a Certain Blindness in Human Beings', p. 158.
30 CIS, p. 39.
31 CIS, p. 38.
32 CIS, p. 37.

he thinks have a chance of being used and thereby literalized'.³³ Freud, along with James, Nietzsche and others, are likened for their spirit of 'playfulness and irony' in grasping language's creative and recreational power. Their aim was not, and could not be, to discover 'The One Right Description',³⁴ for such a reductionist attitude did not make sense in their contingent, rich, and multifaceted worldview. Indeed, their 'lighter', though not naive, view of language speaks of a de-divinised view of reality, within which they believed to be contributing to the development of human society through broadening, instead of narrowing, the 'repertoire of alternative descriptions'.³⁵

The above is the crux of my point. Rorty suggests we adopt a conciliatory attitude to facilitate peaceful coexistence. This is even more clearly expressed in 'Freud and Moral Reflection' (1986/1991), which appeared in a collection devoted to the connections between Freud and pragmatism. As mentioned at the start, Rorty here argues that the difference between the 'energetic' and 'hermeneutic' aspects of psychoanalysis can be read not as opposite poles in tension but as two alternative descriptions. Rorty calls his Davidsonian-Wittgentenian-pragmatist attitude towards contradictory descriptions of psychoanalysis 'eirenic'. He observes how Freud's 'conscious-unconscious distinction cuts across the human-animal and reason-instinct distinctions' in an innovative way that, instead of pointing to representing a fundamental image of self-identity, makes self-knowledge 'a matter of self-enrichment'.³⁶

To further clarify Freud's role in driving the perspective shift Rorty wants to consolidate, he examines conflicting descriptions that can arise within the therapeutic relationship. The analyst and the patient have different purposes and require different methods within the same setting. The analyst's task is to ensure that the treatment proceeds. To

---

33 CIS, p. 38. '[S]omething supposed to replace all other vocabularies, something which claimed to represent reality, but simply [...] one more vocabulary, one more human project, one person's chosen metaphoric'.
34 CIS, p. 39.
35 Rorty, CIS, p. 38. Rorty's interpretation of Freud and James is quite original. Generally speaking, scholars tend to divide James and Freud for their different understanding of the unconscious. See, among others, Gerald Myers, 'James and Freud', *The Journal of Philosophy*, 11 (1990), 593–99, https://doi.org/10.5840/jphil1990871113
36 Rorty, 'Freud and Moral Reflection', p. 150.

achieve this goal, they benefit from considering the patient's narrative and behaviour in terms of stimulus and response, which entails adopting causal models to interpret the conversation's effects. The patient, although oriented toward the same goal, cannot use these models of self-reflection to proceed with the treatment; to safeguard their psycho-physical integrity, they must think of their unconscious life 'in conversational terms':[37]

> These two ways of thinking seem to me alternative tools, useful for different purposes, rather than contradictory claims. I do not think (despite the arguments of, for example, Paul Ricoeur and Roy Schafer) that there is a tension in Freud's thought between 'energetics' and 'hermeneutics.' Rather, the two seem to me to be as compatible as, for example, microstructural and macrostructural descriptions of the same object (e.g., Eddington's table). But to defend my eirenic attitude properly I should offer an account of 'resistance' that chimes with Davidson's interpretation of the unconscious, and I have not yet figured out how to do this.[38]

What Rorty calls 'my eirenic attitude' entails resisting the ideological/exclusive assumption of either perspective, i.e., the energetic or the hermeneutic, in the belief that these are not 'contradictory claims,' but 'alternative' and 'compatible' instruments, 'useful for different purposes'.[39]

By looking at contradictory descriptions as alternative descriptions helpful for differing purposes and actors, Rorty de-potentiates the conflictual dimension that linguistic incoherence can produce. He achieves this through a pragmatist shift in perspective that is not confined to the psychoanalytic framework. Alternative descriptions are not necessarily competitive in an antagonistic sense (i.e., mutually exclusive). They only reveal something about changing realities in different contexts, about different purposes, and much about our mental attitudes. In other words, emphasising the conflictual side of perspectives exposes an absolutist mentality, according to which only one perspective can survive by getting the better of the other. Freud gave us

---

37 Rorty, 'Freud and Moral Reflection', p. 151.
38 Rorty, 'Freud and Moral Reflection', p. 150, emphasis mine.
39 It is worth noting that Rorty links his conciliatory reading of conflicting descriptions of psychoanalysis to the Eddington paradox he used in CIS.

a new technique for achieving a genuinely stable character: the technique of lending a sympathetic ear to our own tendencies to instability, by treating them as alternative ways of making sense of the past, ways that have as good a claim on our attention as do the familiar beliefs and desires that are available to introspection [...] He let us see alternative narratives and alternative vocabularies as instruments for change, rather than as candidates for a correct depiction of how things are in themselves.[40]

Freud thus plays a significant role in Rorty's conciliatory approach. By attentively hearing out conflicting tendencies to reconcile with one's history, Freud sets the stage for Rorty's pragmatist eirenism: a willingness to accept 'alternative narratives and alternative vocabularies as instruments for change'.

Rorty's attention to Freudian psychoanalysis is, then, part and parcel of his attempt to escape the fixed and dichotomic mentality consistent with the Platonic view dominating Western philosophy. '[W]hat Dewey called "a brood and nest of dualisms"',[41] is a reductionist mentality that urges us 'to look for an escape from time and chance',[42] to search for 'universality by the transcendence of contingency'.[43] When it comes to descriptions, a univocal, non-evolving and non-contingent worldview cannot but emphasise contradictions and annihilate practical alternatives. Instead, pragmatist thinking offers 'a hopeful, melioristic, experimental frame of mind' for philosophy and politics.[44] Additionally, Rorty suggests that a lack of solidarity characterises the Platonic view.[45] As argued in PMN, Rorty wishes to substitute the epistemological claim guiding philosophy, centring on the concept of 'commensurability,' with acceptance of 'incommensurability' and a narrative understanding of

---

40 Rorty, 'Freud and Moral Reflection', p. 152.
41 Rorty, PSH, p. xii.
42 Rorty, CIS, p. xiii.
43 Rorty, CIS, p. 25.
44 Rorty, PSH, p. 24.
45 In *Philosophy and the Mirror of Nature*, he recalls, 'I had articulated my historicist anti-Platonism' (Rorty, PSH, p. 12). He also defines Platonism as follows: '"Platonism" in the sense in which I use the term does not denote the (very complex, shifting, dubiously consistent) thoughts of the genius who wrote the *Dialogues*. Instead, it refers to a set of philosophical distinctions (appearance-reality, matter-mind, made-found, sensible-intellectual, etc.): what Dewey called "a brood and nest of dualisms." These dualisms dominate the history of Western philosophy, and can be traced back to one or another passage in Plato's writings. Dewey thought, as I do, that the vocabulary which centres around these traditional distinctions has become an obstacle to our social hopes' (Rorty, PSH, p. xii).

philosophy as one literary genre among others. Only by realising the 'sheer' contingency of scientific and cultural history, our beliefs and desires, and our communities can we aspire to a more solidaristic society. Rorty's historicist-nominalist cultural appeal to turn from philosophy to narrative and from truth to freedom can help imagine how to promote 'human dignity, freedom and peace'.[46] In this view, recognising contingency becomes necessary to promote solidarity, enlarge our sense of who is 'one of us', and turn conflicting views into instruments for positive societal progress.[47] Solidarity, Rorty says, is 'not discovered by reflection'

> but created. It is created by increasing our sensitivity to the particular details of the pain and humiliation of other, unfamiliar sorts of people. [...] This process of coming to see other human beings as 'one of us' rather than as 'them' is a matter of detailed description of what unfamiliar people are like and of redescription of what we ourselves are like. This is a task not for theory but for genres such as ethnography, the journalist's report, the comic book, the docudrama, and, especially, the novel.[48]

Rorty's centring of 'detailed descriptions' and 'redescriptions' of ourselves and others, particularly of the shared experience of human suffering, resonates with James's recognition of our blindness towards other human beings' beliefs and desires,[49] and the Deweyan hope for 'a community in which everybody thinks that it is human solidarity, rather than knowledge of something not merely human, that really matters'.[50]

Contingent communities and pragmatist eirenism

Rorty's last use of James in CIS occurs when Rorty develops his view on the contingency of communities. In a Jamesian attitude, Rorty prefers relying on a persuasive rather than agonistic rhetorical strategy. He wants to show that a vocabulary 'which revolves around notions

---

46 Rorty, CIS, p. 182.
47 It could be interesting to read Rorty's notions of contingency and solidarity in connection with Follett's conception of 'creative experience' resulting from integrating interests. See Mary Parker Follett, *Creative Experience* (New York: Longmans, Green and Co., 1924).
48 Rorty, CIS, p. xvi.
49 Rorty, CIS, pp. 38–39.
50 Rorty, PSH, p. 20.

of metaphor and self-creation rather than around notions of truth, rationality, and moral obligation'[51] works better for a liberal society. He claims that moral and political vocabularies can benefit by abandoning the dichotomic mentality. An ironic attitude towards vocabularies and, at the same time, a faith in the vocabulary of their hopes and desires are: 'the chief virtue of the members of a liberal society'.[52] In holding contingency, irony and solidarity together, Rorty is not saying that his vocabulary ensures 'philosophical foundations of democracy'.[53] In line with the historicist and nominalist cultural perspective he depicted, changing conditions make old descriptions lose efficacy, and new descriptions emerge to replace them.[54] His goal is to offer an up-to-date description of 'the hopes of liberal society' to promote its progress. However, again in an eirenic attitude, Rorty does not want to offer a defence of new descriptions against their enemies; his intention is 'more like refurnishing a house than like propping it up or placing barricades around it'.[55]

Like James, Rorty is aware that his view risks being misread as a form of relativism. The relativistic accusation, however, besides misregarding Rorty's pragmatist inheritance, as Voparil reminds us, overlooks what Rorty thought of the personal commitment towards one's contingent philosophical views: 'one does not simply "find oneself" propounding philosophical arguments; on the contrary, these arguments are part and parcel of what, at the moment of propounding them, one essentially is'.[56] The civic virtue of 'stand[ing] unflinchingly for one's moral convictions' is a matter of identifying oneself with such a contingency'.[57] In other words, in a pragmatist vein, belief is not a matter of fun, but of personal and social transformation.[58]

---

51 Rorty, CIS, p. 44.
52 Rorty, CIS, p. 46.
53 Rorty, CIS, p. 44.
54 'His emphasis on the mortality and irreducibility of vocabularies aims to replace the image of a fixed cultural structure or vocabulary with the image of many different new, impermanent, contingent vocabularies' (Marchetti, 'The Philosophy of Richard Rorty', p. 17).
55 Rorty, CIS, p. 45.
56 Voparil, *Reconstructing Pragmatism*, p. 117.
57 Rorty, CIS, p. 60.
58 Cf. Colin Koopman, 'The Will, the Will to Believe, and William James: An Ethics of Freedom as Self-Transformation', *Journal of the History of Philosophy* 55, 3 (2017), 491–512, https://doi.org/10.1353/hph.2017.0051; Sarin Marchetti, *Ethics and*

Rorty is continually aware of the ethical and political implications of casting the history of culture as contingent and purposeless. This is evidenced by his reading of pragmatists' anti-representationalism as a version of anti-authoritarianism. Their 'anti-representationalist account of belief', he states, 'is, among other things, a protest against the idea that human beings must humble themselves before something non-human, whether the Will of God or the Intrinsic Nature of Reality'.[59]

In this regard, although Rorty's attention turns more frequently and explicitly to Dewey, the affinity with James is impossible to ignore. While James's political thought had an unfortunate destiny,[60] his strenuous effort to challenge the epistemic claims of all forms of philosophical absolutism and moral dogmatism, intent on showing how monolithic theoretical views inevitably involve markedly practical and political concerns, stands close to the Rortyan anti-authoritarian cultural project.[61] Voparil's reading of Rorty and James together shows 'Rortyan irony as a form of anti-authoritarian fallibilism and an instantiation of the pluralist temperament that James most valued'.[62] It is the intertwined connection of epistemic and ethical issues deriving from a pragmatist perspective that these philosophers share. Moreover, the pragmatist push toward positive social change characterises their eirenic strategies—conciliatory and practice-based—to overcome conflicts through promoting, at the same time, contingent-ironical self-reflection and sympathetic-attentive attitudes. What I want to show next is how Rorty's pragmatist eirenic strategy is helpful for de-potentiating the mechanisms of conflict that characterise post-truth societies.

Philosophical Critique in William James (London: Palgrave Macmillan, 2015), https://doi.org/10.1057/9781137541789

59   Rorty, PSH, p. 7.
60   Alexander Livingston, *Damn Great Empires! William James and the Politics of Pragmatism* (New York: Oxford University Press, 2016), https://doi.org/10.1093/acprof:oso/9780190237158.001.0001
61   James reverses the common understanding of the supposedly privileged relationship with experience of the theoretical over the practical by exhibiting how conceptual representation does not provide *full* knowledge of reality. See William James, *Some Problems of Philosophy* (Cambridge, MA, and London: Harvard University Press, 1979), p. 59ff.
62   Voparil, *Reconstructing Pragmatism*, p. 95.

Pragmatist eirenism and the challenges of post-truth society

In key contemporary philosophical and sociological accounts of post-truth communication, Rorty is cast, alongside Jacques Derrida, Michel Foucault and Gianni Vattimo, as a driver of the cultural adoption of the postmodern, specifically pushing an optimistic view of the relativisation of truth. According to these accounts, despite their differences, these philosophers shared an anti-authoritarian sentiment that circulated among intellectuals after the Second World War. In the wake of the humanitarian tragedies that Europe and the US experienced, any strong notion of truth and the firm belief in its possession lost its appeal as it seemed to be doomed to produce violence. This situation affected the relationship between truth and reality by loosening their connection, pushing discourse towards more or less radical constructivism. This cultural process contributed—together with structural processes—to the establishment of a post-truth society.[63]

As shown in the first part of this article, anti-authoritarianism is a key driver of Rorty's cultural and political project and as radical and provocative as his anti-foundational and anti-representational positioning can be. It is also in light of his adoption of contingency that Rorty can get rid of the correspondence theory of truth and claim that 'the world does not provide us with any criterion of choice between alternative metaphors, that we can only compare languages or metaphors with one another, not with something beyond language called "fact"'.[64] Despite Rorty's Nietzschean-inspired focus on metaphors rather than truths, his pragmatist eirenic strategies for facilitating conversations among humanity remain scarcely considered in post-truth societies, particularly in regard to communication conflicts.

---

[63] Giovanni Maddalena and Guido Gili, *The History and Theory of Post-Truth Communication* (Cham: Palgrave Macmillan, 2020), https://doi.org/10.1007/978-3-030-41460-3; Giovanni Maddalena and Guido Gili, 'After Post-Truth Communication', *European Journal of Pragmatism and American Philosophy*, 14.1 (2022), https://doi.org/10.4000/ejpap.2795. On the Lyotard-Rorty quarrel, see Guido Baggio, 'Narrazione e cosmopolitismo etnocentrico', in *La filosofia di Rorty. Epistemologia, etica e politica*, ed. by Giancarlo Marchetti (Milano: Mimesis, 2022), pp. 139–51.

[64] Rorty, CIS, p. 20.

For Rorty, all that matters

> is that if you do believe it, you can say it without getting hurt. In other words, what matters is your ability to talk to other people about what seems to you true, not what is in fact true. If we take care of freedom, truth can take care of itself. If we are ironic enough about our final vocabularies, and curious enough about everyone else's, we do not have to worry about whether we are in direct contact with moral reality, or whether we are blinded by ideology, or whether we are being weakly 'relativistic.' [...] To be a person is to speak a particular language, one which enables us to discuss particular beliefs and desires with particular sorts of people. It is a historical contingency whether we are socialized by Neanderthals, ancient Chinese, Eton, Summerhill, or the Ministry of Truth. Simply by being human we do not have a common bond. For all we share with all other humans is the same thing we share with all other animals—the ability to feel pain.[65]

When we examine Rorty's two claims—firstly, that what all humans share is that they can be hurt and secondly, that what matters is our ability to communicate what we believe to be true, rather than what is actually true—we can gain insights into how Rorty's sophisticated way of prioritising freedom over truth can help us promote solidarity and peaceful coexistence in post-truth societies.[66] In this view, Rorty not only contributed to the emergence of post-truth society but also anticipated some of its shortcomings and envisioned strategic ways to tackle them. These strategies have been overlooked by those thinkers who, even as pragmatists, view Rorty as an ironist but not, as is my point, as an eirenist.

Rorty's usefulness emerges through an examination of two critical aspects of the phenomenon: the role of emotions in shaping beliefs, and the tendency to polarisation of beliefs.

The adjective 'post-truth' became famous in 2016 when the Oxford English Dictionary (OED) selected it as the word of the year. Post-truth identifies the general phenomenon behind fake news. The OED defines post-truth as: 'relating to or denoting circumstances in which objective facts are less influential in shaping public opinion than appeals to emotion

---

65 Rorty, CIS, pp. 176-77.
66 Cf. Eduardo Mendieta, *Take Care of Freedom and Truth Will Take Care of Itself: Interviews with Richard Rorty*, Cultural Memory in the Present (Stanford, CA: Stanford University Press, 2006), https://doi.org/10.1515/9781503620391

and personal belief'. The motivation for choosing this term in 2016 was its widespread employment for describing unexpected political events: 'The concept of post-truth has been in existence for the past decade, but Oxford Dictionaries has seen a spike in frequency this year [in 2016] in the context of the EU referendum in the United Kingdom and the presidential election in the United States. It has also become associated with a particular noun, in the phrase 'post-truth politics'.[67] Since then, many studies of the phenomenon in different domains have flourished.

Post-truth is commonly acknowledged as a philosophically relevant conception and a critical feature of contemporary societies. Its genealogy is associated with the postmodernist program of liberation from traditional objective conceptions of truth and its authoritarian outcomes.[68] Unexpected events like Brexit and Donald Trump's election win in 2016 soon became examples of the social problems that post-truth communication produces in the epoch of new social media. A variety of issues concerning the relationship between politics and media, science and politics, expert knowledge and popular opinion took centre stage after these events, and we are still diagnosing the consequences. Even in disciplines proposing a range of solutions to mitigate the post-truth problem, such as communication studies, most agree that a set of specific characteristics defines the problem-situation: emotions play a significant role in shaping beliefs; the idea of truth is relativised and disconnected from reality; the decline of shame; polarisation of beliefs; and an increase in conspiracy theories. Moreover, some authors have highlighted that post-truth is connected to 'a rise in authoritarianism, the blunting of socially progressive movements and the decline of

---

67 'Post-truth, Adj., Sense 2', *Oxford English Dictionary*, Oxford University Press, July 2023, https://doi.org/10.1093/OED/7768605775

68 As Lee McIntyre puts it, it is the scientific method to be under attack, also because of the new role scientific experts recently played in policy making (Lee McIntyre, *Post-Truth* (Cambridge, MA: MIT Press, 2018), https://doi.org/10.7551/mitpress/11483.001.0001). For a different perspective, see Klaus Benesch, 'Is Truth to Post-Truth what Modernism Is to Postmodernism? Heidegger, the Humanities, and the Demise of Common-Sense', *European Journal of American Studies*, 15.1 (2020), https://doi.org/10.4000/ejas.15619. See also Maurizio Ferraris, *Postverità e altri enigmi* (Bologna: Il Mulino, 2017); Anna Maria Lorusso, *Postverità. Fra reality tv, social media e storytelling* (Rome: Laterza, 2018), https://hdl.handle.net/11585/626637; Maddalena and Gili, *History and Theory*.

democratic scrutiny'.[69] By examining a couple of these characteristics of post-truth, namely the role emotions play in shaping beliefs and the polarisation of beliefs, I hope to present Rorty's alternative perspective clearly and concisely.

The term post-truth, as defined by the OED, refers to the use of emotions and personal beliefs to influence public opinion instead of relying on objective facts. This definition seems to contrast values with facts, unaware of Wilfrid Sellars' critique of the myth of the given, and remains anchored in the traditional dichotomic view that Rorty aimed to abandon.[70] Rorty believed that this view should be replaced with the historicist mentality that was introduced in the twentieth century by pragmatist, continental, and analytic authors he privileged. Rorty's primary reference in discussing the intermingling of facts and values is Dewey. Dewey believed that the fact-value relation was the most pressing philosophical problem at his time, and that James was a 'pioneer' in perceiving that every empirical solution to this problem should be built on the view that 'experience is an intimate union of emotion and knowledge'.[71]

In CIS, Rorty's use of emotions is unsystematic. He refers to emotions for specific purposes, such as analysing the literary connection between style and participatory emotion,[72] and endorsing Sellars' differentiation between moral obligation and benevolence.[73] However, his view of the contingency of moral language and personal and collective consciousness indirectly signals a pragmatist understanding of emotions and their

---

69 Dominic Malcolm, 'Post-Truth Society? An Eliasian Sociological Analysis of Knowledge in the 21st Century', *British Sociological Association*, 55.6 (2021), 1063–79, https://doi.org/10.1177/0038038521994039.
70 Wilfrid Sellars, 'Empiricism and the Philosophy of Mind', in *Minnesota Studies in the Philosophy of Science*, ed. by Herbert Feigl and Michael Scriven (Minneapolis, MN: University of Minnesota Press, 1956), pp. 253–329.
71 John Dewey, 'William James as Empiricist', in *The Later Works of John Dewey, 1925-1953*, vol. 15, ed. by Jo Ann Boydston (Carbondale, IL: Southern Illinois University Press, 1989), pp. 9–17 (p. 17). Rorty's pragmatist move to overcome Enlightenment rationalism aims at retaining Enlightenment liberalism. He acknowledges that philosophers like Dewey (and James) realised the need to abandon the foundational rationalist vocabulary as it became an obstacle to 'a mature (de-scientized, de-philosophized) Enlightenment liberalism' (Rorty, CIS, p. 57).
72 Rorty, CIS, p. 146.
73 Rorty, CIS, p. 196.

role in constructing his 'liberal utopia'. Rorty's definition of the 'liberal ironist' provides insight into this subject:

> I use 'ironist' to name the sort of person who faces up to the contingency of his or her own most central beliefs and desires—someone sufficiently historicist and nominalist to have abandoned the idea that those central beliefs and desires refer back to something beyond the reach of time and chance. Liberal ironists are people who include among these ungroundable desires their own hope that suffering will be diminished, that the humiliation of human beings by other human beings may cease.[74]

According to the contingency framework, we should approach even our most fundamental beliefs and desires with an ironic attitude.

Liberal ironists have a radical contingent outlook because they hold that all emotional attachment and commitment to beliefs and desires are the result of a series of contingencies and, therefore, cannot be grounded in any absolute certainty. The

> citizens of my liberal utopia would be people who had a sense of the contingency of their language of moral deliberation, and thus of their consciences, and thus of their community. They would be liberal ironists—people who met Schumpeter's criterion of civilization, people who combined commitment with a sense of the contingency of their own commitment.[75]

The sense that commitment to contingent beliefs and desires is itself contingent is what Rorty recognises as a 'criterion of civilization'. For Rorty, civilised people can hold space for reflection in personal, social, and political practices. Emphasising the contingency of beliefs and personal and social commitment to those beliefs is a powerful tool for reducing the strength of the affective-emotional dimension and disengaging ourselves and our communities from immediate responses to ideals and ideological identification. In other words, Rorty argues for a mature, responsible, and continually corrigible engagement, acknowledging the intricacy and inseparability of our emotional, reflective, and linguistic practices.[76]

---

74 Rorty, CIS, p. xv.
75 Rorty, CIS, p. 61.
76 Rorty imagines only some people will be continuously ironical towards their beliefs and desires, and these will lead a historicising process. The rest of the community will absorb this ironical attitude as commonsensical nominalism

In Rorty's nominalist and historicist view, emotion is a trait of personal, social and political engagement. His perspective aligns with the non-dualistic pragmatist conception of emotions, in which the epistemic value of emotions can be calibrated through reflective action. James and Dewey believed that emotional habits can be strengthened or weakened through reflection and practice.[77] For Rorty's sophisticated cultural project, articulating the emotional dimension is crucial to cultivating liberal citizens. This is evident from his dual focus on final vocabularies for expressing beliefs and desires and his encouragement to expand each person's set of words to become aware and sensitised to the claims of others.

While pragmatist thinkers understand emotions as psychologically integrated into a more holistic view of human beings, the post-truth society seems to promote a reductionist view of emotional life, stuck in what Rorty refers to as 'the binary oppositions of Western metaphysics'.[78] To adopt a Freudian-analyst perspective of the 'conversation of mankind', social media appears to reinforce stimulus-response mechanisms and overlook the interdependence of facts and values, emotions and cognition. Rorty's pragmatist eirenism helps us rethink the role of emotions, in light of the nominalistic goal of cleansing 'Romanticism of the last traces of German idealism', which means 'eliminating argumentative appeal to the nonpropositional'.[79] The idea is to see human emotional life as enlanguaged, and therefore adaptable to fit new personal and societal narratives. Emotions should not be construed as irrational forces that conflict with logical thinking, but rather as a resource that supports the peaceful coexistence of alternative perspectives that are not necessarily conflicting. Emotions can help us

---

and historicism. This distinction fits with William Curtis's identification of two possible readings of Rorty's irony, either as the shared 'civic virtue' or the 'more active and radical mental habit' performed by liberal ironists. William Curtis, *Defending Rorty: Pragmatism and Liberal Virtue* (Cambridge: Cambridge University Press, 2015), https://doi.org/10.1017/cbo9781316272145, p. 93.

77 On the history of the sociological understanding of hope and its possible developments, see Guido Gili and Emiliana Mangone, 'Is a Sociology of Hope Possible? An Attempt to Recompose a Theoretical Framework and a Research Programme', *The American Sociologist* 54.6 (2022), https://doi.org/10.1007/s12108-022-09539-y

78 Rorty, PSH, p. 24.

79 Rorty, CIS, p. 123.

enlarge our moral identity by reinterpreting various perspectives based on diverse needs, contexts and objectives.[80]

The polarisation of beliefs is the second aspect of post-truth society that can benefit from using a Rortyan framework. As a paradigmatic example, with the Covid-19 pandemic, European countries and the US experienced highly polarised opposition between pro-vax and no-vax supporters, especially on social media.[81] Social networks, even the least appealing to younger generations, such as Facebook, did not allow genuine conversation in the Rortyan sense. Partly because of the algorithmic mechanisms by which they operate, and partly because public discourse was highly politicised, they facilitated radicalisation processes.[82] I touch upon such a complex issue only to notice how Rorty's pragmatist eirenism strategy could also be effective here.

From a Rortyan perspective, the polarising dynamics of social media can nurture the widespread tendency toward insensitivity to others perceived as different. In the post-truth society, where the social fabric is highly fragmented, there is a gradual expansion in the number of people whom, as Rorty puts it, we do not consider 'one of us'.[83] What I have been pointing out is that Rorty thoroughly analyses the Platonic mentality and highlights the risks associated with perceiving viewpoints that are not entirely convergent as *conflicting*. Rorty uses the emblematic

---

80   This view reminds me of Rorty's discourse on the loyalty-justice distinction in the attempt to weaken the idea that they have different sources (reason/feeling). Cf. Richard Rorty, *Philosophy as Cultural Politics* (Cambridge: Cambridge University Press, 2007), https://doi.org/10.1017/cbo9780511812835, p. 52ff

81   This issue benefits from multidisciplinary study ranging from philosophy to sociology, health, environment and political study. Many scientific studies have examined the polarisation of beliefs over the Covid-19 pandemic from different angles. See among others: Julie Jiang, Xiang Ren and Emilio Ferrara, 'Social Media Polarization and Echo Chambers in the Context of COVID-19: Case Study', *JMIRx Med*, 2.3 (2021), https://doi.org/10.2196/29570; Don Albrecht, 'Vaccination, Politics and COVID-19 Impacts', *BMC Public Health*, 22.96 (2022), https://doi.org/10.1186/s12889-021-12432-x; Jonathan T. Rothwell, Christos A. Makridis, Christina M. Ramirez and Sonal Desai, 'Information, Partisanship, and Preferences in a Pandemic', *Frontiers in Public Health*, 11 (2023), https://doi.org/10.3389/fpubh.2023.1019206

82   See, for instance, studies on echo chamber and filter bubbles such as Cass R. Sunstein, *#Republic: Divided Democracy in the Age of Social Media* (Princeton, NJ: Princeton University Press, 2017), https://doi.org/10.1515/9781400884711; Eli Pariser, *The Filter Bubble: What the Internet Is Hiding from You* (New York and London: Penguin Books, 2011), https://doi.org/10.3139/9783446431164

83   Rorty, CIS, p. xv, p. 191.

examples of the antagonism in Freudian scholarship between materialist and hermeneutic conceptions of the unconscious, as well as Eddington's philosophical paradox, to show how alternative framings, which coexist peacefully on the practical level and enrich relevant debates, can come to be contrasted on the theoretical level for mere theoretical reasons. More than that, this mutual exclusion is the consequence of the short-circuit of the reductive, dichotomous mentality we are still trapped in.

Rorty's eirenic strategy for preventing radicalisation and fanaticism in a post-truth society involves enlarging our moral vocabulary by getting in touch with others' lived or imaginary stories. Rorty uses a term deeply in tune with James's notion of direct knowledge, for he invites us to enlarge our 'acquaintance' to impact our sensitivity and responsiveness.[84] The eirenic lessons he takes from James are: 1) not to create false oppositions, in the sense of abstract oppositions that imply an oversimplified view of ourselves and the world; and 2) to actively exercise sympathetic attention towards others' conditions to increase our sensitivity towards a growing number of people.[85] Accordingly, creating personal bonds helps eliminate abstract generalisations and avoid the risk of adopting antagonism as a basic stance. By increasing our sensitivity to others' beliefs, desires, and sufferings, we can contribute to the progressive establishment of a sympathetic and eirenic attitude toward their ways of living and suffering. His pragmatist recipe thus differs from Habermas's idea that 'rationality' and 'universality' are the 'social glue' that philosophy must supply to build bridges between liberal citizens.[86] He prefers, instead, to bring in 'contextualism and perspectivalism' and the conviction that, in the contingent and changing framework he portrayed, sensitivity should be recovered and trained as an antidote to damaging divisions.

---

84 Rorty, CIS, p. 80. Of course, there should be other conditions to make responsiveness feel and act upon, but "acquaintance" remains necessary.
85 This view shares Voparil's accurate interpretative reading of Rorty and James as 'philosophers of agency' in the much more subtle and nuanced sense in which, for them, epistemic and ethical concerns are deeply intertwined. See Voparil, *Reconstructing Pragmatism*, p. 119.
86 Rorty, CIS, p. 83; cf. Michael Bacon and Nat Rutherford, 'Rorty, Habermas, and Radical Social Criticism', in *The Ethics, Epistemology, and Politics of Richard Rorty*, ed. by Giancarlo Marchetti (New York and London: Routledge, 2021), pp. 191–208, https://doi.org/10.4324/9780429324734-14

Rorty's sophisticated use of irony may fail to convey the active and democratic aspect of his cultural project. Using irony can potentially limit the effectiveness of his liberal proposal by creating a sense of elitism and detachment from core beliefs and emotional attachment. Rorty connects irony with curiosity toward other people's descriptions and vocabularies. By being ironic about our final vocabularies and curious about those of others, we can avoid concerns about not having access to moral truth, being clouded by ideology, or being too relativistic. Rorty encourages personal and collective efforts to be more attentive to others and embrace their perspectives, rather than promoting neutrality or relativism. The term 'eirenism' conveys this *practice of combining irony and curiosity* to counter the tendency to see things in opposition, sometimes with violent outcomes. Using pragmatist eirenism as a framework retains the benefits of adopting an ironic approach while also helping ironism reach its full pragmatist potential in fostering social change and promoting peaceful coexistence. More specifically, pragmatist eirenists can adopt a clear stance while remaining reconciled with the fact that there are many ways of seeing.

In CIS, Rorty seeks an integration between contingency thinkers, specifically those who support an intimate and creative understanding of the self, and those more interested in social justice and solidarity. 'Most ironists', he says,

> confine this longing to the private sphere, as [...] Proust did and as Nietzsche and Heidegger should have done. Foucault was not content with this sphere. Habermas ignores it, as irrelevant to his purposes. The compromise advocated in this book amounts to saying: Privatize the Nietzschean-Sartrean-Foucauldian attempt at authenticity and purity, in order to prevent yourself from slipping into a political attitude which will lead you to think that there is some social goal more important than avoiding cruelty.[87]

Within this conciliatory perspective, the active attention paid to cultivating 'authenticity and purity' in personal self-transformation is not only a matter of 'irresponsible subjectivism', but a way 'to prevent yourself from slipping into a political attitude which will lead you to think that there is some social goal more important than

---

87 Rorty, CIS, p. 65.

avoiding cruelty'. The clash with the contingency of beliefs, desires, and commitments helps rebound harsh ideological contraposition in favour of a 'liberal reformist political culture'[88] that aspires to integrate demands progressively by cultivating the enlargement of our moral identity. In a post-metaphysical and post-religious society, peace can be built on a practical level, which implies considering human beings in their entirety, including the possibility that they may change their minds.

Rorty's eirenist goal is to imagine possible ways to enlarge our mentalities and contribute to a growing sense of community with concrete fellow humans. However, unlike the Kantian project, the starting point is the 'incommensurability' of perspectives, not universal principles based on a shared natural human essence. The only recognised authority, if one can say it with Haffenden, is the authority of suffering,[89] which is a shared one and should further support that process of epistemic and ethical comprehension of the constitutive limits of the human form of life.

Conclusion

Reconsidering Rorty's cultural project in light of his eirenic attitude sheds light on his effort to reconcile and integrate alternative perspectives in favour of a vision of social progress that holds the need to resort to violence as an extreme ratio. His eirenic proposal is profoundly pragmatist in its attempt to outgrow the dichotomic mentality embodied in conflicting vocabularies of social and political action. Adopting a Rortyan view in post-truth society means considering peace as a possible hope, and progressively achievable in the long run. Powerful eirenic tools for achieving it are acquaintance and imagination. If 'persons and cultures are, for us, incarnated vocabularies',[90] then 'the liberal ironist needs as much *imaginative acquaintance* with alternative final vocabularies as possible'.[91] His use of

---

88 Rorty, CIS, p. 64.
89 John Haffenden, *The Life of John Berryman* (London: Routledge and Kegan Paul, 1982), p. 149.
90 Rorty, CIS, p. 80.
91 Rorty, CIS, p. 92, emphasis mine.

the term 'acquaintance', besides speaking for the Jamesian inheritance, is programmatic of his urge to substitute hope for knowledge. In an ever-changing, unpredictable world, for Rorty, there is no sense in thinking about 'intellectual and moral progress [...] as a matter of getting closer to the True or the Good or the Right, but as an increase in imaginative power'. Imagination is 'the cutting edge of cultural evolution [...] the source both of new scientific pictures of the physical universe and of new conceptions of possible communities'.[92]

His idea of 'imaginative acquaintance' orients toward a kind of knowledge that does not have personal edification as its unique goal. The challenge is about understanding the actual and possible humiliation of people using alternative final vocabularies. Indeed, for ironists,

> nothing can serve as a criticism of a final vocabulary save another such vocabulary; there is no answer to a redescription save a re-re-redescription. Since there is nothing beyond vocabularies which serves as a criterion of choice between them, criticism is a matter of looking on this picture and on that, not of comparing both pictures with the original. [...] Ironists read literary critics, and take them as moral advisers, simply because such critics have an exceptionally large range of acquaintance. They are moral advisers not because they have special access to moral truth but because they have been around. They have read more books.[93]

In Rorty's view, such learning can help increase our sensitivity to others' suffering, expand the boundaries of our enlanguaged experience, and foster a more and more inclusive, caring and peaceful human community.

Rorty's eirenic attitude can work as an activist commitment/appeal for peace in a highly polarised post-truth society. In particular, his sophisticated proposal to edify a mature, sympathetic and increasingly enlarging sensitivity challenges reductionist conceptions of emotion and ideological identification, undermining the dualistic and antagonistic mentality. More specifically, I have tried to show how Rorty's blurring of the division between reason and feeling can foster redescription of emotional habits as enlangued attitudes and, as such, corrigible. The need to articulate (and re-articulate) emotional life is evident from Rorty's use of vocabularies to express beliefs and

---

92 Rorty, PSH, p. 87.
93 Rorty, CIS, p. 80.

desires. Moreover, for Rorty, expanding each person's set of words can help one become more sensitive to the others' claims. Emotional-affective ties, thus reconsidered, can be seen as tools that aid the peaceful coexistence of alternative perspectives by helping to focus on and value distinct aspects of the conversation. They can enlarge our moral identity by helping us interpret unfamiliar claims and goals in familiar terms and, vice versa, by reconsidering our familiar beliefs and desires. Moreover, in a society where social media records habits, reactions, and interests, the risk is high that alternative viewpoints are oversimplified and, if not entirely convergent, are seen as conflicting. Adopting a habit of engaging with different perspectives in real life, literature, and social media is important to avoid becoming mentally closed off.[94] As Rorty says, in conversation, we can draw on 'an immense reserve army of common beliefs and desires'.[95] Of course, this does not mean sheltering ourselves from all possible conflicts and violence. However, to coexist peacefully, it is important to avoid abstracting and absolutising points of disagreement, to value the numerous subjects and aspects of agreement, to consider them in light of the priority of peaceful coexistence, and, finally, to think about visions that appear to be conflicting in non-exclusive terms.

Rorty's conciliatory view of alternative visions is a utopian yet deeply pragmatic eirenist cultural project. It capitalises on the epistemic and moral fallibilism of pragmatism and the Jamesian recognition that openness to others is a sympathetic attitude to exercise daily to counter the mechanisms of enmity that post-truth society fosters. Rorty seems well aware that if we do not personally and socially cultivate the irony and curiosity that come from a contingent and sympathetic approach to learning, the outcome of overcoming an authoritarian, representationalist conception of knowledge may yield undesirable and equally authoritarian results. Seen in light of pragmatist eirenism, Rorty's utopian cultural project reveals its melioristic drive, rooted in the ungroundable hope that its imaginative efforts might reach out

---

94 For a comprehensive understanding of Rorty's views on the role of literature, the 'literary' and 'literary culture', see Elin D. Huckerby, 'The Takeover by a Literary Culture: Richard Rorty's Philosophy of Literature' (Doctoral Thesis, University of Cambridge, 2021), https://doi.org/10.17863/CAM.76906
95 Rorty, PSH, p. 53.

to later generations and lead them to the common cause of peaceful coexistence.

My contention is thus that this word should be adopted into our pragmatist vocabulary. It captures an important aspect of Rortyan pragmatism and usefully extends his notion of ironism. Being 'ironic' towards others or their preferred vocabularies can come across as dismissive. Approaching others from an eirenic stance entails being brave enough to adopt a position, remain mindful of the other's right to advance their 'incommensurable' position, be at peace with this tension and appreciate its productive potential.

6. Creative Doubts against Authoritarian Certainty: Rorty through Reparative Critique

Heidi Salaverría

[O]ur shared ability to suffer humiliation [...]

[H]uman solidarity is based on a sense of a common danger, not on a common possession or a shared power.

Richard Rorty[1]

We have to be brave and curious and not fearful and suspicious.

Eddie Izzard[2]

Rorty's model of the autonomy of the self is deeply conflictual: the more it asserts itself through self-creation, the more cruelty it entails; the more it sensitises itself to these dangers, the weaker and more easily humiliated its own position becomes. A similar tension is still found in debates around the self in contemporary aesthetic theory. While modernist traditions, following Kant, focused on the autonomy of the subject, many postmodernist theories focus on the impact otherness has on the decentred, constructed subject. Interestingly, aspects of Rorty's philosophy resonate profoundly with a strand of theory that seeks to overcome such a dichotomous construal, namely, reparative critique. Rorty, too, rejects oppositional framings. With Freud, he rejects the

---

1   Richard Rorty, *Contingency, Irony and Solidarity* (Cambridge: Cambridge University Press, 1989), https://doi.org/10.1017/cbo9780511804397, p. 91, hereafter CIS.
2   Eddie Izzard, 'Eddie Izzard at the 2022 Equality Utah Allies Gala', *YouTube* (31 January 2023), https://www.youtube.com/watch?v=nOyye_ldJoA

idea 'that art is *really* sublimation or philosophical system-building *merely* paranoia, or religion *merely* a confused memory of the fierce father',³ and thus that there is a separate aesthetic realm apart from the non-aesthetic. In both standpoints, he implicitly aligns with what the 'reparative position' represents: an intermediary position that avoids the binary logic of a 'paranoid position'. Rorty's model of self-creation can be understood as fluctuating between two modes. Still, we can gain a clearer understanding of what he is proposing by highlighting the reparative aspect of his thought and its thrust to overcome the violent logic of the 'paranoid'.

By reparative critique, I mean newer theoretical developments relying on Melanie Klein, as developed by Eve Kosofsky Sedgwick, Maggie Nelson, Susan Best and, more recently, in the context of political philosophy, Judith Butler. Reparative critique, also in politics, seeks a promising third alternative to both 'paranoid reading and 'negative aesthetics' (encompassing aesthetics in the tradition of critical theory, such as Th. W. Adorno, but particularly postmodernist theories, such as J. F. Lyotard's elaborations on the sublime).⁴

However, reparative does not mean a depoliticised doctoring away of symptoms, which would only stabilise the *status quo* of unresolved problems within societies. Instead, recognition and thus valorising of conflictual ambivalences, ambiguities, and, as I want to stress, of creative doubts (which I differentiate from other forms of doubt) is central to the reparative mode. Moreover, in reparative critique, creative and nurturing components are revealed precisely by *working through* relational tensions of self and other, such as the tension between empathy and aggression.

This approach thus resonates with Rorty's thoughts on the struggle between self-creation and (self-)doubts. As I will argue, examining

---

3   CIS, p. 39.
4   Cf. Eve Kosofsky Sedgwick, 'Paranoid Reading and Reparative Reading, or, You're So Paranoid, You Probably Think this Essay is About You', in *Touching Feeling. Affect, Pedagogy, Performativity* (Durham, NC: Duke University Press, 2003), pp. 123–51, https://doi.org/10.2307/j.ctv11smq37.9. See also Maggie Nelson, *On Freedom. Four Songs on Care and Constraint* (New York: Vintage, 2021), p. 26. For more details on 'negative aesthetics' and the proposed alternative of an aesthetics of doubting, see: Heidi Salaverría, 'The Beauty of Doubting', in *Between the Ticks of the Watch. Exhibition Catalogue*, ed. by Solveig Øvstebo and Karsten Lund (Chicago, IL: The Renaissance Society at the University of Chicago,2017), pp. 153-83 (pp. 163–66).

Rorty in light of the reparative critique can therefore help clarify the relation between self-creation and solidarity in his work. It makes a case for embracing the *political importance and reparative potential of non-humiliating, creative doubts* while avoiding the fallacy of scepticism. It sheds new light on Rorty's distinction between private self-creation and public solidarity, and can serve as a valuable resource for pragmatism more broadly. One of my key claims is that doubting, especially creative or imaginative doubting, is more readily deployed than irony to oppose authoritarian certainty (which Rorty explicitly wants to do). Moreover, doubting helps us overcome humiliation. Put the other way around: certainty as well as what I will call 'authoritarian doubts' are incompatible with solidarity, because they seek to evade or deny dependency and humiliability.

Paranoid and reparative autonomy

In Rorty's work, our striving for self-creation is a conflictual process: autonomy entails self-assertion while remaining continuously aware of the dangers of one's own self-assertion. The more the self affirms itself through aesthetic self-creation, the more cruelty it possibly exerts ('the dimly felt connection between art and torture'); the more it sensitises itself to these dangers, the weaker and more humiliable its position becomes.[5]

This seemingly unresolved problem is made apparent in his figure of the liberal ironist, which insists on both self-creation and self-doubt, making it not only the most conflicted figure in CIS but also widely contested (in part, by Rorty himself). It seems to embody an inconsistent process of creative doubting. However, I want to suggest that this process remains inconsistent as long as it is bound to a problematic (modernist, authoritarian, heroic, genius) model of autonomy—one that Rorty sometimes appears to hold onto.[6] That is, a misguided fantasy

---

5   CIS, p. 146; Salaverría, 'Prophetische Zweifel und der "dunkel erahnte Zusammenhang von Kunst und Folter"–zur politischen Ästhetik Rortys', in *Handbuch Richard Rorty*, ed. by Martin Müller (Wiesbaden: Springer, 2023), pp. 933–47, https://doi.org/10.1007/978-3-658-16253-5_57

6   Alan Malachowski in his recent critique even claims that Rorty 'places the imagination *completely* outside the sphere of disciplined criticism and practice', and from this point of view problematises the relation between contingency and

of autonomy as independence, which, in attempting to maintain that independence, paradoxically remains dependent on others by trying to suppress that dependency. To put it in terms of G. W. F. Hegel's lord-bondsman dialectic: the lord's seeming independence is dependent on those in bondage made dependent on him. Self-creation that is parasitic on less autonomous selves becomes authoritarian if *it tries to deny that dependency*. Such denial, which implies a denial of contingency, of doubtfulness and humiliability, is a source of cruelty. As I will show, this problematic model can be described in terms of the paranoid position, the counterposition to the reparative.

Reparative critique elucidates this problem and can help resolve this apparent conflict in some of Rorty's writings. The reparative position acknowledges dependence on others. It thereby establishes a different, more permeable kind of autonomy, reducing projections and even finding joy in the process. It reevaluates doubt. When, for example, the trans activist Alok describes the trans movement as a 'love letter to the world' and how some straight people are threatened by queer people because 'we have the audacity to love the parts of ourselves that other people hate in themselves', that would be an example of converting torments into liberation in the reparative spirit, thereby welcoming doubts.[7]

Klein paves the way for a model of autonomy rendered less authoritarian by acknowledging relational dependence (I am reading Klein's model in a pragmatic way, much as Rorty reads Freud).[8] It is this self-understanding that is epitomised by the reparative position, in

---

autonomy as genius in Rorty. See Malachowski, 'Imagination over Reason: Rorty's Romance with Contingency', in *Handbuch Richard Rorty*, pp. 799–813, https://doi.org/10.1007/978-3-658-16253-5_48 (p. 808). There seems to be, I agree, a tension between claims such as '[s]ocialization [...] goes all the way down' (Rorty, CIS, p. 185), and 'imaginativeness goes all the way down', Rorty, *Philosophy as Poetry* (Charlottesville, VA, and London: University of Virginia Press, 2016), p. 13. But I think that these tensions can be resolved by the reparative reading I am proposing in that socialisation and imagination meet at the intersection of creative doubts.

7 Alok Vaid-Menon, in conversation with Jamie Lee Curtis, Upfront Ventures, 'Jamie Lee Curtis Interviews ALOK on the World Beyond the Gender Binary 2023 Upfront Summit', *YouTube* (10 March 2023), https://youtu.be/hWAs_2oGNB8?t=2

8 The advantages of Klein's model over Freud's are that her model is less hierarchical, linear and patriarchal than Freud's, and that she focusses more on the relationality of the self and its affects. See Amy Allen, *Critique on the Couch: Why Critical Theory Needs Psychoanalysis* (New York: Columbia University Press, 2021), https://doi.org/10.7312/alle19860

contrast to the paranoid outlook.⁹ These two positions are considered as two different poles in human behaviour, not as pathological clinical diagnoses. The paranoid position is characterised by experiencing oneself as in a quasi-symbiotic, unresolved, and aggressive love-hate relation to the world and to others. Its defence mechanism is splitting. On a socio-political level, the worldwide growing ideologies of the far right and of conspiracy can serve as an example of how the paranoid position manifests. In these dynamics, one's own fears and aggressions are not perceived and recognised as such, but are split off, and projected 'into' others (e.g., it manifests as the racist fantasies of white supremacists).¹⁰ Yet, whatever one has split off remains one's own fantasy, and thus it persists. This is why the projection 'returns' to the self in the form of paranoia, and in pathologically extreme cases as persecutory delusion. Tragically, one is haunted by one's own fears and aggressions, which one tried to get rid of in vain. All forms of structural discrimination (racism, sexism, classism, queerphobia, etc.) can be portrayed as partaking in a paranoid dynamic in this sense.

Thus, the paranoid position, driven by projection, seeks to maintain autonomy and separateness while it actually remains entrapped within its fear of being influenced by others; it is held captive by fantasies of others (thus it depends on them) in its obsessive efforts to break free of them. Arguably, Rorty's strong poet (a term he borrows from Harald Bloom) partially adopts this position when he fears he will remain only a replica of old vocabularies.¹¹

Whereas the socio-political examples I have given suggest that the paranoid position applies to the far right, Eve Kosofsky Sedgwick diagnoses tendencies in part of the academic left as paranoid—not necessarily discernible in the content of their writing, but in their affective posture. According to her, the paranoid 'practice' (as she calls it) is characterised by what Paul Ricoeur dubbed the 'hermeneutics

---

9   Melanie Klein, 'Notes on Some Schizoid Mechanisms', in *The Writings of Melanie Klein*, ed. by Roger Money-Kyrle, 5 vols (New York: The Free Press, 1984), III, 1–24. To simplify, in what follows, I will refer to them as the paranoid and reparative position, although the extended terms are paranoid-schizoid and depressive or reparative.
10 Klein, 'Notes', p. 8.
11 Salaverría, *Prophetische Zweifel*, p. 935.

of suspicion' (which Rorty refers to as well).¹² Sedgwick typifies this practice as *anticipatory*, a *strong theory*, a theory of *negative affect* (particularly the fear of being humiliated), and one that relies on unveiling (e.g., in dogmatic readings of Freud, Marx or Derrida, where reality is structured by an alleged necessary and hidden logic).¹³ Instead, the reparative practice favours *weak theory*, accepts *positive affect*, is willing to be *surprised* and believes in *production* rather than discovery.¹⁴ Rorty's anti-representationalist and historicist stress on the possibility of redescription, his abjuration of the idea of Reality-discovery in any form, and description of his writing as 'weak thought'¹⁵ imply that his position partly aligns with the reparative position.

As mentioned, Rorty's model of self-creation is best understood as fluctuating *between* the two practices. What I am proposing, then, is that the seeming paradox of assertive self-creation on the one hand and the weakening (self-)doubts on the other can be overcome by modifying the mentioned problematic model of the self that Rorty partly perpetuates. It can be reconstrued as a creative or imaginative process involving temporarily loosening, and thereby losing, the violent grip of the self (in the paranoid sense) in order to find new reparative redescriptions. I agree with Tracy Llanera in that a 'closer look at Rorty's writing reveals that self-creation is best achieved when one *loses* the self to *create* the self'.¹⁶ But I propose, *contra* Llanera, to take more into account the ambivalent elements of this process of self-creation as 'self-overcoming'. In this, I align partly with Bjørn T. Ramberg on what 'disruption of one's self-understanding' calls for: 'a tentative move toward restating one's practical understanding of what one is here and now, and what one may be in the process of making of oneself'.¹⁷

---

12   Rorty, CIS, p. 57. Sedgwick, 'Paranoid Reading and Reparative Reading', p. 124.
13   Sedgwick, *Paranoid Reading*, p. 124, p. 130.
14   I have inverted Sedgwick's negative descriptions of paranoid reading, p. 130.
15   Richard Rorty, *Essays on Heidegger and Others* (Cambridge: Cambridge University Press, 1991), III, 6.
16   Tracy Llanera, *Richard Rorty: Outgrowing Modern Nihilism* (New York: Palgrave Macmillan, 2020), https://doi.org/10.1007/978-3-030-45058-8, p. 144. Llanera 'proposes taking self-creation and solidarity as the primary redemptive paths from egotism. These two liberal ideals centralize our efforts toward becoming less self-satisfied and more other-oriented'. Ibid.
17   Rorty, CIS, p. 29. Bjørn T. Ramberg, 'Irony's Commitment: Rorty's Contingency, Irony and Solidarity', *The European Legacy*, 19 (2014), 144–62, https://doi.org/10.1080/10848770.2014.876197 (p. 157).

Creative doubting

A range of objections have been raised against the figure of the liberal ironist, particularly against its incessant doubting. One argument against self-doubt is that it pulls the rug out from under the self, and thus is self-destructive. Rorty responded to J. B. Schneewind's well-known critique by even taking back his idea of the liberal ironist in the sense of a too 'anguished existentialist adolescent [...] ever conscious of the abyss', to instead advocate for the possibility of being be both a 'romantic self-creator' and an 'unruffled pragmatist [...] placid Deweyan [...] not much troubled by doubt'.[18] However, cutting out those doubts contradicts Rorty's emphasis on the value of those idiosyncrasies and obsessions that drive 'our own half-articulate need to become a new person, one whom we as yet lack words to describe'.[19] In other words, we need to go through an idiosyncratic moral struggle in order to reposition ourselves; we have a 'moral obligation' to find out 'about our unconscious motives'.[20] To invoke José Medina, we need 'beneficial epistemic friction' to prevent self-complacency.[21] Such complacency leads, Rorty argues in a description of the figure of the 'egotist', to a self-satisfaction that not only hinders self-creation, but also regard for others and the development of solidarity.[22]

Instead of cutting out those struggling doubts, we need to explore and reevaluate their characteristics: neither are they limited to the private sphere nor to individuals, as Rorty himself underlines when discussing political movements—in this case, feminism—and highlights the collective creation of new vocabularies. He agrees with Marilyn Frye that 'there probably is no distinction, in the end, between imagination and courage' and that you can describe the creative process as 'a sort

---

18 Rorty, 'Reply to J. B. Schneewind', in *The Philosophy of Richard Rorty: The Library of Living Philosophers, Volume XXXII*, ed. by Randall E. Auxier and Lewis E. Hahn (Chicago and Lasalle, IL: Open Court, 2010), pp. 506–09, p. 506.
19 Rorty, CIS, p. xiv.
20 Rorty, CIS, p. 32; Rorty, 'Freud and Moral Reflection', in *The Rorty Reader*, ed. by Christopher J. Voparil and Richard J. Bernstein (Malden: Wiley-Blackwell, 2010), pp. 259–79, p. 261 and 264.
21 José Medina, *The Epistemology of Resistance: Gender and Racial Oppression, Epistemic Injustice, and Resistant Imaginations* (Oxford: Oxford University Press, 2013), https://doi.org/10.1093/acprof:oso/9780199929023.001.0001, p. 303.
22 Rorty, 'Redemption from Egotism: James and Proust as Spiritual Exercises', in *The Rorty Reader*, pp. 389–406.

of flirtation with meaninglessness [...] trying to plumb abysses which are generally agreed not to exist'.[23] This not only underscores that the separation between the private and the public is more permeable than Rorty sometimes suggests. It also shows that creative doubting can be collective, and as a process of constructively working through old and new, is indispensable.[24] 'For meaninglessness is exactly what you have to flirt with', Rorty reiterates, 'when you are in between social, and in particular linguistic practices—unwilling to take part in an old one but not yet having succeeded in creating a new one'.[25] It also shows that Rorty is sympathetic to plumbing abysses. However, not as an 'anguished existentialist adolescent', which alludes to an immature, maybe even pretentious pose, but instead as someone who understands the importance of facing up to gaps in the space of reasons, and is willing to expand it through courage and imagination. And both courage and imagination point to constructively enduring an uncertain situation, e.g., not yet having an established linguistic practice, yet not giving up.[26]

Such positive reassessments of doubting reveal another vital, productive component of creative doubting: *doubting is not all suffering*. The 'flirtation' with meaninglessness implies *promise and hope*, and even *pleasure*.[27] To make a sharp distinction between happy-ego-confirming self-creation and unhappy-ego-undermining doubts would be a caricature. The persevering resistance against those positive elements in doubting might stem from the fact that they are incompatible with a paranoid-heroic-egotistical image of the self, which remains deeply ingrained in Western societies. The antidote, however, is not to conjure a totalising notion of alienation (as some negativistic theories might propose), which would rather fit Sedgwick's paranoid reading, but a

---

23 Marilyn Frye, *Politics of Reality* (Trumansburg/New York: The Crossing Press, 1983), p. 154. Quoted in: Rorty, 'Feminism and Pragmatism', in *The Rorty Reader*, pp. 330–51 (pp. 341–42). (In this paper, Rorty comments approvingly some of Sedgwick's reflections, p. 348.)
24 See also Nancy Fraser, 'From Irony to Prophecy to Politics', in *Feminist Interpretations of Richard Rorty*, ed. by Marianne Janack (University Park, PA: Penn State University Press, 2010), pp. 47-55.
25 Rorty, *Feminism and Pragmatism*, p. 342.
26 See Michael Bacon who also makes a case for doubting 'in terms of redescription' and refers as well to expanding the logical space: 'Rorty, Irony and the Consequences of Contingency for Liberal Society', *Philosophy and Social Criticism*, 43.9 (2017), 953–65, https://doi.org/10.1177/0191453716688365
27 Salaverría, *The Beauty of Doubting*, pp. 153–83.

'willingness to substitute imagination for certainty', 'throwing oneself into the process of unpredictable change', thereby 'increasing sensitivity' and gain a 'better ability to deal with doubts about what we are saying'.[28]

Critics have articulated other arguments against Rorty's insistence on the need for (self-)doubts, ranging from Richard Bernstein's worry that Rorty's account is 'infected with epistemological terminology' and thus runs the risk of being misunderstood as scepticism, to Jonathan Lear's reproach of a 'lack of commitment', which Ramberg has discussed.[29] One advantage of (self-)doubt over irony is indeed that in everyday language, irony is associated with some kind of detachment and indifference (which, if gradually increased, manifests as sarcasm and cynicism). Thus, while irony has a long philosophical and literary, particularly romantic conceptual history, it is in the pragmatist ethos to emphasise the continuity between philosophy and everyday language. Secondly, stressing doubt over irony might prevent some objections against ironism as a position incompatible with genuine commitment.[30] More importantly, the notion of *doubt* is more readily deployed to oppose authoritarian *certainty*-claims, whereas irony suggests opposing earnestness.

Bernstein's critique is surprising as he knows better than most that pragmatism renounces the traditional divisions of philosophy, and thus that doubts are not confinable to an epistemological sphere.[31] On

---

28 Rorty, *Pragmatism as Anti-Authoritarianism*, ed. by Eduardo Mendieta, Robert Brandom (Cambridge, MA: Harvard University Press, 2021), https://doi.org/10.2307/j.ctv33mgbns, p. 142, p. 135.

29 Richard J. Bernstein, *Ironic Life* (Cambridge and Malden: Polity, 2016), p. 46, 52, 129, n. 22; Jonathan Lear, *A Case for Irony* (Cambridge, MA: Harvard University Press, 2011), https://doi.org/10.4159/harvard.9780674063143, p. 39; see also Ramberg, *Irony's Commitment*, p. 155; for more details see Salaverría, *Prophetische Zweifel*, pp. 938-41.

30 See Bacon who also sees the compatibility of 'commitment to one's beliefs while at the same time acknowledging some measure of doubt'. Rorty, *Irony*, p. 961.

31 More than that, Bernstein replied to an essay I had written on the aesthetic dimension of exemplary *doubts* and its proximity to reflective judgements in Kant (at the intersection of Dewey, Kant and Arendt in Pragmatism), and he agreed with the link I drew (relying on Bernstein's writing) between Kant's Third Critique and Dewey. See Bernstein's analysis in 'A Reply to Heidi Salaverría', in *Confines of Democracy. The Social Philosophy of Richard Bernstein: Essays on the Philosophy of Richard Bernstein*, ed. by Ramón del Castillo, Ángel M. Faerna and Larry A. Hickman (New York: Brill/Rodopi, 2015), pp. 169-70, https://doi.org/10.1163/9789004301207_019

the contrary, the power of Rorty's notion of doubting lies precisely in its holistic impact. Valorising creative self-doubts, as I propose, moreover helps correct a misguided tendency in pragmatism, namely to think of doubts as a necessary, yet disagreeable *transitional* state of problem-solving, en route to attaining new beliefs. As I have suggested elsewhere, and as Dewey himself insinuated, we need to endure and even *enjoy* the intermediate state between doubting and believing, the experimentation between doubting and what Peirce calls abduction. This helps us better explore possible alternatives in the given situation, a process I call *creative* or *imaginative doubting*.[32]

Several passages in Rorty can be used to demonstrate how his perspective aligns with what I am proposing. He states, for example, that the greatness of philosophers such as Plato and Kant is to be found in 'confronting us with their own *double-mindedness*'.[33] Rorty rejects the metaphysical posture which comes with 'the quest for the kind of grandeur that becomes possible only when doubt is eliminated'.[34] Thus, when we remove heroism from self-creation, we are left with redescriptions still susceptible to future doubts.[35] This differs from

---

32   Salaverría, 'Enjoying the Doubtful. On Transformative Suspensions in Pragmatist Aesthetics', *European Journal of Pragmatism and American Philosophy*, 4.1 (2012), https://doi.org/10.4000/ejpap.791; Salaverría, 'The Beauty of Doubting', 153–83; Salaverría, 'Vague Certainty, Violent Derealization, Imaginative Doubting. Reflections on Common Sense and Critique in Peirce and Butler', *European Journal of Pragmatism and American Philosophy*, 12.2 (2020), https://doi.org/10.4000/ejpap.2102

33   I found this quote in an unpublished manuscript by Rorty and want to stress the interesting term 'double-mindedness'. It can be translated to German as 'Zwiespältigkeit'. In my book on pragmatism, I describe Rorty's notion of the self as 'Zwietracht des Selbst', a 'discorded self'; Salaverría, *Spielräume des Selbst. Pragmatismus und kreatives Handeln* (Akademie-Verlag: Berlin, 2007), pp. 167–90, https://doi.org/10.1524/9783050047232. See Rorty, *Die Schönheit, die Erhabenheit und die Gemeinschaft der Philosophen* (Frankfurt/Main: Suhrkamp, 2000), p. 27, p. 27 (n. 10); Rorty (n.d.), 'Rational Beauty, Non-discursive Sublimity, and the Community of Philosophers', *drafts 1988 and undated* (Special Collections and Archives, The UC Irvine Libraries, Irvine, California. 30.08.2023), box 11, folder 8, Richard Rorty Papers. MS-C017, emphasis added. See also Rorty, CIS, p. 9.

34   Rorty, 'Grandeur, Profundity, and Finitude', in *Philosophy as Cultural Politics* (Cambridge: Cambridge University Press 2007) pp. 73–89, https://doi.org/10.1017/cbo9780511812835.006, p. 79.

35   Rorty is not always clear in his position towards heroism, see e.g., CIS, p. 60. Elin Danielsen Huckerby comments that although Rorty argues against heroism, 'he would have benefitted from stating this rejection of the quest-narrative form more plainly than he did'. I agree. Huckerby, 'The Takeover by a Literary

self-enlargement in the sense of self-aggrandisement, because sometimes it is beneficial to take things back, unlearn things, or *stop* doing things, etc.

Such willingness for self-criticism, however, should not be confused with shame or guilt. From a reparative position, Nelson has criticised a posture in political aesthetics that is too sure of right and wrong, which Grant Kester dubbed the 'orthopaedic aesthetic', a variation of negative aesthetics. This is the view 'that there is something wrong with us that requires artistic intervention to fix [...] with the twist that now the so-called left is often cast [...] in the repressive, punitive position, with the right-wing morality police appearing newly [...] enthralled by disinhibition, lawlessness, debauchery, and "freedom and fun"'.[36] Best has argued (in the field of visual arts) that the 'affect of shame usually terminates interest and thereby forecloses on attention and any possibility of prolonged viewing'.[37] Works of art achieve more by leaving a reparative space for the viewer. I want to add that non-humiliating doubt opens up those possibilities not only for the arts.

While we need to emphasise the need to endure (and partly to enjoy) doubts, and see them as more than a necessary evil, doubting is not a permanent condition, never 'radical *and* continuing', as Rorty later admitted in his reply to Schneewind.[38] If that were the case, you would either be dealing with, in Peirce's words, artificial 'paper-doubts', or with agonising self-doubts.[39] If they were radical and continuing, they should be better described as internalised humiliation, or, as I call them, *authoritarian doubts*.[40] Authoritarian doubts primarily result from direct or structural violence—for instance, when they cause you to hate your body shape or the colour of your skin. Klein describes this process as

---

Culture: Richard Rorty's Philosophy of Literature' (Doctoral Thesis, University of Cambridge, 2021), https://doi.org/10.17863/CAM.76906, p. 42.

36 Maggie Nelson, *On Freedom*, pp. 23–24.
37 Susan Best, *Reparative Aesthetics: Witnessing in Contemporary Art Photography* (New York: Bloomsbury, 2016), https://doi.org/10.5040/9781474277839, p. 6. She makes the case for a non-shaming art history by analysing four contemporary artists of the Global South working with art photography.
38 Rorty, CIS, p. 73 (emphasis added). 'Reply to J. B. Schneewind', in *The Philosophy of Richard Rorty*, pp. 506–09 (p. 506).
39 Charles S. Peirce, *The Collected Papers of C.S. Peirce*, 8 vols, ed. by C. Harsthorne, P. Weiss and A. Burks, (Cambridge, MA: Harvard University Press, 1938–59), V, 514.
40 Salaverría, *Vague Certainty*, pp. 27–36.

projective identification: giving in to the (e.g., sexist or racist) paranoid projections others have construed around you. Instead, doubting plays a central role in *transforming and thereby overcoming humiliation* through the redescription of formerly unresolved conflicts, as described earlier.

My suggestion is to distinguish between different forms of doubting, depending on one's position in society. Political movements often are fuelled by *anti-authoritarian doubts* capable of transforming humiliation into empowerment—doubts about authoritarian narratives (including those internalised as authoritarian doubts), be it with regard to class, sex, race or their intersection. Consolidating one's position, in these cases, e.g., in recent years, within movements such as BLM, Ni una Menos, and #MeToo, can *create doubts in others* (regarding dominant narratives) that serve to encourage solidarity with the cause of one's movement. However, even while consolidating the movement's collective self, you need to practice self-doubting to unlearn your previously naturalised self-hatred (a practice of dismantling internalised *authoritarian doubts*, understood as doubts instilled by authoritarian narratives about your self). These are distinct from *acknowledging doubts*, in which you (as part of a dominant or privileged group within society) recognise and mourn your own cruelty (e.g., in the form of indifference) towards others, thereby transforming yourself, overcoming shame and evolving a higher sense of solidarity. This kind of doubting aligns with what Ramberg calls *shakenness*.[41] These are, again, different from *creative* or *imaginative doubts*, in which you explore your own obsessions and idiosyncrasies (be it in the arts, philosophy, science, or, in Rorty's vocabulary, the vast field of self-creation). Of course, there are overlaps.[42]

Authoritarian certainty through sublime purification

In an engagement with what Rorty calls Freud's 'wackiest' book, *Moses and Monotheism*, he describes pragmatism as a 'liberation from the primal father'.[43] He even places Freud's theory of the origin of conscience and of the superego in the tradition of 'the anti-authoritarian strain which motivated Dewey'. In doing so, he applies Freud's 'story of how social

---

41 Ramberg, *Irony's Commitment*, p. 160.
42 See Salaverría, *Vague Certainty*, pp. 8–9, 27–41.
43 Rorty, *Pragmatism as Anti-Authoritarianism*, pp. 10–11.

cooperation emerges from parricide' to the Western 'onto-theological tradition' (a term he borrows from Heidegger).[44] Through a process of metaphysical purification, the original totem is first humanised in Polytheism, followed by the figure of the fatherly god in 'the great patriarchal monotheisms' in which 'the murdered father was restored to his rightful role as one who demanded unconditional obedience, although he was now banished from the earth to the sky'.[45] Rorty goes on to imagine that, for Freud, Platonism would have represented a depersonalised form of this monotheism. Ultimately, Rorty's anti-essentialist interpretation of Freud comes down to this: 'The analogy between ceasing to believe in Sin and ceasing to believe that Reality has an intrinsic nature'.[46] In other words, his critique of the Western tradition proposes that even its epistemological claims remain bound to authority and that this authority is considered as something sublime, pure. From this perspective, pragmatists are considered somehow *impure*, 'their metaphysically inclined opponents suggest, *shameless* in their willingness to revel in the mutable and impermanent',[47] particularly, then, in what one could call 'dirty doubts'.[48] One fascinating aspect of this story is that it is told in relational terms or, put differently, in terms of a struggle for recognition—even its traditional epistemological side.

This is also where the connection between authoritarian purification and violence (specifically, cruelty and humiliation) takes effect: Rorty underpins his anti-authoritarian trajectory by opposing the 'neurotic Cartesian quest for certainty' based on dualist separations.[49] Speaking instead with Klein: it is a splitting of theory and practice, resulting in a splitting off of mere/impure doubtable belief from unchanging/pure knowledge. But the primary objective of Deweyan and Rortyan pragmatism is to overcome this tradition *because it is humiliating*: 'The idea of a non-human authority and the quest for sublimity are both

---

44 Rorty, *Pragmatism as Anti-Authoritarianism*, p. 10, 11, 27.
45 Rorty, *Pragmatism as Anti-Authoritarianism*, p. 12.
46 Rorty, *Pragmatism as Anti-Authoritarianism*, p. 1.
47 Rorty, *Pragmatism as Anti-Authoritarianism*, p. 14, see also 'Aesthetic Cruely, Dirty Doubts', in Salaverría, *The Beauty of Doubting*, pp. 158–60.
48 Salaverría, *The Beauty of Doubting*, pp. 158–60.
49 Rorty, 'Pragmatism, Relativism, and Irrationalism,' in *The Rorty Reader*, pp. 111–22 (p. 112); see also Dewey, *The Quest for Certainty. A Study of the Relation of Knowledge and Action*, *The Later Works of J. Dewey, 1925–1953*, vol. 4, ed. by J. A. Boydston (Carbondale and Edwardsville, IL: Southern Illinois University Press, 1984).

products of self-abasement'.⁵⁰ Humiliation is something humans inflict upon themselves by clinging to one side of the dualism, hoping to be provided with purity, while instead being plagued by the constant reminder of their impurity.

Two things become clearer now. One is the full extent of the central role humiliation plays in view of this historical onto-theological dimension, which explains why the only negative universalist claim Rorty ever makes is 'our shared ability to suffer humiliation'.⁵¹ That is because, simply put, the self needs others (internalising their subjectivity, their vocabularies) to emerge.⁵² Humiliation reverses this process, thereby (partly) undoing the self. The other is the central role *certainty* plays as the peak of the humiliating metaphysical quests, which makes even more plausible the importance of *doubting as an anti-authoritarian countermovement*.

Viewed from a Kleinian perspective, the process of purification can be described as a process of paranoid splitting and externalisation: the fantasy of sublime (self-)certainty can only be attained and maintained by identifying with some non-human authority. Translated into the field of negative or anti-aesthetic theory, the sublime is located in otherness, not within the self. This is why, from this perspective, the arts transcend the self and confront it with something ungraspable, unavailable. For Lyotard, the sublime is only a 'negative presentation' of the absolute, an 'obscure debt', an 'enslavement to the *aistheton*', which subjects to the 'law of alterity', described in terms of 'shock', 'sacrifice and disaster'.⁵³ The *diagnosis* (which I share) of a misled violent model of autonomy leads to a *vision* (which I do not share) in which this violence is transferred from the self to a quasi-sacral otherness of art that then is considered to be overwhelming in a humiliating way.⁵⁴ On the other hand, theories

---

50 Rorty, *Pragmatism as Anti-Authoritarianism*, p. xxix.
51 Rorty, CIS, p. 91.
52 See e.g., Vincent Colapietro, referring here to Butler, 'Toward a Pragmatic Conception of Practical Identity', in *Transactions of the Charles S. Peirce Society*, 42.2 (2006), 173–205, https://doi.org/10.1353/csp.2006.0019 (p. 185).
53 Jean-François Lyotard, *The Inhuman: Reflections on Time* (Stanford, CA: Stanford University Press, 1991), p. 136, p. 127; Lyotard, *Postmodern Fables* (Minneapolis, MN: University of Minnesota Press, 1999), p. 243. For a critique on Lyotard, see Jacques Rancière, 'The Sublime from Lyotard to Schiller: Two Readings of Kant and their Political Significance', *Radical Philosophy*, 126 (2004), 8–15 (p. 10, p. 8).
54 There are some tensions between Rorty's critique of the quest for the metaphysical sublime as 'ineffable', 'incommensurable with the past' while 'ironist novelist are not interested in incommensurability' (Rorty, CIS, p. 101 and 126), and his claim

of beauty stemming from Kant's approach locate aesthetic experience within the self. Now, there are two options: either they hold on to the idea of purity, in which case the impure has to be split off as well, or they *integrate the impure (including aggressions) within the self*. The latter could be described as reparative.

With Sedgwick, this reparative position 'is the position from which it is possible in turn to use one's own resources to assemble or "repair" the murderous part-objects into something like a whole—though, I would emphasize, *not necessarily like any preexisting whole*'.[55] If it were not too static, one could speak of a Kintsugi-self (instead of a fantasy of the self, taking up Rorty's critique of a 'model of Parmenides' well-rounded sphere') in which mended cracks, instead of being concealed, are brought out as the most precious golden parts of the reconfigured whole.[56] But of course, a self is not a vase. Reconfiguration means living and working through redescriptions. With Sedgwick, the 'ethical possibility' it 'inaugurates' has to do with 'the very fragile concern to provide the self with pleasure and nourishment in an environment that is perceived as not particularly offering them'.[57]

A concept of beauty that holds on to purity, however, contains paranoid elements in the sense of outsourcing impurity to others. Speaking with Pierre Bourdieu: the Kantian seemingly disinterested (hence, autonomous or free) pleasure of beauty turns out to be

---

that self-creation and solidarity are 'equally valid, yet forever incommensurable' almost sounding Lyotardian (Rorty, CIS, p. xv, emphasis added). However, in the spirit of Rorty's overall trajectory of 'curing us from our "deep metaphysical need"', I propose a more malleable relation between self-creation and solidarity (ibid., p. 46).

55 Sedgwick, *Paranoid Reading*, p. 128.
56 Rorty, 'Deconstruction and Circumvention', *Critical Inquiry*, 11.1 (1984), 1–23, https://doi.org/10.1086/448273 (p. 8). Rorty uses the metaphor to discuss Jacques Derrida who 'loves to show that whenever a philosopher lovingly shapes a new model of Parmenides' well-rounded sphere, something will always stick, or leak, out'. It fits the picture of the paranoid position failing to uphold its self-contained entity because of its entanglement with authority. The 'dream of philosophy turns into nightmare just at its climax: [...] when the sphere is rounding itself off nicely, [...] something goes horribly wrong. Self-referential paradox appears; the unintelligible repressed returns as the condition of the intelligible' (p. 9). However, as Rorty rightly points out, describing this dynamic in a necessitarian way would be self-contradictory, and, I would add, remain within the paranoid logic. It is more helpful to describe these processes, as Rorty proposes, as tragicomedies, which is more in accordance with the reparative position.
57 Sedgwick, *Paranoid Reading*, p. 137.

interest-led (hence, heteronomous or unfree), insofar as it creates class distinction. 'The tastes of freedom can only assert themselves as such in relation to the tastes of necessity, which are thereby brought to the level of the aesthetic and so defined as vulgar'.[58] For example, visitors to an art exhibition can feel superior to the lower classes who—allegedly— simply do not get it. The supposedly special ability to make autonomous aesthetic judgements becomes a status symbol of distinction. And the ability of the 'genius-monster' to create art—and thus to create oneself, even more so. 'The poets claimed for art the place in culture traditionally held by religion and philosophy'.[59] I have suggested elsewhere that this kind of cultural capital is tied, in a Bourdieuian way, to certainty-distinction: aesthetic joy that stabilises the self-certainty of one's own autonomy-authority by *feeding* on the uncertainty of those who allegedly do not know what to feel or think. 'It confers the self-certainty which accompanies the certainty of possessing cultural legitimacy, and the ease which is the touchstone of excellence [...] which bourgeois families hand down to their offspring as if it were a heirloom'.[60] As mentioned, this is not an epistemological form of certainty, but rather a political-aesthetic one, as it secures exclusiveness and distinction through authority, accompanied by the aggressive feeling of a *right* to self-certainty. The 'search for self-enlargement' that Rorty sees as the counterposition to the misguided 'search for purity' in this sense runs the danger of remaining within the problematic purity logic, which Rorty criticises.[61]

Self-creation and humiliation

Rorty's description of autonomy remains ambivalent. On the one hand, there is a playful, reparative tendency in that redescriptions of strong poets 'play into each other's hands'; their 'metaphors rejoice in one another's company'.[62] In a utopian society, where 'both the world and the self have been de-divinized', there would be no need for rivalry.[63]

---

58 Pierre Bourdieu, *Distinction. A Social Critique of the Judgment of Taste* (Cambridge, MA: Harvard University Press, 1984), p. 56.
59 Rorty, CIS, p. 161, p. 3.
60 Bourdieu, *Distinction*, p. 66. For a more detailed account see Salaverría, *Vague Certainty*, pp. 23–24.
61 Rorty, *Freud and Moral Obligation*, p. 269.
62 Rorty, CIS, p. 39.
63 Rorty, CIS, p. 40.

On the other hand, Rorty strikes an almost belligerent tone in conjuring the options self-creation is left with in the face of radical contingency: in face of the 'final victory of metaphors of self-creation over metaphors of discovery', the power we have left is to be able to 'appropriate by adopting and then transforming' the language of other persons ('for example [...] parents, gods, and poetic precursors'), thereby 'becoming identical with the threatening power and subsuming it under our own more powerful selves'.[64] This comes to read as fitting the paranoid position when we see that the remedy to overcome this fear is to do to others what they fear most themselves. In other words: self-creation through humiliation of others. Others can be other persons, but they can also be the past, which in one passage Rorty surprisingly personalises: 'The hope of such a poet is that what the past tried to do to her she will succeed in doing to the past: to make the past itself, including those very casual processes which blindly impressed all her own behavings, bear *her* impress'. And, he adds that success in this matter means saying to the past 'Thus I willed it' (citing Nietzsche), and 'giving birth to oneself' (citing Bloom).[65]

In its most nefarious extreme of this model, which Rorty so drastically depicts and urgently warns us against, torturers hope (!) that people can 'experience the ultimate humiliation of saying to themselves, in retrospect, [...] "I no longer have a self to make sense of"'.[66] The reason is that, in that case, I am inhabited by fantasies of someone else who invaded my own subjectivity, substituting it with *their description of me*. Those invasive substitutions make my self-understanding incoherent. For Klein, this happens in projective identification:[67] when those you project into *identify* with that projection, i.e., when a woman begins to believe she is to blame for the man's sexual assault she suffered, or when a person of colour begins to feel inferior to white people, thereby giving in to such a dynamic. As Ta-Nehisi Coates puts it: 'A thing has happened to someone. And the way that society talks about it, they *make* the thing that's happened *into the person*'.[68] Worst case, the thing made into the

---

64 Rorty, CIS, p. 40.
65 Rorty, CIS, p. 29. See also Heidi Salaverría, *Spielräume des Selbst*, pp. 174–82.
66 Rorty, CIS, p. 179.
67 Klein, 'Notes', p. 8.
68 Ta-Nehisi Coates, *Interview with Oprah Winfrey on The Water Dancer* (Oprah's Book Club: Club Apple TV, 2019).

person is declared their truth and therefore the justification for future humiliations (apparent in turns of phrases such as 'see? I told you, this is how women/blacks/queers/Jews, etc. *really* are'). In such a case, you start to believe what you cannot believe, which is an impossible thing to do. Your integrity, in the sense of an inner resting-place, to take a term from William James, is gone. Instead, there is perpetual inner conflict between impossible options, because redescriptions by someone else have been implanted into you like an alien soul. Therefore, you no longer know how to be yourself. Again, here I do not have any form of constructive doubting in mind, but rather what I call authoritarian doubting, an internalisation of humiliation.

Many times, humiliation leads to another form of splitting, in which someone humiliated for a trait of their core identity starts to degrade others who share that same degraded trait, in order to somehow keep it away from them, for example, when women try to outsource their inflicted self-hatred—particularly towards their own body—by degrading the bodies of other women, which then again can be used for patriarchal narratives, e.g., of women being incapable of real solidarity or friendship.

Humiliation leads, as Rorty puts it, referencing Judith Shklar and Elaine Scarry, to 'making the things that seemed most important to them look futile, obsolete, and powerless'.[69] Complete humiliation can be seen as externalising all of those 'impure' dependency-parts into someone else. In George Orwell's *1984*, the refined torturer O'Brien ends up with 'doublethink', which, as Rorty adds, is something O'Brien 'has mastered', as a 'deliberately induced schizophrenia', yet 'in the unconscious way in which those with split personalities can switch'.[70] I doubt that you can master it deliberately, because there is no god's eye perspective from which to orchestrate this switching. Doublethink remains within the paranoid logic in the two senses of doing to others what he fears most they will do to him (splitting off) and in the sense of actually fighting with his own fantasies. With Klein, the 'torturer's hope' can be explained in that the 'object of the exercise [...] to tear a mind apart', particularly fulfils the perverted hope of externalising one's own, dreaded doublethink. The torturer's authoritarian autonomy *feeds* on this breaking of the autonomy

---

69 Rorty, CIS, p. 89.
70 Rorty, CIS, p. 187, p. 187 (n. 20).

of others (giving in to the humiliation, believing what they cannot believe), thereby fantasising himself into a god-like position.[71]

Alas, this he needs others for, which is why the exercise has to be repeated, again and again, as if, in a twisted manner, the 'sound of the tearing' of those he breaks, were a consolation, were empathy with his own abjected doublethink. More harmlessly, Nabokov's description of his ideal readers as 'a lot of little Nabokovs' fits within this logic, as does the traditional male fantasy of 'giving birth to oneself' in bypassing the mother and the whole issue of dependency by erasing her from the picture, which is what, according to Klein, the infant does in his paranoid-schizoid fantasy.[72] In that sense, the symbolic patricide is preceded by a matricide.

As my discussion has shown, self-creation in its quest for autonomy runs the danger of cruelty, when intent on purification—that is, the disentanglement from impure dependency—the self shifts to identify with the authoritarian, sublime position of certainty. It turns from a bondage position, afraid of the punishing lord, to embodying the lord-position itself, because the 'highest hopes are for union with something beyond human [...] which has the authority *to free one from guilt and shame*'.[73] This union becomes easier, according to Rorty, when the authority is depersonalised. Then 'proper respect for a de-humanized father-figure is shown not by obedience to him but by an attempt to become identical with him'.[74] Historically, the price for this yearned freedom from the possibility of humiliation has been to split off (marginalise) those declared less autonomous. Rorty himself concedes: 'In our society, straight white males of my generation—even earnestly egalitarian straight white males—cannot easily stop themselves from feeling guilty relief that they were not born women, or gay, or black'.[75] Autonomy is always relationally constructed.

My overall point is that we have ignored the cost of claiming our autonomy at the expense of the oppression of others for too long.[76]

---

71 Rorty, CIS, p. 179.
72 Rorty, CIS, p. 163.
73 Rorty, *Pragmatism as Anti-Authoritarianism*, p. 10, emphasis added.
74 Rorty, *Pragmatism as Anti-Authoritarianism*, pp. 13–14.
75 Rorty, *Feminism as Pragmatism*, p. 224, Salaverría, *Vague Certainty*, p. 25.
76 For an analysis of the political and economic side of this externalisation, see: Stephan Lessenich, *Living Well at Others' Expense: The Hidden Costs of Western*

The historical moment when Romanticist ideas of purified autonomy and aesthetics reached their peak coincided with the era of colonial expansion and enslavement. As long as we continue to repress this 'dark side' of our pursuit of unbounded freedom—as long as we persist in warding off what is uncomfortable in our collective and individual past—this darkness will return to persecute us.

Reparative solidarity

With Rorty, we have to acknowledge that solidarity 'is based on a sense of a common danger, not on a common possession or a shared power'.[77] And, as he convincingly argues, the source of this kind of empathy is not the identification with any pure authority, but, on the contrary, with 'impure,' concrete, particular descriptions of those humiliated, because we can relate to these. Identification with 'humanity as such' not only seems impossible because of its abstraction, but furthermore, it might be 'an awkward attempt to secularize the idea of becoming one with god'.[78] In other words, it might be the ego decorating itself with abstract morality to assume an untouchable position.

Therefore, '[w]e have to start from where *we* are', but at the same time '[i]t is the "we" of the [liberal] people who have been brought up to distrust ethnocentrism'.[79] In the case of Western societies, permeated by the onto-theological tradition and its dark colonial legacy, we must doubt the misguided model of autonomy based on humiliating others in the quest for sacrosanct self-*affirmation*. Rorty's proposal to expand our 'we-intentions' (a term he takes up from Wilfrid Sellars), continually including more 'others' into our 'we', would be problematic if it meant a process of collective self-affirmation, which is why Rorty describes his position as 'being consciously provincial'.[80] In the Rortyan model, being ethnocentric or even provincial does *not mean being relativist or self-congratulatory* (that would be egotistic). On the contrary, it means adopting a *self-questioning posture* to counteract hubris and chauvinism.

Prosperity (Oxford: Polity Press, 2019).
77 Rorty, CIS, p. 91.
78 Rorty, CIS, p. 198.
79 Rorty, CIS, p. 198.
80 Rorty, CIS, p. 170 (n. 2).

Therefore, we need 'human solidarity [...] as the self-doubt' of people who have learned to give up the idea of a higher authority and instead doubt 'their own sensitivity'. To create 'an ever larger and more variegated *ethnos*', in this sense, means learning to listen to others without exoticising them, but instead with growing 'curiosity about possible alternatives'.[81] That would be a reparative position. It allows for the positive affect of ambivalence, thereby acknowledging non-humiliating doubts: through political movements, cultural and artistic practices, journalistic reports, and so on.[82]

Being colonised by the vocabulary of others (what the strong poet fears so much) is what marginalised people experience daily. Taking seriously into account the position of those marginalised and humiliated can create doubts in the face of authoritarian certainty, thereby broadening solidarity. In this sense, as Eduardo Mendieta proposes, Rorty's ironism is 'active, activist, critical, forward-looking'. We should 'create ever more critical pictures of what we have turned into and what we have failed to become', thereby abandoning 'narrow, cruel, exclusivist versions of our old and inherited "we", whose outer perimeter is drawn and redrawn from the perspective of the marginalized people, from the perspective of those we have been socialized to think of as "they" rather than "we"'.[83] Mendieta speaks of the 'power of irony'. I hope to have shown why it is no sophistry that I prefer the power of doubting (though I agree with the trajectory of his argument of 'confessed ethnocentrism').[84]

Butler has argued that the 'hatred that follows from non-negotiable dependence', which Rorty describes in his onto-theological reading of Freud, can be overcome by 'making reparations'.[85] The source of empathy, hence solidarity, lies in acknowledging the painful experiences of loss and deprivation we share with those we love and are dependent on. 'Even as I have sympathy for another, perhaps for the reparation that another never received for a loss or for a deprivation, it seems that I am,

---

81 Rorty, CIS, p. 198.
82 Cf. Rorty, CIS, p. xvi.
83 Eduardo Mendieta, 'Introduction', in *Take Care of Freedom and Truth will take Care of Itself: Interviews with Richard Rorty* (Stanford, CA: Stanford University Press, 2005), https://doi.org/10.1515/9781503620391, p. xxii.
84 Ibid.
85 Judith Butler, *The Force of Nonviolence: An Ethico-Political Bind* (Verso: London/New York, 2021), p. 92, p. 91.

at the same time, making reparation for what I never had, or for how I should have been cared for'.[86] The paranoid position tries to resolve frustration and anger through splitting, submitting others by making them dependent. The reparative position embraces those feelings as *catalysts* and works them through by 're-enacting some unmourned losses or some unfulfilled wishes, [...] how in treating others well and securing their happiness, we, each of us, replay our grievances against those who did not love us well enough or whose good love we unacceptably lost'.[87] Solidarity in this sense overcomes internalised humiliation by *respecting dependence*, not as submissiveness, but as a need for others, however, without either 'taking over that place' of the other or 'becoming engulfed' by them.[88] This need for others is *used as a motor* to re-enact constructively, redescribe it into a less painful version—*not denying* it, but on the contrary, *integrating it* into a more complete, less violent picture as an 'ambivalent form of the social bond'.[89]

Interpreting Rorty this way is in accord with Christopher Voparil's suggestion of 'cultivating responsive sensibilities toward others and the details of their lives, as well as the need for a willingness to alter one's beliefs'.[90]

What I am proposing aligns with yet another aspect of Rortyan redescriptions: acknowledging dependencies on others in a welcoming way, because there are 'no lives which are not largely parasitical on an un-redescribed past and dependent on the charity of as yet unborn generations'.[91] From the reparative perspective, Sedgwick advocates that this could be a temporality in which 'generational relations don't always proceed in this [Oedipal] lockstep'.[92] Creating doubts about the authoritarian certainty of the onto-theological tradition Rorty so convincingly criticises can produce 'surprising gestalt switches'.[93] In the words of Joseph Litvak, whom Sedgwick quotes, the reparative approach has 'a lot to do with loosening the traumatic, inevitable-seeming

---

86 Butler, *The Force of Nonviolence*, p. 91.
87 Butler, *The Force of Nonviolence*, p. 89, p. 90.
88 Butler, *The Force of Nonviolence*, p. 87.
89 Butler, *The Force of Nonviolence*, p. 96.
90 Christopher Voparil, 'Rorty and James on Irony, Moral Commitment, and the Ethics of Belief', *William James Studies*, 12.2 (2016), 1–30 (p. 17).
91 Rorty, CIS, p. 42, p. 41.
92 Sedgwick, *Paranoid Reading*, p. 147.
93 Cf. Rorty, CIS, p. 78.

connection between mistakes and humiliation' and that 'a lot of queer energy [...] goes into [...] practices aimed at taking the terror out of error, at making the making of mistakes sexy, creative, even cognitively powerful'.[94] In this sense, there is a reparative component in the creative 'individual brush strokes of unprofessional prophets and demiurges' which Rorty describes as being so inspirational to us *precisely because of their imperfection*.[95]

This mistake-friendly approach allows for the double-mindedness of acknowledging doubts towards the past (both historically and individually) without converting into resentful or cruel doublethink. It allows for solidarity through listening to the critique and anti-authoritarian doubts of others without feeling humiliated, and for opening up to self-creative doubts inspired by the new, without lapsing into the heroism of finding purified certainty (although never be too sure of that).

---

94 Sedgwick, *Paranoid Reading*, p. 147.
95 Richard Rorty, *Achieving our Country. Leftist Thought in Twentieth-Century America* (Cambridge, MA: Harvard University Press, 1989), p. 133. Thanks to Elin Danielsen Huckerby for pointing out this quote to me.

7. Rortyan Irony as Civic Virtue in Our Myside Society

Martin Müller

The liberal ironist in our fragmented public sphere

The figure of the 'liberal ironist' and the concept of irony are central to Richard Rorty's *Contingency, Irony and Solidarity* (CIS), his main contribution to political philosophy. Both have attracted much criticism.[1] This chapter provides an overview and discussion of this criticism, focusing on a partial redescription of the liberal ironist in the light of what I call serene fallibilism and the relationship between Rortyan irony and conversability. Rorty's own corrections in his later work and the interpretations of leading Rorty scholars are considered, which is significant as there is almost no reference to the concept of irony as the awareness of contingency after CIS. Moreover, the depiction of irony in CIS is somewhat muddled.[2] With it, Rorty got into trouble even with his most generous and amicable readers, such as Michael Williams and J. B. Schneewind, and toward the end of his life, Rorty conceded that his 'description of the liberal ironist was badly flawed'.[3] In a reply

---

1 For a summary of the main lines of criticism see Michael Bacon, 'Rorty, Irony and the Consequences of Contingency for Liberal Society', *Philosophy and Social Criticism*, 43.9 (2017), 954–65, https://doi.org/10.1177/0191453716688365 (pp. 954–58).

2 William Curtis, *Defending Rorty: Pragmatism and Liberal Virtue* (Cambridge: Cambridge University Press, 2015), https://doi.org/10.1017/cbo9781316272145, p. 93.

3 Richard Rorty, 'Reply to Schneewind', in *The Philosophy of Richard Rorty*, ed. by Randall Auxier and Lewis Hahn, The Library of Living Philosophers 32 (Chicago

to Schneewind, published in 2010, Rorty writes that his 'attempt to imagine a composite figure called "the liberal ironist"—half Mill, half Nietzsche—was misguided'.[4]

So, given this self-assessment, should we not simply say goodbye to irony? Is the catchy claim 'irony is over' and the equally catchy call for a return to realism perhaps right after all? While this might seem like an easy way out of our predicament, a nostalgic return to 'Truth' and 'Reality' in times of post-truth politics is not only inconsistent but politically useless, and maybe even dangerous in view of today's fragmented public sphere.

In contrast, Rortyan irony, understood as a civic virtue that leads to openness and conversability, is an important resource for a renewal of democratic discourse in our 'Dark Years',[5] especially in view of the latest research in moral psychology, which suggests that our current predicament is best described as a 'myside society'. According to scholars like Keith Stanovich and others, we still value truth and facts—but only when they support our views, that is, the views of the moral tribe we are a member of: 'We believe in *our* truth, in *our* news [...] What our society is really suffering from is myside bias: [...] We are not living in a post-truth society—we are living in a myside society'.[6] In this situation, the figure of the liberal ironist as an ideal of citizenship is timelier than ever. Rortyan irony has political 'cash value',[7] which makes it worth salvaging rather than abandoning. Therefore, this chapter offers a partial redescription of the notion of irony that Rorty commended to us in CIS. With this project, I am joining those Rorty scholars who argue that there

---

and Lasalle, IL: Open Court Press, 2010), pp. 506–08 (p. 506); Bjørn T. Ramberg, 'Irony's Commitment: Rorty's Contingency, Irony and Solidarity', *The European Legacy*, 19 (2014), 144–62, https://doi.org/10.1080/10848770.2014.876197 (p. 147).

4   Rorty, 'Reply to Schneewind', p. 506.
5   Richard Rorty, *Philosophy and Social Hope* (New York: Penguin Books, 1999), p. 243.
6   Keith E. Stanovich, *The Bias That Divides Us: The Science and Politics of Myside Thinking* (Cambridge, MA/London: MIT Press, 2021), https://doi.org/10.7551/mitpress/13367.001.0001, p. ix. Stanovich (p. 9) defines the myside bias as follows: '[It is] the bias that occurs when we evaluate evidence, generate evidence, and test hypotheses in a manner favorable toward our own prior opinions and attitudes'. For more on the diagnosis of a tribalist myside society see for instance: Joshua Green, *Moral Tribes: Emotion, Reason, and the Gap Between Us and Them* (New York: Penguin, 2013).
7   William James, *The Writings of William James a Comprehensive Edition*, ed. by John J. McDermott (Chicago, IL: University of Chicago Press, 1977), p. 388.

is something valuable in Rorty's account of irony; like them, I aim to work out the public value of Rortyan irony for democratic society.[8]

Pragmatism, fallibilism and political virtue

As Carol Nicholson has argued, the varieties of pragmatism, from Peirce to Rorty, cannot be easily defined as a philosophical school with a shared system of thought or method. Nevertheless, the common denominator is a specific fallibilistic and melioristic attitude or mentality: the pragmatic habit of mind or 'temperament'.[9] On Nicholson's reading, which I follow here, 'pragmatism is a radical shift in our way of thinking, rather than in the content of our thought'.[10] Richard Bernstein thus champions a pragmatic way of thinking when he champions fallibilism as a genuine alternative to foundationalism and religious fundamentalism.[11] In Bernstein's words: 'fallibilism, in its robust sense, is not a rarified epistemological doctrine. It consists of a set of virtues'.[12]

Without referring to Nicholson and Bernstein, but following this assessment, William Curtis shows convincingly that Rorty is most fruitfully understood as 'a proponent of liberal virtue ethics'.[13] The primary concern of his pragmatic liberalism is with what practical habits and character traits are demanded by democratic citizenship, and

---

8   See Bacon, 'Rorty, Irony and the Consequences', pp. 954–55.
9   James, *The Writings of William James*, p. 363 Also, according to Rorty, pragmatism is the expression of a 'hopeful, melioristic, experimental frame of mind': Rorty, PSH, p. 24.
10 Carol Nicholson, 'Education and the Pragmatic Temperament', in *The Cambridge Companion to Pragmatism*, ed. by Alan Malachowski, Cambridge Companions to Philosophy (Cambridge: Cambridge University Press, 2013), https://doi.org/10.1017/cco9781139022132, pp. 249–71 (p. 269).
11 By 'mentality' Bernstein means 'a general orientation—a cast of mind or way of thinking—that conditions the way we approach, understand and act in the world': see Richard J. Bernstein, *The Abuse of Evil: the Corruption of Politics and Religion since 9/11* (Malden, MA: Polity Press, 2005), p. 18.
12 Bernstein, *The Abuse of Evil*, p. 29. Bernstein stresses that the clash of mentalities between robust fallibilists and absolutists in search for certainty cuts *across* the religious/secular divide: see p. 104.
13 Curtis, *Defending Rorty*, p. 4 Curtis openly admits that Rorty never refers to himself as a virtue theorist (p. 22). For an approving assessment of Curtis reading of Rorty's (political) work as vitally important and original, see Susan Dieleman, 'Defending Rorty: Pragmatism and Liberal Virtue, Written by William M. Curtis', *Contemp. Pragmat.*, 13.4 (2016), 441–44, https://doi.org/10.1163/18758185-01304006 and Bacon, 'Rorty, Irony and the Consequences', p. 956.

among these is irony: 'The upshot of Rorty's wide-ranging project [...] is the necessity of liberal virtues, especially the virtue of irony, for the success of liberal culture and society'.[14]

In a similar vein, John Pettegrew asserts not only that the virtue of irony should be an important aspect of pragmatism but that, even if the concept of irony in CIS is difficult to deploy as a political construct, 'Rorty's ironist is salvageable and continues to serve pragmatism'.[15] Even Bernstein, for a long time a friendly but harsh critic of Rorty's merely 'inspirational liberalism',[16] has reevaluated Rorty's figure of the liberal ironist. In his book *Ironic Life*, he champions the virtue of irony and offers a more sympathetic re-reading of Rorty's redescription. According to Bernstein, the liberal ironist in CIS is a politically valuable utopian figure who serves pragmatic fallibilism.[17]

Following these reassessments, the remainder of this chapter first offers an overview of Rorty's liberal ironist and her combination of private irony and public solidarity. It includes a discussion of the relationship between the two senses of irony in CIS, distinguished by Curtis, Pettegrew, and other renowned Rorty scholars: fallibilist and romantic, which, in turn, serves as a basis for the partial redescription of Rortyan irony that I want to advance. Secondly, this chapter addresses the nature of ironic doubt in Rorty's definition of the ironist. Referring to Bernstein in particular, I emphasise the interpretation of irony as an anti-foundationalist virtue: a serene fallibilism beyond essentialism and epistemological scepticism that entails not only awareness of contingency, but commitment, open-mindedness and creativity.

Rorty's version of pragmatism is, at its heart, a philosophy of conversation. The final part of this chapter connects the description of the ironist in CIS as dependent on communication with others to Rorty's later construal of the love of Truth as conversability. Thus, Rortyan irony can be redescribed as entailing the civic virtue of conversability across

---

14   Curtis, *Defending Rorty*, p. 260. See also p. 25.
15   John Pettegrew (ed.), *A Pragmatist's Progress?: Richard Rorty and American Intellectual History*, American Intellectual Culture (Lanham, MD: Rowman and Littlefield, 2000), pp. 104, 118.
16   Richard J. Bernstein, 'Rorty's Inspirational Liberalism', in *Richard Rorty*, ed. by Charles Guignon and David R. Hiley (Cambridge: Cambridge University Press, 2003), pp. 124–38, https://doi.org/10.1017/cbo9780511613951.007
17   Richard J. Bernstein, *Ironic Life* (Cambridge: Polity Press, 2016), pp. 46–53.

the boundaries of discursive communities. In conclusion, I argue, in line with the focus of this volume on the relevance and usefulness of CIS, that the civic ideal of the liberal ironist is a promising alternative to the (understandable) call for a return to truth-talk in times of a fragmented public sphere. Rortyan irony can be partly redescribed as a serene fallibilism and as related to the civic virtue of conversability. Importantly, these represent alternatives to truth-talk.

The figure of the liberal ironist and the two senses of irony in *Contingency, Irony and Solidarity*

In CIS, Rorty outlines the utopia of a democratic anti-foundationalism with the motto 'substitute Freedom for Truth'.[18] He has thus drawn the consequences of his anti-representationalism and his ethnocentrism for moral thought and politics.[19] 'Contingency' is his anti-metaphysical combat term against all attempts to escape from finitude. He promotes the experiment of learning to live without certitude. For Rorty, the virtue required for this experiment is irony, understood as an awareness of contingency.

Rorty redescribes the concept of irony in an idiosyncratic way as the virtue of a serene awareness of three contingencies: language, the self, and the political community.[20] From the recognition of the contingency of language follows, according to Rorty, not only an awareness of the contingency of the self, but also of political community. Even the values and institutions of the liberal community of justification are 'only' a contingent result of its cultural history.[21]

Ironism understood in this new way is vital to Rorty's vision of a post-metaphysical utopia. At the same time, however, the liberal sense of solidarity remains intact within it. Furthermore, awareness of contingency heightens the recognition of the fragility of the liberal institutions and our consciousness of the need to defend them: 'The

---

18 Richard Rorty, *Contingency, Irony and Solidarity* (Cambridge: Cambridge University Press, 1989), https://doi.org/10.1017/cbo9780511804397, p. xiii. See also p. 176.
19 Cf. Richard Rorty, *Philosophy and the Mirror of Nature* (Princeton, NJ: Princeton University Press, 1979); Richard Rorty, *Objectivity, Relativism, and Truth* (Cambridge: Cambridge University Press, 1990).
20 Rorty, CIS, pp. xv, 9, 46, 61, 73.
21 Rorty, CIS, pp. 3–69.

fundamental premise of this book is that a belief can still regulate action, can still be thought worth dying for, among people who are aware that this belief is caused by nothing deeper than contingent historical circumstance'.[22] Building on Joseph Schumpeter's criterion of a civilised person as one who can combine commitment with a sense of the contingency of their own commitment, Rorty sketches in CIS the vision of a pragmatic balance between irony and engagement.[23]

> The heroine of CIS, the liberal ironist, embodies this pragmatic balance: I borrow my definition of 'liberal' from Judith Shklar, who says that liberals are the people who think that cruelty is the worst thing we do. I use 'ironist' to name the sort of person who faces up to the contingency of his or her own most central beliefs and desires—someone sufficiently historicist and nominalist to have abandoned the idea that those central beliefs and desires refer back to something beyond the reach of time and chance. Liberal ironists are people who include among these ungroundable desires their own hope that suffering will be diminished, that the humiliation of human beings by other human beings may cease.[24]

The utopian figure of the liberal ironist is aware of the historical contingency of her socialisation. She also understands her central beliefs and needs—Rorty speaks here of her 'final vocabulary'[25]—as contingent.

In Rorty's idiosyncratic new version of the concept of irony, irony is thus primarily focused on one's own assumptions and vocabularies. However, it is understood not only as a virtue of serene acceptance of contingency, but at the same time as a sense of the project of autonomy through linguistic self-creation.[26] In accordance with the romantic concept of *Bildung* or 'edification', which is already developed in the final part of *Philosophy and the Mirror of Nature*,[27] the goal of the ironist's aesthetic way of life is self-creation instead of self-knowledge.[28] Consequently, the prevailing definition of freedom in Rorty's utopian, post-metaphysical liberal society is no longer insight into (rational) necessity, but 'freedom

---

22 Rorty, CIS, p. 189 See also pp. xv, 9, 73, 190, and Rorty, PSH, p. 250.
23 Rorty, PSH, p. 61.
24 Rorty, CIS, p. xv.
25 Rorty, CIS, p. 73.
26 Rorty, CIS, pp. 9, 46, 61.
27 Rorty, PMN, p. 360; Rorty, CIS, p. 92.
28 Rorty, CIS, pp. 25–29.

as recognition of contingency'.²⁹ This recognition is the prerequisite for a creative approach to the question of one's own identity.

Ironists, according to Rorty, experiment playfully with the plurality of their network of beliefs and desires. The decentring and contingency of the self is thus not a reason for despair, but an opportunity for creativity, or for testing out ever-new self-descriptions.³⁰ So, Rorty's transformative redescription of the self includes not only an emphasis on decentring and contingency. The active component of the self, the liberal ironist as the heroine of Rorty's book, can distance herself from her own socialisation *and* recreate herself through self-description. By the virtue of irony, Rorty refers to consciousness of one's own contingency and, at the same time, the capacity for autonomy through ongoing linguistic self-creation. His conception of irony connects to the romantic demand that one should live poetically.

The paradigmatic figure of this romantic conception of autonomy is, for ironists, the strong poet: 'In my view, an ideally liberal polity would be one whose culture hero is Bloom's "strong poet" rather than the warrior, the priest, the sage, or the [...] scientist'.³¹ The powerfully creative poet, who uses words as no one before her have used them, is even declared to be the 'archetypal human being'.³² For Rorty, the aesthetic mode of existence of the productive artist is the paradigm of individuality. His strong romantic impulse is most evident in this vision of an authentic life through poetic self-creation.³³

But irony also has a dark side for Rorty, who is arguably the most important thinker of irony in contemporary philosophy. It consists above all in the danger of cruelty through humiliation of others that arises from strong projects of linguistic self-creation through redescription.³⁴ Hence, Rorty insists on its privatisation: 'Irony seems

---

29 Rorty, CIS, p. 26.
30 Rorty, CIS, pp. 39–40.
31 Rorty, CIS, p. 53.
32 Rorty, CIS, p. 34.
33 For a reading of Rorty's thinking as fragile coexistence of pragmatism *and* Romanticism see Martin Müller, *Private Romantik, öffentlicher Pragmatismus?: Richard Rortys transformative Neubeschreibung des Liberalismus*, Edition Moderne Postmoderne (Bielefeld: Transcript, 2014) and Martin Müller, *Richard Rorty: A Short Introduction* (Wiesbaden: Springer VS, 2022), https://doi.org/10.1007/978-3-658-38838-6
34 CIS, pp. 89–90.

inherently a private matter'.³⁵ Contrary to what some critics claim, irony does not fail to ground solidarity in Rorty's account. Rather, it urges a liberal containment of irony. Rorty combines ironism and ethnocentric liberalism. In his liberal utopia, the limits placed on irony constitute an updated version of John Stuart Mill's Harm Principle. What Rorty advocates in CIS, is a differential conception of ethics in which private irony coexists with public solidarity.

The solidarity of the liberal ironist is a matter of her practical identity, acquired as a loyal member of the liberal community with which she identifies. Rorty conceives his ideal citizen as both an ironist and an ethnocentrist. She has internalised the liberal distinction between the private and the public, and she is an ironist only in her private life. She is also the 'embodiment' of Rorty's differential yet interlinked conception of ethics and politics. The precondition of her combination of a private ethics of self-creation and a public one of solidarity is that her final vocabulary is split into a (large) private and a public part. Both come together to constitute the liberal ironist's identity—without having a special relation to each other.³⁶ Liberal ironists consider their project of linguistic self-creation, and *a fortiori* the pursuit of sublimity, irrelevant to the sphere of politics. In the latter, for them, it is only about expansion of (communicative) solidarity and about democratic experimentalism and reformism within the existing liberal institutions.³⁷

The liberal ironist embodies Rorty's cultural-political proposal of a new ideal of virtue for our pluralistic, liberal societies. Through his utopian vision of the ideal citizen, he radicalises the art of separation already practised in liberal societies daily. Following Isaiah Berlin's pluralism, Rorty recommends a new, convincing pragmatist ideal of wisdom for the (intellectual) citizens of liberal societies. It includes the thesis that the successful balance between responsibility for oneself and responsibility for others cannot be the result of theoretical insight, but of practical knowledge.³⁸

---

35 Rorty, CIS, p. 87.
36 Rorty, CIS, pp. 91–92, 100, 120–21.
37 Rorty, CIS, pp. 63–65, 84–85, 173–75. See also Richard Rorty, *Philosophy as Cultural Politics* (Cambridge: Cambridge University Press, 2007), https://doi.org/10.1017/cbo9780511812835, pp. 102–03.
38 Rorty, CIS, pp. xv, 93, 120.

The presentation of the liberal ironist in CIS has attracted much criticism. Several commentators, including Curtis and Pettegrew, have noticed tensions or a fluctuation in Rorty's use of 'irony' and 'ironist'.[39] For the purpose of this chapter, two main issues are especially relevant: first, Rorty introduces 'irony' in the introduction as a universal civic virtue: 'One of my aims in this book is to suggest the possibility of a liberal utopia: one in which ironism, in the relevant sense, is universal'.[40] However, in part two, chapter four of the book, he seems to assume an elitist restriction of irony to intellectuals only: 'In the ideal liberal society, the intellectuals would still be ironists, although the nonintellectuals would not. The latter would be commonsensically nominalist and historicist'.[41] Secondly, he commends not only, as explained already above, the privatisation of irony, but also 'making a firm distinction between the private and the public'.[42]

Following the suggestions of Pettegrew and Curtis, it has become common in Rorty scholarship to distinguish two senses of irony used in CIS to resolve these apparent contradictions: moderate irony as civic virtue and its pure or radical romantic version.[43] Curtis captures the

---

39 Bacon, 'Rorty, Irony and the Consequences', p. 954; Bernstein, *Ironic Life*, p. 132 (n. 42).
40 Rorty, CIS, p. xv.
41 Rorty, CIS, p. 87. See also p. 89: 'The ironist is the typical modern intellectual'. Gascoigne rightly emphasises that the figure of the liberal ironist represents a new self-image that the intellectual readers of CIS are invited to adopt: see Neil Gascoigne, *Richard Rorty: Liberalism, Irony and the Ends of Philosophy*, Key Contemporary Thinkers (Cambridge: Polity, 2008), p. 180.
42 Rorty, CIS, p. 83. This standard liberal distinction is Rorty's key practical distinction and its rigid use in CIS remained a major point of controversy. But by now there is an increasing consensus in Rorty scholarship that its softening up is not only required but possible (see Martin Müller, 'General Introduction to the Handbuch Richard Rorty', in *Handbuch Richard Rorty*, ed. by Martin Müller (Wiesbaden: Springer Fachmedien Wiesbaden, 2022), pp. 1–30, https://doi.org/10.1007/978-3-658-16260-3_80-1 (pp. 23–25)). In substance, this insight is already present in CIS. For example, the importance of socialization is vehemently emphasized (e.g., Rorty, CIS, p. 185). Also, the social role of the figure of the strong poet as acknowledged legislator of society presupposes the connection between the private and the public (e.g., Rorty, CIS, pp. 24–26, 37; Rorty, ORT, pp. 72, 121). For a 'friendly amendment' (Brandom) of Rorty's use of the public-private distinction see John P. Anderson, 'Achieving Rorty's New Private-Public Divide', in *Handbuch Richard Rorty*, pp. 865–82, https://doi.org/10.1007/978-3-658-16260-3_51-1
43 Pettegrew (ed.), *A Pragmatist's Progress?*, pp. 107–08; Curtis, *Defending Rorty*, pp. 93–99, 163.

difference nicely: 'The first sense is the civic virtue that all liberal citizens should ideally possess because it helps them be tolerant, adaptable, and just. The second sense is the more active and radical mental habit that "ironist intellectuals" exhibit as they challenge the conventional wisdoms of the cultural domains in which they work'.[44]

In the first, moderate sense, 'irony' is Rorty's label for the typical pragmatist themes of anti-foundationalism and fallibilism. It is commended as a civic virtue for all liberal citizens because it fosters open-mindedness and tolerance. In this fallibilist sense, Rortyan irony is uncontroversial, at least among pragmatists.[45] William Curtis even asserts: 'Perhaps the most significant, and controversial, contribution that Rorty makes to liberal political thought is to emphasize the importance of a sense of irony as a crucial virtue for liberal citizenship'.[46] Not only Curtis, but also Pettegrew and Bernstein focus on this first sense of Rortyan irony.

In contrast, several Rorty scholars try to work out in various ways the political role of its second, more radical sense. This second sense focuses on the idea of linguistic self-creation.[47] However, as Bacon rightly asserts, these two senses of irony are not in conflict with each other. The distinction between the two senses of irony should not be drawn too sharply, as the two senses exist on a continuum.[48]

---

44 Curtis, *Defending Rorty*, p. 93. Ramberg ('Irony's Commitment', p. 153) speaks of political and existential perspective on irony. Chris Voparil distinguishes its moderate version and a more acute, hyper-version: Christopher Voparil, 'Rorty and James on Irony, Moral Commitment, and the Ethics of Belief', *William James Studies*, 12.2 (2016), 1–30 (p. 8).

45 Even Hilary Putnam, who (mis)reads Rorty as a relativist, asserts that 'Rortyans [...] may be more tolerant, less prone to fall for various varieties of religious intolerance and political totalitarianism': see Hilary Putnam, *Realism with a Human Face*, ed. by James Conant (Cambridge, MA: Harvard Univ. Press, 1992), p. 24.

46 Curtis, *Defending Rorty*, p. 5.

47 See, among others, Michael Bacon, *Richard Rorty: Pragmatism and Political Liberalism* (Lanham, Plymouth: Lexington Books, 2007); Tracy Llanera, *Richard Rorty: Outgrowing Modern Nihilism* (Basingstoke: Palgrave Macmillan, 2020), https://doi.org/10.1007/978-3-030-45058-8, E. D. Huckerby, 'Finely Aware and Ironically Responsible: Rorty and the Functions of Literature', *Studium Ricerca*, 120.2 (2024), 22–37, Voparil, 'Rorty and James'; Christopher Voparil, 'Rorty's Ethics of Responsibility', in *A Companion to Rorty*, ed. by Alan Malachowski, Blackwell Companions to Philosophy 73 (Hoboken, NJ: Wiley Blackwell, 2020), pp. 490–504, https://doi.org/10.1002/9781118972199.ch30

48 Bacon, 'Rorty, Irony and the Consequences', pp. 961–62. Curtis's position is in this regard not clear. For him, Rorty 'inadvertently implies and conflates two different

This assessment can be made plausible by looking closer at the comprehensive definition of the ironist as intellectual in the above-mentioned chapter four of CIS, where this figure is defined in terms of three conditions:

> I shall define an 'ironist' as someone who fulfills three conditions: (1) She has radical and continuing doubts about the final vocabulary she currently uses, because she has been impressed by other vocabularies, vocabularies taken as final by people or books she has encountered; (2) she realizes that argument phrased in her present vocabulary can neither underwrite nor dissolve these doubts; (3) insofar as she philosophizes about her situation, she does not think that her vocabulary is closer to reality than others, that it is in touch with a power not herself. Ironists who are inclined to philosophize see the choice between vocabularies as made neither within a neutral and universal metavocabulary nor by an attempt to fight one's way past appearances to the real, but simply by playing the new off against the old.[49]

Curtis makes this clear: 'on this definition, it is apparent that there is much more to being an "ironist" than mere acceptance of contingency and being fallibilistic'.[50] Building on this interim result, what follows is my own variation on the project of reading Rortyan irony in its full sense as ethically and politically useful for liberal democracy. Following Bernstein, I first discuss irony more deeply as an anti-foundationalist virtue of serene fallibilism, which moves beyond essentialism and epistemological scepticism. However, the focus then shifts to its partial redescription as a civic virtue of conversability across the boundaries of discursive communities.

Serene fallibilism over epistemological scepticism: Irony as public virtue of openness and creativity

The pragmatic alternative to foundationalism is not scepticism or relativism, but fallibilism. According to Hilary Putnam, 'that one can be fallibilistic and antiskeptical is perhaps the unique insight of American

---

and conflicting senses of irony'. But he also states that, 'the two senses of irony exist on a continuum'. See Curtis, *Defending Rorty*, p. 93.
49 Rorty, CIS, p. 73.
50 Curtis, *Defending Rorty*, p. 95.

Pragmatism'.⁵¹ The meaning of fallibilism is nicely illustrated in Wilfried Sellars' view of science: science is not rational because it has a foundation, but because it is a self-correcting enterprise.⁵² According to Bernstein, pragmatist fallibilism is 'the belief that any knowledge claim, or more generally, any validity claim [...] is open to ongoing examination, modification, and critique'.⁵³ Bernstein is championing the political stance of fallibilism as one of the key features of the pragmatic ēthos. The following discussion of the nature of ironic doubt for the liberal ironist builds on his assertion that Rorty is 'one of the most forceful and eloquent defenders of pragmatic fallibilism'.⁵⁴

According to Bernstein, Rorty offers a novel or even idiosyncratic definition of irony, one that is not particularly concerned with the traditional definition of irony or with the popular view that the ironist is someone who is detached and avoids commitment. Rortyan irony is to be interpreted as a variation of the pragmatic theme of fallibilism as a mentality, which Bernstein himself wants to foster.⁵⁵ Referring here to Bernstein in particular⁵⁶, and arguing against the serious criticisms levelled by Williams and Schneewind, I emphasise a reading of Rorty's redescription of irony as a fallibilistic anti-foundationalist virtue of serene fallibilism, which moves beyond essentialism and epistemological scepticism. Understood in this way, it entails not only awareness of contingency but also commitment, open-mindedness, and creativity.

Rortyan irony as self-irony is defined by a particular relation to one's 'final vocabulary'. Rorty uses this notion to designate the set of words with which individuals justify their actions, beliefs, and lives. It is final because, as he puts it, 'if doubt is cast on the worth of these words, their user has no noncircular argumentative recourse. Those words are as far as he can go with language; beyond them there is only

---

51 Hilary Putnam, *Words and Life*, ed. by James Conant (Cambridge, MA: Harvard University Press, 1994), p. 152.
52 Wilfrid Sellars, *Empiricism and the Philosophy of Mind*, Minnesota Studies in the Philosophy of Science 1 (Cambridge, MA: Harvard University Press, 1997), p. 79.
53 Bernstein, *The Abuse of Evil*, p. 28.
54 Bernstein, *The Abuse of Evil*, 127 (n. 6).
55 Bernstein, *Ironic Life*, pp. 7, 116–20.
56 For this reading of irony as important epistemic virtue of fallibilism see also Voparil, 'Rorty and James', p. 2: 'Rortyan irony is best read as a form of antiauthoritarian fallibilism'.

helpless passivity or a resort to force'.⁵⁷ The notion of 'final vocabulary' has attracted criticism, most prominently by Williams, for it evokes a strong suggestion of Cartesian epistemic scepticism, rooted in the very foundationalist picture of epistemology that pragmatists reject. 'Nothing', Williams asserts, 'is immune from revision. As a pragmatist, Rorty should have no truck with the language of "finality"'.⁵⁸ Williams also criticises Rorty's depiction of the ironist, especially with reference to the notion of 'radical and continuing doubts'. With reference to classic epistemological expressions like 'doubt' (in condition one) and 'argument' (in condition two) of this depiction, Rorty is falling prey again to sceptical modes of thinking and therefore failing to defend the fallibilist pragmatist properly: 'Rorty's irony is scepticism under another name'.⁵⁹ This, according to Williams, is the most ironic result of the depiction of the ironist in CIS.⁶⁰

Several Rorty commentators have defended Rorty's 'ironic fallibilism toward one's own beliefs'.⁶¹ According to Bacon, for instance, in Rorty's construct of a 'final vocabulary', 'finality' does not mean 'permanency'. Rather, finality indicates that we have gone as far as we can go with language *for now*.⁶² Moreover, for Bjørn Ramberg, Rorty's notion of finality does not refer to the argumentative realm but to the existential experience of finitude: 'What Rorty is trying to talk about [...] is a practical shortfall—our experience of it, and our coping with it. Concretely existing, with a cultivated ability for ironic experience, we are brought up against the finality of our vocabularies as a *present practical limit*'.⁶³ Bernstein, in his above-mentioned reassessment of Rortyan irony, emphasises that its main point is, after all, to question the illusory idea of the possibility of a final ahistorical justification of our

---

57   Rorty, CIS, p. 73. One is reminded of Wittgenstein saying: 'If I have exhausted the justifications, I have reached bedrock and my spade is turned. Then I am inclined to say: "This is simply what I do"'. (Ludwig Wittgenstein, *Philosophische Untersuchungen. Philosophical Investigations*, trans. by G. E. M. Anscombe (New York: The Macmillan Company, 1953), § 217, p. 85.
58   Michael Williams, 'Rorty on Knowledge and Truth', in *Richard Rorty*, ed. by Guignon and Hiley, pp. 61–80 (p. 78) See also pp. 72, 76–77.
59   Williams, 'Rorty on Knowledge and Truth', p. 76.
60   Williams, 'Rorty on Knowledge and Truth', pp. 76–79. See also Bernstein, *Ironic Life*, p. 46.
61   Curtis, *Defending Rorty*, p. 9.
62   Bacon, 'Rorty, Irony and the Consequences', p. 960.
63   Ramberg, 'Irony's Commitment', p. 159.

ultimate values: 'When Rorty speaks of a "final vocabulary," he certainly does not mean that it rests on a firm foundation, or even that it remains constant. This is just what he is criticising'.[64]

At the same time, Ramberg must agree that the nature of the 'radical and continuing doubts' in Rorty's depiction of the ironist is clearly at the heart of the issue.[65] Rorty himself has admitted that this expression in CIS is misleading because it suggests precisely the idea of a Cartesian 'comprehensive doubt'. He stresses, therefore, firstly, that the ironist is not asserting methodical doubts but is open to alternative vocabularies, as she is aware of the contingency of her own. Secondly, and more importantly, is the difference between the Cartesian 'paper doubt' (Peirce) and the real doubt of the ironist that guides her (communicative) practice as it leads to her greater willingness to listen to others. Therefore, Rorty concludes that he should have spoken of 'perpetual readiness for radical doubt' or of an 'extraordinary degree of openness to suggestions for change'.[66]

This shift towards self-correction aligns with Bernstein's fallibilist reinterpretation of the Rortyan ironist: despite some misleading formulations, Rorty should not be interpreted as making a standard epistemological point about doubts. Bernstein maintains that Rorty's point is a matter of how one believes or doubts. Moreover, the Rortyan ironist is aware of the plurality of final vocabularies and that there is no standpoint outside and above these vocabularies from which to evaluate them. Moreover, Bernstein reads Rortyan irony not only as a powerful way of exposing the illusion of foundationalism; he also captures its creative dimension: 'Rorty's ironist, at her best, wants to liberate us from the dead weight of past vocabularies and open up space for the imaginative creation of new vocabularies'.[67] One of Rorty's key motivations for keeping irony alive is, according to Bernstein, to foster our creative freedom and to keep open human possibilities: 'That is,

---

64 Bernstein, *Ironic Life*, p. 32.
65 Ramberg, 'Irony's Commitment', p. 158. On the oddity of Rorty's invocation of 'radical doubt' see also Gascoigne, *Richard Rorty*, pp. 177–78.
66 Richard Rorty, 'Erwiderung auf Ulrich Baltzer', in *Hinter den Spiegeln: Beiträge zur Philosophie Richard Rortys mit Erwiderungen von Richard Rorty*, ed. by Thomas Schäfer, Udo Tietz and Rüdiger Zill, Suhrkamp Taschenbuch Wissenschaft, 1522, 1st edn (Frankfurt am Main: Suhrkamp, 2001), pp. 49–55 (pp. 52–53). My translation.
67 Bernstein, *Ironic Life*, p. 52.

new, creative ways of shaping ourselves and establishing solidarity with our fellow human beings. Irony, then, is *not* merely a rhetorical trope [...] but rather a proposal for how *we*—or *some of us*—might live our lives'.[68]

Bernstein's interpretation of Rortyan irony is convincing. However, he only touches upon the existential context of linguistic self-creation by redescription, as discussed above. Regarding Bacon and Ramberg's interpretations,[69] it is important to stress that their horizon is the context of the 'radical and continuing doubts' of the ironist, and her romantic conception of autonomy as linguistic self-creation. That is, what they bring to the fore is that the ironist as intellectual is not only an antifoundationalist but also a romantic self-creator. She is concerned with linguistic self-creation by redescription in order to come to terms with the contingency of her final vocabulary: 'Private autonomy can be gained by redescribing one's past in a way which had not occurred to the past'.[70] The aim of the ongoing creative redescription of the 'blind impresses' of their lives is, for Rortyan ironists, to become the best selves they can:[71] to achieve autonomy as authenticity. Liberal ironists are

> trying to get out from under inherited contingencies and make [their ...] own contingencies, get out from under an old final vocabulary and fashion one which will be all [their ...] own. The generic trait of ironists is that they do not hope to have their doubts about their final vocabularies settled by something larger than themselves. This means that their criterion for resolving doubts, their criterion of private perfection, is autonomy rather than affiliation to a power other than themselves. All any ironist can measure success against is the past—not by living up to it, but by redescribing it in his terms, thereby becoming able to say, 'Thus I willed it'.[72]

Hence, if one considers not only the often-criticised definition of the ironist but also its context in chapter four of CIS, it becomes clear that Rorty is not to be interpreted as making a standard epistemological point about doubts at all.

---

68 Bernstein, *Ironic Life*, p. 34.
69 Bacon, 'Rorty, Irony and the Consequences', pp. 958–60; Ramberg, 'Irony's Commitment', pp. 153–56.
70 Rorty, CIS, p. 101.
71 Rorty, CIS, p. 80.
72 Rorty, CIS, p. 97.

Taking this into account weakens Schneewind's criticism of Rorty's description of irony. However, Schneewind does point to an important dimension of Rorty's irony that has not been addressed so far: 'The ironist is not looking for truth in choosing a final vocabulary. She is creating, not discovering. What is the point of doubt here? The answer may be that [...] she is a nostalgic fallibilist'.[73] For Schneewind, the Rortyan ironist is regressive because she is not a 'calm fallibilist' but is still troubled by a disappointed nostalgia for the illusory sense of certainty and the anxieties that accompany self-creation. 'Irony as realization that there are many vocabularies opens doors to self-creation, but irony as doubt and its anxieties changes nothing to the project. Rorty has not gotten us beyond Mill'.[74]

The existentialist anxieties Schneewind is referring to plague the ironist: she worries that her final vocabulary is never properly her own but only that of Martin Heidegger's 'Man'. Rorty himself alludes to Jean-Paul Sartre's existentialism for an explanation of the ironist's fragile or rootless position:

> [Her] renunciation of the attempt to formulate criteria of choice between final vocabularies, puts [her] in the position which Sartre called 'meta-stable': never quite able to take [herself] seriously because always aware that the terms in which [she describes herself] are subject to change, always aware of the contingency and fragility of [her final vocabulary], and thus of [her self].[75]

Furthermore, the impulse for her continuous creative search for autonomy by redescription is driven by a specific anxiety: 'This is what Harold Bloom calls "the strong poet's anxiety of influence", his "horror of finding himself to be only a copy or a replica"'.[76]

At the same time, while the existentialist process of self-creation that Rorty develops in light of Nietzsche and Freud is a tentative and

---

[73] J. B. Schneewind, 'Rorty on Utopia and Moral Philosophy', in *The Philosophy of Richard Rorty*, pp. 479–505 (p. 492).

[74] Schneewind, 'Rorty on Utopia and Moral Philosophy', pp. 493–94. Bernstein comes to the same conclusion that Rorty's description of the ironist suggests some sort of existential anguish but does not delve into this question: see Bernstein, *Ironic Life*, p. 47.

[75] Rorty, CIS, pp. 73–75.

[76] Rorty, CIS, p. 24. On this, see especially Bacon, 'Rorty, Irony and the Consequences', p. 960 and Ramberg, 'Irony's Commitment', p. 156.

necessarily never-completed project, it is also a sometimes heroic endeavour. Thus, the 'pathos in finitude' would probably be ineliminable, even for the strong poet, the hero for Rortyan ironists.[77] There are several passages in which Rorty distinguishes his figure of the ironist from the tragic heroism of the existentialists.[78] Yet, in his reply to Schneewind, he agrees with his criticism: 'My description of the liberal ironist was badly flawed. I conflated two quite different sorts of people: the unruffled pragmatist and the anguished existential adolescent. I made it sound as if you could not be an antifoundationalist and a romantic self-creator without becoming a Sartrean, ever conscious of the abyss. But one can be both and remain [...] a placid Deweyan'.[79]

Bacon has rightly pointed out, however, that 'Rorty's mistake, as he came to see it, rather was to associate ironic fallibilism and Romanticism with existentialism'.[80] This association is not necessary. Contrary to Rorty's own reading of the liberal ironist, there is textual evidence in CIS that suggests Rorty's utopian figure can be interpreted as a model of pragmatist civil virtue, freed from any existentialist anguish. Thus, her project of self-creation through redescription would become a pragmatic and even playful process, devoid of sentimental nostalgia. Still, we are left with the problem of the two different senses of irony—fallibilistic and romantic—that seem to be at work in chapter four of CIS. I want to turn to the public role of Rortyan irony in both senses—fallibilistic and romantic—as described in that part of CIS.

Rorty's utopian figure is explained not only in terms of contingency and self-creation but also through a juxtaposition of irony with common sense and 'the metaphysician'. Following Heidegger's view of metaphysics as essentialism, the latter is, according to Rorty,

> someone who takes the question 'What is the intrinsic nature of (e.g., justice, science, knowledge, Being, faith, morality, philosophy)?' at face value. [The metaphysician] assumes that the presence of a term in his own final vocabulary ensures that it refers to something which *has* a real essence.[81]

---

77 Rorty, CIS, pp. 40–43.
78 See for instance Rorty, CIS, pp. xiii, 22, 39, 42, 111, 137.
79 Rorty, 'Reply to Schneewind', p. 506.
80 Bacon, 'Rorty, Irony and the Consequences', p. 962.
81 Rorty, CIS, p. 74.

Metaphysicians are still plagued by the 'quest for certainty' (Dewey) and believe that philosophical argumentation can ground and secure their final vocabularies and their political convictions in a theory of human nature or rationality. 'The ironist, by contrast, is a nominalist and a historicist. She thinks nothing has an intrinsic nature, a real essence'.[82] She calls into question the pretence of the metaphysician that we can break out of our vocabularies through logical argument and know reality as it really is.[83] Unlike the metaphysician who aims at inferring what is real, 'her [the ironist's] method is redescription rather than inference'.[84]

As an ironist, she is aware of the contingency of our values, of these as results of the poetic achievements of strong poets. She reminds her fellow citizens of it again and again. For her as a liberal, the invocation of ahistorical entities is not only futile but also tends to be politically dangerous for liberal democracy. So, Rortyan irony performs the anti-authoritarian function of a 'deep theory filter' against essentialising theories. As Ramberg furthermore says, 'When successfully executed, it serves liberalism in the specific sense that it provides an antidote to the temptations of radicalism of any stripe. Ironism matters politically insofar as it counters the urge for sweeping social change guided by a vision framed in terms of deep theory'.[85]

Generally, the driving impulse of the anti-essentialising therapy of the ironist in CIS is a Deweyan democratic anti-authoritarianism that challenges any notion of non-human authority.[86] For Rorty, essentialist philosophy is a form of authoritarianism because it is directed toward an authority beyond the realm of discourse. 'Truth', 'objectivity', 'nature' and 'reality' are only philosophical surrogates of God, he argues. Rorty's

---

82 Rorty, CIS, p. 74. Rorty consistently uses the feminine form of the ironist in contrast to the masculine metaphysician. This gender coding, of course, serves to provoke liberal *malestream* thinkers.
83 Bernstein, *Ironic Life*, p. 36.
84 Rorty, CIS, p. 78.
85 Ramberg, 'Irony's Commitment', p. 152. For the notion of 'deep theory' see also Rorty, PSH, pp. 117–18: 'There is no such thing as human nature, in the deep sense in which Plato and Strauss use this term'. Consistently, philosophy as a theory of the human being in Rorty's utopian society of liberal ironists is relegated to the private sphere. For more on the provocative division of labour between philosophy and literature in CIS, see Müller, *Private Romantik* and *Richard Rorty*.
86 Richard Rorty, *Pragmatism as Anti-Authoritarianism*, ed. by Eduardo Mendieta, Robert Brandom (Cambridge, MA: Harvard University Press, 2021), https://doi.org/10.2307/j.ctv33mgbns, pp. xxxiii, 1–2.

wish is to leave all these 'obsequious Names of God' behind,[87] and to stop feeling responsible to a non-human authority.[88] Rorty understands his ironist redescription of liberalism and pragmatism, with its focus on the social practice of justification, as an emancipatory alternative. The strong ethico-political motive for his transformative project is a 'deep humanism'.[89] His cultural-political goal is a radical secularisation or 'de-divinization' of our democratic culture.[90] In it, no non-human authority beyond the human consensus is sought and recognised any more. Human consensus alone is authority in all public affairs.[91]

Rorty advocates for a discursive pluralism that celebrates the diversity of vocabularies and places them on an equal footing. In his ideal liberal culture, there is equality between all cultural spheres. The goal is tolerance and diversity. Even the natural sciences do not have a special *epistemic* position. This epistemic anti-authoritarianism seems more relevant today than ever, in light of what Rorty called the danger of 'arrogant scientism',[92] as well as the still-dominant essentialist framing of democratic discourse.

The creative contribution of CIS is on the level of justification. Rorty's guiding methodological thesis is that democracy is prior to philosophy.[93] The 'negative' side of this priority thesis is that liberal democracy cannot be theoretically justified; it can only be formulated. However, on the Rortyan view, it does not need a 'strong' justification; seeking it is even harmful for democratic practice. Identification with one's own contingent political community of justification is sufficient—thus its controversial 'positive' side. A philosophical justification of liberalism is thus neither possible nor necessary, only its articulation 'in the service of democratic politics'.[94] Consequently, Rorty's democratic anti-foundationalism does not seek to justify liberalism, but instead proposes a culturally and

---

87 Rorty, *Philosophy as Cultural Politics*, p. 134.
88 See, for some examples, Rorty, *Pragmatism as Anti-Authoritarianism*, p. 1; Rorty, CIS, pp. 21–22, 189.
89 Richard J. Bernstein, 'Richard Rorty's Deep Humanism', *New Literary History*, 39 (2008), 13–27, https://doi.org/10.1353/nlh.0.0012
90 Rorty, CIS, p. 45. See also Rorty, *Pragmatism as Anti-Authoritarianism*, pp. xxxii–xxxiii.
91 Among others, see Rorty, *Pragmatism as Anti-Authoritarianism*, pp. xxxii–xxxiii.
92 Rorty, PCP, p. 136.
93 Rorty, ORT, pp. 175–96.
94 Rorty, CIS, p. 196.

politically motivated redescription that better aligns with the values of liberal society.

This redescription, which has irony as its starting point, is also eminently relevant for methodological reflection in contemporary political theory. According to Rorty's broad characterisation of metaphysics, most of the contemporary liberal thinkers, such as Jürgen Habermas, are still 'liberal metaphysicians',[95] even if they do not think of themselves as such.[96] Critical theory *and* radical thought risk falling back into essentialism without the reflexivity that comes with irony.[97]

According to Jonathan Lear's strong case for irony, 'The point of Socratic irony is not simply to destroy pretenses, but to inject a certain form of not-knowing into polis life. This is a way of teaching virtue. Socratic ignorance is thus an embrace of human open-endedness'.[98] Unfortunately, Lear does not recognise that this is exactly the creative, exploratory and disruptive public role played by the Rortyan ironist as well.[99] With her attitude of moral openness, the ironist seeks to pierce through the crust of convention. Therefore, her irony is primarily in opposition to the complacency of common sense of her linguistic community:

> The opposite of irony is common sense. For that is the watchword of those who unselfconsciously describe everything important in terms of the final vocabulary to which they and those around them are habituated. To be commonsensical is to take for granted that statements formulated in that final vocabulary suffice to describe and judge the beliefs, actions and lives of those who employ alternative final vocabularies.[100]

---

95 Rorty, CIS, pp. 46, 115.
96 On this see Bernstein, *Ironic Life*, pp. 46, 115.
97 For a case for the methodological relevance of Rorty for contemporary political thought see Clayton Chin, *The Practice of Political Theory: Rorty and Continental Thought*, New Directions in Critical Theory (New York: Columbia University Press, 2018), https://doi.org/10.7312/chin17398. Chin's focus is on the metatheoretical level and on Rorty's later conception of pragmatist philosophy as 'cultural politics'. Unfortunately, he does not consider the relevance of Rortyan irony.
98 Jonathan Lear, *A Case for Irony*, Tanner Lectures on Human Values (Cambridge, MA, and London: Harvard University Press, 2011), https://doi.org/10.4159/harvard.9780674063143, p. 6.
99 For a discussion of Jonathan Lear's inspiring case for irony, which unfortunately presents a superficial reading of Rorty's notion of irony see Bernstein, *Ironic Life*, pp. 15–28.
100 Rorty, CIS, p. 74. See Ramberg, 'Irony's Commitment', pp. 148, 156.

In contrast, Rortyan ironists, as intellectuals, maintain a kind of reactive distance from the shared final vocabulary of their moral community or tribe. Their specific doubts are an expression of their alienation from them.[101] At the same time, their 'ironism [...] results from awareness of the power of redescription'.[102] Therefore, they remind their fellow citizens that the prevailing common sense is the contingent product of previous redescriptions. The ironist contrasts them with the redescriptions she is trying to create for herself.[103] In light of this important public role for Rortyan irony, Ramberg's conclusion should be heeded: 'Such liberal ironists may be hard to be, but they are good to have around'.[104]

Rorty's philosophy of conversation and the connection between (romantic) irony and democratic conversability

A key premise for articulating the public role of the romantic side of Rortyan irony—in contrast, then, to Rorty's own strategy of privatising it—is noticing that the ironist, in her existential project of linguistic self-creation, is dependent on communication with others: 'The *liberal* ironist needs as much imaginative acquaintance with alternative final vocabularies as possible, not just for her own edification, but in order to understand the actual and possible humiliation of the people who use these alternative final vocabularies'.[105] According to Rorty, ironists need to communicate with others because only conversation enables them to handle the doubts about their final vocabulary, to keep themselves together, that is, to keep their web of beliefs and desires coherent enough to enable them to act. As Christopher Voparil has noted, one of the underappreciated aspects of Rortyan irony is the extent to

---

101 Rorty, CIS, p. 88. This way, Rortyan irony serves as an antidote to the myside bias. See Stanovich, *The Bias That Divides Us*, p. 85: 'To avoid myside bias, we need to distance ourselves from our convictions'.
102 Rorty, CIS, p. 89.
103 Rorty, CIS, pp. 61, 87–88.
104 Ramberg, 'Irony's Commitment', p. 160. Ramberg also emphasizes that irony is not just a corrective antidote to metaphysics but to any petrified common sense too. Hence, against Neil Gascoigne's view that the last ironist goes with the last metaphysician (Gascoigne, *Richard Rorty*, p. 182), Ramberg rightly states that irony as serene virtue of critical open-mindedness remains a necessary antidote even for a pragmatist common sense: 'This is why irony... never ceases, even in a Rortyan utopia'. See Ramberg, 'Irony's Commitment', pp. 152, 156, 158.
105 Rorty, CIS, p. 92. My emphasis.

which the ironist needs others and what her moral imperative is.[106] CIS is quite explicit about it: 'The ironist [...] desperately needs to *talk* to other people, needs this with the same urgency as people need to make love'.[107] 'Our doubts about our own characters or our own culture can be resolved or assuaged only by enlarging our acquaintance'.[108]

This emphasis on the importance of conversational encounters for ironists is a reflection of the general significance of conversation in Rorty's anti-authoritarian pragmatism. Rorty seeks to replace representationalist philosophy as epistemology with a philosophy of conversation that focuses solely on the practice of justification. 'Conversation is the highest good for discursive creatures', according to Rorty.[109] In his version of a philosophy of conversation, communicative solidarity, rather than truth or objectivity, is the supreme ideal. Even the cautionary use of 'true' does not exhort us to strive for objective truth as opposed to merely contextualised justification. It simply requires a willingness to defend our views, even to an audience that may disagree with us. The goal, he argues, must be to extend the reach of the communicative 'we' ever further.

The learned openness of Western culture to other voices does not need 'truth' to serve as a normative, context-transcending reference point.[110] Rorty proposes that we instead posit, as its functional replacement, a

---

106 Voparil, 'Rorty's Ethics', p. 497.
107 Rorty, CIS, p. 186.
108 Rorty, CIS, p. 80. Taking this need of the ironist as a starting point, Voparil, 'Rorty and James', reads, with recourse to William James, Rortyan irony as key concept of a liberal ethics of attention and responsiveness that combines epistemic modesty and willingness to listen and learn from others with ethical responsiveness. Although I am very sympathetic with this project, it runs against the basic anti-foundationalist thrust of CIS. Furthermore, irony *qua* irony cannot serve as its 'ground'. Surely, it does lead to tolerance and willingness to respect and to listen also to the other side but only the *liberal* ironist is, additionally, attentive to hitherto unperceived forms of suffering through her project of enlarging her acquaintance with other final vocabularies. See my emphasis in the above quote (CIS, p. 92). See also the following noteworthy passage restricting relevant interlocutors for ironists to 'people intelligent enough to understand what one is talking about—people who are capable of seeing how one might have these doubts because they know what such doubts are like, people who are themselves given to irony' (CIS, p. 187).
109 Richard Rorty, 'Response to Dennett', in *Rorty and His Critics*, ed. by Robert Brandom, Philosophers and Their Critics 9 (Malden, MA, and Oxford: Blackwell, 2000), pp. 101–08 (p. 105).
110 Rorty, ORT, pp. 2, 21–23, 204; Richard Rorty, *Truth and Progress* (Cambridge: Cambridge University Press, 1998), https://doi.org/10.1017/CBO9780511625404, pp. 51–54.

commitment to keep the conversation of culture open. In *Philosophy and the Mirror of Nature*, Rorty stated that the ultimate goal of philosophy is to keep this conversation going.[111] And in CIS, he sketches a truly democratic culture in which freedom—that is free conversation—has replaced truth as the normative guiding ideal. Free discourse is not a means to truth, but it becomes a goal in itself.[112]

Long before the debate about post-truth politics in times of a fragmented public sphere, Rorty was criticised for debunking truth in his conversational pragmatism. Akeel Bilgrami and Daniel Dennett, for instance, argued that the refusal to value truth leads to subversive and dangerous relativism.[113] According to both, Rorty's postmodernism cannot distinguish between the frivolous and the serious, and therefore cannot identify 'bullshitters'.[114] Rorty addresses this charge indirectly by focusing on the importance of the democratic virtue of conversability. For this, he builds on his redescription of 'love of Truth as simply conversability'.[115]

Rorty views conversability not as an instrumental virtue, but as an intrinsic good, associated with tolerance and a lack of fanaticism.[116] His redescription is motivated, again, by the democratic anti-authoritarianism discussed above: 'Pragmatists construe the love of Truth as an attitude toward one's fellow beings rather than as an attitude toward something non-human'.[117] For Rorty, the distinction between the frivolous and the serious is an important *practical* distinction between 'incurious cultists and more conversable sorts of people'.[118] For him, the test for 'bullshitters' is not philosophical but sociological. The relevant question is not: 'Do

---

111 Rorty, PMN, pp. 377–79.
112 Rorty, CIS, pp. xiii, xvi, 84.
113 For the never-silent (but false) reproach of relativism see esp. Putnam, *Realism with a Human Face*, pp. 22–25.
114 Akeel Bilgrami, 'Is Truth a Goal of Inquiry?: Rorty and Davidson on Truth', in *Rorty and His Critics*, ed. by Brandom, pp. 242–62 (pp. 260–61); Daniel C. Dennett, 'Postmodernism and Truth', *The Proceedings of the Twentieth World Congress of Philosophy*, 8 (2000), 93–103.
115 Richard Rorty, *Is "Post-Modernism" Relevant to Politics?: Spinoza Lectures* (Assen: Van Gorcum, 1997), p. 26.
116 Rorty, *Is "Post-Modernism" Relevant to Politics?*, pp. 25–27.
117 Rorty, *Is "Post-Modernism" Relevant to Politics?*, p. 8. It is worth noting that Rorty not only preached the ideal of conversability but, as the author could experience himself, lived by it even in exchanges with unknown interlocutors.
118 Rorty, 'Response to Dennett', p. 104.

you value truth?' but rather 'Are you curious about other views?'. To sort the serious from the bullshitters, behavioural evidence is crucial: 'Bullshitters are distinguished by being unconversable, incurious, and self-absorbed'.[119] In other words, 'bullshitters' can be identified by their (group-)egotism. So for Rorty, the relevant *moral* probity is independent of the philosopher's debate about Truth and Reality. It is whether one does one's honest best to break out of one's own parochial political vocabulary and to attempt a fusion of horizons. What matters in democratic discourse is intellectual curiosity. So, one must ask: 'Who is willing to go to considerable effort to build conversational bridges?'.[120]

The liberal ironist's value lies in this: she exemplifies exactly the democratic virtue of conversability required in situations where discourse across incommensurable vocabularies is necessary to continue public deliberation. Her irony—consciousness of the contingency of her final vocabulary and of the power of redescription—makes a difference in her communicative practice. Afraid of being stuck in the vocabulary in which she was brought up, she tries to get acquainted with as many strange people and communities as possible.[121] Her irony leads to greater open-mindedness and a willingness to respect and listen to the other side, not only in dialogue with foreign cultures but also with other discursive communities in general.[122]

The connection between Rortyan irony and the democratic virtue of conversability is especially relevant given the structural transformation of the public sphere following the rise of social media. The public sphere becomes increasingly splintered into segregated semi-publics with serious consequences for the deliberative process of forming opinions in a democracy. The polarising fragmentation into 'echo chambers' and 'filter bubbles' enforces not only extreme partisan bias but also hinders shared conversation across the boundaries of opposing discursive communities within democratic society.[123] According to the science journalist David Roberts, this 'leads to what you might call *tribal epistemology*: information is evaluated based not on conformity to common standards of evidence

---

119 Rorty, 'Response to Dennett', p. 105.
120 Rorty, 'Response to Dennett', p. 105. See 104–06.
121 Rorty, CIS, p. 80.
122 Rorty, 'Erwiderung Baltzer', pp. 52–53.
123 See, among others, Jürgen Habermas, *Ein neuer Strukturwandel der Öffentlichkeit und die deliberative Politik* (Berlin: Suhrkamp Verlag, 2022).

or correspondence to a common understanding of the world, but on whether it supports the tribe's values and goals and is vouchsafed by tribal leaders'.[124]

In view of this development, Rorty's lifelong preoccupation with questions of metaphilosophy and the ethical dimension of 'abnormal' discourse between incommensurable vocabularies is more relevant than ever.[125] This is especially true of his linguistic communitarianism.[126] Turning the focus to the practice of justification, Rorty is addressing the crucial importance of communicative communities in questions of truth and facts.[127] Following Rorty, Voparil rightly notes that '[l]oyalties can— and do—trump facts'. Therefore, the often called-for return to truth or to facts in this situation of a fragmented public sphere is understandable but not effective because 'anywhere deeply fractured interpretive communities exist, the appeal to facts goes nowhere'. We fail to reach agreement not primarily because of a lack of orientation towards facts. Most in need of recovery, in the so-called post-truth world, is not our relation to objective reality, but to our fellow citizens. In the tribalist myside-society we inhabit, we need to expand communicative solidarity beyond our parochial loyalties.[128]

Rorty asked the *now* crucial political questions for ensuring open conversation beyond the boundaries of our tribal communities of justification, and revive democratic life: 'What are the limits of our community? Are our encounters sufficiently free and open? Has what we have recently gained in solidarity cost us our ability to listen to

---

124 David Roberts, 'Donald Trump and the Rise of Tribal Epistemology', *Vox* (19 May 2017), https://www.vox.com/policy-and-politics/2017/3/22/14762030/donald-trump-tribal-epistemology
125 Because of Rorty's emphasis on this dimension in general, and on the moral rather than methodological character of the choice between vocabularies in particular, William Curtis (*Defending Rorty*, p. 54) sees Rorty rightly as 'virtue *epistemologist*' (my emphasis).
126 Müller, 'General Introduction', pp. 6–7.
127 Consider, for example, the (in-)famous provocative formulation in PMN that truth is no 'more than what our peers will, *ceteris paribus*, let us get away with saying' (p. 176), or his claim that even the reputed 'hardness of facts as an artefact produced by our choice of language game ... is simply the hardness of the previous agreements within a community about the consequences of a certain event' (ORT, p. 80).
128 Christopher Voparil, 'The Truth Doesn't Matter', *The Boston Globe* (7 June 2017), https://www.bostonglobe.com/ideas/2017/06/07/the-truth-doesn-matter/I4fY2nu99KnViMINTkIOCP/story.html

outsiders who are suffering? To outsiders who have new ideas? [...] With what communities should you identify, of which should you think of yourself as a member?'.[129] At the same time, Rorty's ethics of inclusivity consistently stresses the importance of open conversation beyond the borders of tribal justification communities and identity groups. For him, striving for an overarching common conversational community is not only a prerequisite for a functioning democracy, it 'pretty much *is* democratic politics'.[130]

To keep the democratic conversation going across the borders of segregated justification communities, despite our ideological differences, we need reforms of the (digital) infrastructure of the public sphere.[131] Moreover, we need to foster the civic virtues that are required in our situation. As Rorty rightly states, 'civility is not a method, it is simply a virtue'.[132] Already in PMN, he advocates 'getting into conversation with strangers' as a 'new virtue'.[133] For the urgent project of fostering the democratic virtue of conversability, the figure of the ironist of CIS, with her characteristic conversability, serves as a contemporary civic ideal. We urgently need more ironists because it is 'the ironist [who] spends her time worrying about the possibility that she has been initiated into the wrong tribe, taught to play the wrong language game'.[134]

Regarding the Rortyan project of fostering irony, two qualifying remarks are required. First, irony can serve as a valuable resource in our dark times, but it is a virtue that, like any virtue, requires cultivation. Accordingly, Rorty does not only preach virtue, his 'bourgeois liberalism' is well aware of the mundane 'materialist' base of liberal institutions and virtues.[135] He therefore stresses the need for practical measures, such as general education, security and prosperity, as social conditions for liberal irony.[136] Rorty's version of liberalism emphasises the importance of deepening and broadening social solidarity as the basis of liberal

---

129 Rorty, ORT, p. 13.
130 Richard Rorty, 'Universality and Truth', in *Rorty and His Critics*, ed. by Brandom, pp. 1–30 (p. 9).
131 Cf. Habermas, *Ein neuer Strukturwandel*.
132 Richard Rorty, *Consequences of Pragmatism: (Essays: 1972-1980)* (Minneapolis, MN: University of Minnesota Press, 1982), p. 202.
133 Rorty, PMN, p. 319.
134 Rorty, CIS, p. 75.
135 Rorty, ORT, p. 198.
136 Rorty, CIS, pp. xiv, 84-85.

democracy. Tirelessly, Rorty promoted 'old-fashioned' leftist egalitarian politics of reform within liberal democracy.[137]

Secondly, the project of fostering irony as conversability does not mean that only the voters of populist politicians must learn finally to listen to the liberal 'good guys'. Both sides of the political spectrum tend to restrict the conversation to their own justification 'tribe'. Therefore, conversability in *both* directions is required. For example, we cosmopolitan liberals must not look down upon the 'deplorable' losers in our own national democracies. Instead, we need to take their loss of social hope seriously and, if still possible, initiate a serious conversation with them. Rorty warned against the dangers of not doing so—against cultural chauvinism and neglecting increasing social inequality. As early as 1997, he predicted that this would make the rise of right-wing populism and the election of a 'strong man' increasingly likely.[138]

Rortyan irony as ideal civic virtue of a serene fallibilism and of conversability

Section three of this chapter provided an overview of Rorty's account of irony and of the controversial figure of the liberal ironist who combines private irony and public solidarity. Assuming a softening of the split between the public and the private, this figure presents a plausible proposal for a new self-image for the citizens of liberal societies. Additionally, the common distinction in Rorty scholarship between two senses of irony in CIS—fallibilist and romantic—is critically discussed. I have offered a redescription of Rortyan irony based on a rejection of a sharp distinction between these.

The fourth section contained a discussion of the notion of final vocabulary and of the nature of ironic doubt in Rorty's definition of the ironist. Referring to Bernstein in particular, I emphasised the interpretation of Rortyan irony as an anti-foundationalist virtue of a serene fallibilism, beyond essentialism and epistemological scepticism, that entails not only awareness of contingency, but also open-mindedness and creativity. I argue that Rortyan fallibilistic irony is still

---
137 See e.g., 'Back to Class Politics', pp. 252–54, in Rorty, PSH.
138 Richard Rorty, *Achieving Our Country: Leftist Thought in Twentieth-Century America* (Cambridge, MA: Harvard University Press, 1998), pp. 87–88.

and remains politically useful against the 'bad faith'[139] of essentialist theories of human nature and any form of petrified common sense. Specifically, it serves as an 'antidote' against the above-mentioned tribe-based myside bias. Therefore, the liberal ironist, with her sense of the fragility of democratic institutions, is not only a useful personification of the fallibilist attitude central to pragmatists but also a convincing civic ideal. The combination of anti-foundationalism and democratic commitment of CIS is a necessary remedy against foundationalists and (pseudo-)radicals of any stripe.

Rorty's version of pragmatism is, at its heart, a philosophy of conversation. Section five connected the description of the ironist in CIS as dependent on the communication with others, with Rorty's later construal of the love of Truth as conversability. The result is that Rortyan irony can be redescribed as leading to the public virtue of conversability across boundaries of discursive communities. The fallibilist civic ideal the liberal ironist embodies, represents, therefore, also a promising alternative to the (understandable) call for a return to truth-talk in times of a fragmented public sphere. Her virtue of conversability is desperately needed to foster democratic community beyond partisan justification-communities.

In sum, the liberal ironist of CIS remains a politically useful utopian figure. Furthermore, a properly redescribed Rortyan irony in *both its senses* is a valuable resource in our dark times. Its political 'cash value' is (moral) tolerance, open-mindedness, creativity and conversability. Therefore, one can agree with Rorty that irony is, next to solidarity, the 'chief virtue of the members of a liberal society'.[140]

---

139 Rorty, CP, p. 109. With reference to Jean-Paul Sartre, any essentialism is for Rorty a kind of 'bad faith', as an attempt to turn oneself into a thing and to slough off the moral responsibility for choice among the vocabularies we employ.

140 Rorty, CIS, p. 46.

8. Irony as Hope and the Future of the Humanities

Bryan Vescio

Of the three terms Richard Rorty introduced in the title of his 1989 book *Contingency, Irony and Solidarity*, the one that has provoked by far the most resistance and that is currently in the most danger is irony.[1] That is partly because it is the one Rorty himself has come closest to renouncing. In one of the last pieces he wrote before his death from pancreatic cancer in 2007, a posthumously published reply to J. B. Schneewind's essay in *The Philosophy of Richard Rorty* (2010), Rorty responds to Schneewind's criticisms of his concept of irony by straightforwardly admitting that it was poorly conceived. While he stops short of disavowing the concept entirely, he concedes that it is deeply flawed, as is the distinction between the public and the private that he likewise introduced in CIS. Many critics surely felt vindicated by this reply, since the book's distinction between the public and the private and its celebration of irony have inspired the most opposition to it, even among those who otherwise admire Rorty's work and share his basic pragmatist commitments.[2]

Those of us who, on the other hand, find in Rorty's account of the private ironist intellectual a more or less precise description of what

---

1   Rorty, Richard, *Contingency, Irony and Solidarity* (Cambridge: Cambridge University Press, 1989), https://doi.org/10.1017/cbo9780511804397. Hereafter CIS.
2   Writers who embrace pragmatism but who reject Rorty's distinction between the public and the private are too numerous to mention individually. A characteristic discussion can be found in Richard Shusterman, *Practicing Philosophy: Pragmatism and the Philosophical Life* (London: Routledge, 1997). William Curtis also has a useful discussion of a number of readers sympathetic to Rorty who nevertheless object to his public/private distinction on pp. 103–06 of his book.

attracts us to the academic humanities cannot be so enthusiastic about this apparent late career turn away from irony. Because I so closely identify the conception of private irony in CIS with what I most value in the humanities, I hope to accomplish two things in this chapter: first, to remedy the deficiencies in Rorty's idea of irony by reinterpreting it, using suggestions from his own works including CIS; and second, to explain how doing so makes this book a valuable resource in the effort to rescue the humanities from the much-discussed 'crisis' in which they are currently embroiled. The way forward on both fronts, I will argue, is to substitute hope for doubt as the source of Rortian irony.

Commentators who hope to defend Rorty, and specifically his concept of irony, from his critics often do so by assigning irony, against Rorty's explicit wishes, a fairly direct and central role in advancing Rorty's democratic politics. A case in point is William Curtis's 2015 book *Defending Rorty: Pragmatism and Liberal Virtue*, whose effort to distinguish between Rorty's 'critical, therapeutic subproject' and 'his constructive, explicitly normative, utopian subproject' partly inspires the present volume.[3] Curtis quotes John Dewey's insistence that democratic political institutions must be accompanied by a culture that inculcates habits and values in citizens that support those institutions. He argues that Rorty's philosophy contributes to such a culture by identifying the 'virtues' that it must encourage in democratic citizens, chief among them what Curtis calls 'the civic virtue of irony'. This virtue, which Curtis associates with fallibilism and believes is instilled through a liberal arts education, makes people 'more likely to be good democratic citizens' because 'they will be less likely to insist on the righteous certainty of their political agendas and lord political power over their opponents, and more likely to be politically circumspect, moderate, and tolerate a range of political differences'.[4] At times, he insists that cultivating this virtue is important enough actually to bring about the liberal utopia that Rorty envisions: 'What is to be gained by adopting this attitude of ironic, apparent "double-think"? Nothing less than "liberal utopia"'.[5]

---

3   William Curtis, *Defending Rorty: Pragmatism and Liberal Virtue* (Cambridge: Cambridge University Press, 2015), https://doi.org/10.1017/cbo9781316272145, p. 34.
4   Curtis, *Defending Rorty*, p. 83.
5   Curtis, *Defending Rorty*, p. 37.

Rorty is, to put it mildly, less optimistic about the potential contributions of irony to democratic politics. In CIS, he famously relegates irony to the private sphere and warns against adopting it as the public rhetoric of a democratic society. He says that the activities of private ironists only occasionally and accidentally contribute to public projects of solidarity. Elsewhere, Rorty writes, in a passage Curtis also quotes, that philosophical ideas in general, like his conception of irony, tend to 'make some practical differences' only 'sometimes' and 'in the long run'.[6] In my reconstruction of his concept of irony, I hope to do full justice to these reservations, which are born of Rorty's pragmatist subordination of theory to practice and his robust sense of the distinction between public and private. Like Curtis, I think a sense of irony is cultivated by a liberal education, and in particular a humanistic one. But I will argue for a much more modest constructive project for which a rehabilitated version of Rorty's concept of irony can be used: a defence of the humanities that itself tempers our expectations of their ability to bring about a liberal utopia. The constructive project for Rorty's pragmatism I will recommend is that if, for the reasons Rorty suggests in CIS, irony cannot serve as the public rhetoric for liberal democracy in general, a confluence of accidental circumstances today might make it just the public rhetoric the humanities need.

In his contribution to *The Philosophy of Richard Rorty*, Schneewind makes a powerful case against the version of irony Rorty describes in CIS. His case hinges on the first of the three conditions Rorty claims ironists must meet in the following passage:

> I shall define an 'ironist' as someone who fulfills three conditions: 1.) She has radical and continuing doubts about the final vocabulary she currently uses, because she has been impressed by other vocabularies, vocabularies taken as final by people or books she has encountered; 2.) she realizes that argument phrased in her present vocabulary can neither underwrite nor dissolve these doubts; 3.) insofar as she philosophizes about her situation, she does not think that her vocabulary is closer to reality than others, that it is in touch with a power not herself.[7]

---

6 Richard Rorty, 'Hilary Putnam and the Relativist Menace', in Richard Rorty, *Truth and Progress* (Cambridge: Cambridge University Press, 1998), pp. 43–62, https://doi.org/10.1017/cbo9780511625404.003, p. 45.

7 Rorty, CIS, p. 73.

Schneewind has no problem with the second or third of these conditions, which are just standard expressions of anti-foundationalism, but he believes that the idea that an ironist 'doubts' her final vocabulary creates problems for Rorty. Schneewind's criticisms arise from asking the question all pragmatists must ask about these doubts: 'The "crackerbarrel pragmatist" in me wants to ask what difference in her life is made by her doubt. What exactly is the ironist doubting?'.[8] If the doubts have no practical effect on her life at all, then they are what Peirce would have called 'make-believe doubts', which is to say that for a pragmatist, they are not really doubts at all.[9] The practical consequences that doubts typically have, by definition, are to make us less inclined to act on our beliefs, which pragmatists consider to be, in James's phrase, 'rules for action'. So if the ironist's doubts do make a practical difference to her life, Schneewind points out that they must make her less inclined to act on her most deeply held beliefs, and this must apply to the public as well as the private beliefs she formulates in her final vocabulary: 'If she is an antifoundationalist, then she takes *all* her beliefs to be ungrounded and so tied to time and contingency. How then will she confine her doubt to her *private* final vocabulary?'.[10]

This is where Rorty appears to run into a contradiction, since his central argument in CIS is that irony and liberalism are not incompatible, either for a utopian liberal society or for individual citizens of it; one can be both an ironist and a fully committed liberal citizen. All citizens of the liberal utopia Rorty sketches in his book are commonsensical anti-foundationalists, who, in the words of Joseph Schumpeter, 'realise the relative validity of [their] convictions and yet stand for them unflinchingly'.[11] But ironists are more than just anti-foundationalists because they also meet condition 1 above: they have 'radical and continuing doubts' about their deepest convictions, and to have such

---

8   J. B. Schneewind, 'Rorty on Utopia and Moral Philosophy', in *The Philosophy of Richard Rorty*, ed. by Randall Auxier and Lewis Hahn, The Library of Living Philosophers 32 (Chicago and Lasalle, IL: Open Court Press, 2010), pp. 479–505 (p. 491).
9   See Charles Sanders Peirce, 'The Fixation of Belief', in *Charles Sanders Peirce: Selected Writings (Values in a Universe of Chance)*, ed. by Philip P. Wiener (New York: Dover, 1958), pp. 91–112.
10 Schneewind, 'Rorty on Utopia and Moral Philosophy', p. 491.
11 Rorty, CIS, p. 46. Rorty is quoting Isiah Berlin *Four Essays on Liberty* (Oxford University Press, 1969), p. 172, on which Berlin quotes Joseph Schumpeter.

doubts must mean that they cannot be fully committed liberals. So the dilemma Schneewind finds in Rorty is this: either an ironist's doubts are purely make-believe because they have no pragmatic effects at all, or they seriously undermine liberal convictions, thus compromising the whole argument of CIS.

A related problem Schneewind finds with Rorty's conception of irony also hinges on its supposed origins in doubt. Specifically, he points out that the very idea of 'doubting' one's entire final vocabulary does not make sense in Rorty's terms: 'Has the ironist who asks if she has the wrong vocabulary mistaken a question that makes sense about a particular point inside common sense morality for one that makes sense when asked about the whole of it?'.[12] The point Schneewind has in mind here is Rorty's rejection of 'the idea that there can be reasons for using languages [or vocabularies] as well as reasons within language for believing statements'.[13] This is what Robert Brandom has called Rorty's 'vocabulary vocabulary', which he considers to be Rorty's most original contribution to philosophy: the view that there can only be inferential relations between beliefs within vocabularies, and not between vocabularies themselves, which is to say that there can be no criteria of choice for adopting a vocabulary.[14]

But Schneewind's point is that if there can be no reasons for adopting one vocabulary over another, then there also cannot be doubts about a vocabulary: a doubt is a worry that a belief within a vocabulary is not sufficiently justified, but one cannot worry that a vocabulary—which by definition cannot be justified—is sufficiently justified. Schneewind concludes that because irony is what distinguishes Rorty's account of self-creation from older versions of that idea found in writers like Montaigne, Kant and Mill, he really has not moved beyond these thinkers at all.

One would expect a fierce defence of irony in Rorty's reply to Schneewind in the same volume, but instead he seems to capitulate almost entirely. He writes, 'Reading Schneewind's contribution to this

---

12 Schneewind, 'Rorty on Utopia and Moral Philosophy', p. 494.
13 Rorty, CIS, p. 48.
14 See Robert B. Brandom, 'Vocabularies of Pragmatism: Synthesizing Naturalism and Historicism', in *Rorty and His Critics*, ed. by Robert B. Brandom (Oxford: Blackwell, 2000), pp. 156–83.

volume has made me realize that my description of the liberal ironist was badly flawed. I conflated two quite different sorts of people: the unruffled pragmatist and the anguished existentialist adolescent. I made it sound as if you could not be an antifoundationalist and a romantic self-creator without becoming a Sartrean, ever conscious of the abyss'.[15] Schneewind suggests that Rorty's ironist doubt really only amounts to nostalgia for lost foundations, something that has no place in the liberal utopia Rorty imagines: 'If Rorty's utopia ever arrives, no one will have had the sort of upbringing that generates ironic nostalgia. If no one thinks ordinary language gets the world right, or that some better language might, Rorty's ironist will vanish'.[16] Again, Rorty concurs, writing, 'Schneewind is right that all antifoundationalism can do, when it comes to the moral life is "to take the nostalgia out of fallibilism"'.[17] Finally, he concedes that Schneewind 'is right in saying that my description of the liberal ironist does not get us beyond Mill. Neither does my distinction between the public and the private'.[18] Not only do these concessions call into question Rorty's description of the 'liberal ironist' in CIS, but they appear to leave little work for the middle term in the title to do at all. It is notable that Rorty's language avoids taking back the notion of irony altogether, but his reply to Schneewind certainly raises the question of what is left of it. Can anything be salvaged of this idea, and is it worth it to try?

I want to answer yes on both counts, and Rorty himself provides clues for how to rehabilitate irony in CIS. In a discussion of Foucault, Rorty says that his 'yearning' for autonomy is what should 'be reserved for private life' in his liberal utopia: 'Autonomy is not something which all human beings have within them and which society can release by ceasing to repress them. It is something which certain particular human beings hope to attain by self-creation, and which a few actually do'.[19] This word 'hope' is used a number of times in the book to describe this necessarily private quest for autonomy, most notably when Rorty explicitly attributes the ironist's efforts at redescription to a kind of hope: 'We ironists hope, by this continual redescription, to make the best

---

15 Richard Rorty, 'Reply to Schneewind', in *The Philosophy of Richard Rorty*, pp. 506–08 (p. 506).
16 Schneewind, 'Rorty on Utopia and Moral Philosophy', p. 493.
17 Rorty, 'Reply to Schneewind', p. 507.
18 Rorty, 'Reply to Schneewind', p. 506.
19 Rorty, CIS, p. 65.

selves for ourselves that we can'.²⁰ The persistence of the word 'hope' in Rorty's descriptions of the ironist's motives and activities suggests a revision of his definition of irony that might well allay the reservations he shares with Schneewind about the term.

Instead of saying that anti-foundationalism leaves the ironist with 'radical and continuing doubts' about her final vocabulary, Rorty could with equal justice have said that her realisation of the contingency of the vocabularies she has inherited—and thus the fact that they are subject to change—has led her to *hope* for a future self that is better than her current one. This hope, which we have seen Rorty invoke explicitly elsewhere in his book, is equally inspired by the fact that the ironist 'has been impressed by other vocabularies, vocabularies taken as final by people or books she has encountered'.²¹ As Rorty stresses throughout CIS, the contingency of a final vocabulary entails that it is 'final' only 'in the sense that if doubt is cast on the worth of these words, their user has no noncircular argumentative recourse',²² not in the sense that it is immune from time and chance. If an ironist embraces this contingency and also has been impressed by other final vocabularies she has encountered, she can hope for a better future iteration of herself, a better final vocabulary one day, without necessarily casting doubt on the worth of her current one. This hope is tantamount to the desire Nietzsche famously found to be the source of religion in *On the Genealogy of Morals*: 'the desire to be different, to be in a different place'.²³ Harold Bloom has identified this same desire as the motive for literature in *Agon*, so it would be a natural choice for Rorty's definition of the ironist, since his book places both that figure and Bloom's conception of poetry at the centre of the poeticised culture he hopes will accompany his liberal utopia.²⁴

Reinterpreting irony as entailing this hope but not necessarily any particular doubts about either one's final vocabulary or one's beliefs removes Schneewind's epistemological and practical concerns about the term while preserving the role Rorty assigns it in CIS. The vague,

---

20   Rorty, CIS, p. 80.
21   Rorty, CIS, p. 73.
22   Rorty, CIS, p. 73.
23   Friedrich Nietzsche, *Basic Writings of Nietzsche*, ed. by Walter Kaufman, Modern Library Classics (New York: Modern Library, 1968), p. 556.
24   Harold Bloom, *Agon: Towards a Theory of Revisionism* (Oxford: Oxford University Press, 1982), p. 91.

non-epistemic hope I described above undermines neither an entire vocabulary nor any particular beliefs the way Schneewind worries that irony must. Rorty writes, 'if languages are historical contingencies, rather than attempts to capture the true shape of the world or the self, then to "stand unflinchingly for one's moral convictions" is a matter of identifying oneself with such a contingency'.[25] The point of Schneewind's criticism is that if irony is conceived as doubt, then an ironist must indeed flinch, and that means flinching even from the moral convictions Rorty associates with liberalism. But an ironist who merely hopes vaguely that someday the contingencies of life will transform her into someone better need not flinch from any particular commitments, including her commitment to liberalism.

This suggestion is wholly consistent with Rorty's remark that 'ironists do not see the search for a final vocabulary as (even in part) a way of getting something distinct from this vocabulary right'.[26] They cannot worry that their current final vocabulary is 'wrong' in this sense either; rather, they know that they will probably talk differently someday, and they hope that when they do they will see themselves as in some way better, though they know that they will have no criteria for judging themselves so. Irony as hope also escapes the concern about 'make believe doubt' because it has discernible practical consequences, the ones Rorty assigns to irony throughout CIS: if you have the hope to be different or elsewhere you will voraciously seek out new texts, conversation partners, and experiences in the hope of redescribing and recontextualising them— or, if you are especially lucky, being redescribed or recontextualised by them. An ironist culture defined by hope would look precisely like the one Rorty describes as defined by doubt, only without the philosophical deficiencies that make the latter implausible.

However, is an irony founded on hope rather than doubt still worthy of the name? Schneewind quotes a later interview in which Rorty describes his distinctive use of the term 'irony': 'Irony is often associated with indifference and distance. I have tied something else to this word. I wanted to point to the insight that every self-inventor is always a creation of time and contingency'.[27] The reason Rorty cannot associate irony with

---

25 Rorty, CIS, p. 60.
26 Rorty, CIS, p. 75.
27 Rorty, CIS, qtd. on p. 492.

indifference and distance is because his view of the self is derived from Davidson, who rejects the picture of the self in which 'human beings are not simply networks of beliefs and desires but rather beings which *have* those beliefs and desires'.[28] If a self consists of nothing but its beliefs and desires, there is no way to distance oneself from them.

Richard J. Bernstein's book *Ironic Life* (2016) explains why a conception of irony founded on both this anti-foundationalist view and hope rather than doubt nevertheless belongs within the tradition of philosophical thinking about irony by tracing continuities between theorists of irony from Socrates (through the interpretations of Gregory Vlastos and Alexander Nehamas) to Kierkegaard and contemporary theorists like Jonathan Lear and, of course, Rorty himself. The common thread among all these thinkers, according to Bernstein, is the treatment of irony as '*not* merely a rhetorical trope, but rather a proposal for how *we—or some of us*—might live our lives'.[29] He approvingly cites Schneewind's criticisms of Rorty's definition of irony, noting of his use of the word 'doubt' that 'it is "ironic" that his characterization of the ironist is infected with epistemological terminology'.[30] Bernstein thinks these criticisms can be deflected by insisting that Rorty 'is not making a standard epistemological point about doubt. Because there is a plurality of final vocabularies—and it is always possible to create new final vocabularies—it simply makes no sense to speak as if there is one and only one final vocabulary'.[31] But Bernstein's amendment of Rorty is just a restatement of the ironist's acceptance of contingency, and he observes later in his book that 'recognizing this contingency is not sufficient for identifying the "ironist"'.[32] The revision of Rorty's first condition of irony he suggests, though, does not really go beyond that recognition: 'Instead of describing the ironist as "having radical and continuing doubts", Rorty would have been clearer—and prevented misunderstanding—if he had simply said that the ironist knows that her final vocabulary is the result of all sorts of historical contingencies, and that other contingencies generate other final vocabularies'.[33] One

---

28 Rorty, CIS, p. 10.
29 Richard J. Bernstein, *Ironic Life* (Cambridge: Polity Press, 2016), p. 34.
30 Bernstein, *Ironic Life*, p. 46.
31 Bernstein, *Ironic Life*, p. 32.
32 Bernstein, *Ironic Life*, p. 116.
33 Bernstein, *Ironic Life*, p. 47.

problem with this suggested revision is that this is pretty much what the second and third conditions already say, but another is that Bernstein is simply trading one epistemological term, 'doubt', for another, 'knows'. He makes a similar epistemological claim when he says that Rorty's 'irony becomes a powerful way of exposing illusion',[34] specifically the illusion of necessity and finality. An even better solution is the one I have offered: rewriting condition 1 not as an epistemic condition, whether of doubt or of knowledge, but as a non-epistemic condition of hope.

For Bernstein, Rorty's conception of irony is bound to other historical conceptions in part because it extends Kierkegaard's version of irony, and exchanging epistemological terms like doubt for hope makes it work even better for this purpose. Bernstein notes that Kierkegaard's discussion of irony is critical of what he calls 'pure irony', the kind of 'radical determinate negation' which deprives the ironist of any firm ground to stand on: 'The more one pushes this ironic stance to its extreme, the more it becomes clear that it is unstable and paradoxical. If the ironist is to be thoroughly consistent, he must turn his irony against his own ironic stance'.[35] For Bernstein, Kierkegaard's innovation is that he found a way beyond this 'sheer emptiness or the seduction of determinate

---

34 Bernstein, *Ironic Life*, p. 33.
35 Bernstein, *Ironic Life*, p. 89. One objection to thinking of irony in terms of hope rather than doubt might be that it seems to remove this sense of negation from the concept. But the hope to be different, to be elsewhere, carries the same sense of alienation that animates Kierkegaard's sense of irony. For Rorty, this hope is specific to the aspiring strong poet's hope to escape the language of the tribe, and in CIS, he notes that the strong poet knows that their fondest hope will always remain 'a project rather than a result' because of both the inevitability of death and the inevitably social nature of language: 'The strong poet's fear of death as the fear of incompletion is a function of the fact that no project of redescribing the world and the past, no project of self-creation through imposition of one's own idiosyncratic metaphoric, can avoid being marginal and parasitic' (CIS, pp. 40–41). This knowledge is the negative side of irony as hope and the source of the strong poet's perpetual restlessness. But it is also specific to the private hope for originality and autonomy: the public hope for solidarity faces no such insuperable practical obstacles. So it is clear that this negative or self-critical aspect of irony can indeed be confined to the private sphere in a way that Schneewind rightly claims irony as doubt cannot. Irony as hope can be so confined because the reservations it entails are not about a final vocabulary but rather about the peculiar project of the strong poet. For the Davidsonian reasons Rorty cites, no one, not even a strong poet, can put their entire final vocabulary up for grabs at once. In this light, a liberal ironist is just someone who can affirm with Rorty that when it comes to the hope for public solidarity 'Western social and political thought may have had the last *conceptual* revolution it needs' (CIS, p. 63) in the form of liberalism,

negation' to a view of irony grounded in 'a swerve to ethical passion: freely choosing what we are to become'. 'But it is possible for each of us', Bernstein writes, summarising this view, 'to *freely* actualize ourselves as ethical human beings, and thereby move beyond the unstable negativity of pure irony'.[36] The problem with Kierkegaard's view, though, is that it renders this kind of irony a completely inward condition with only purely subjective criteria for determining whether one has moved from 'pure irony' to 'ethical irony': 'There is no outward sign to determine when the ironist has made the internal move to become an ethicist (and thereby to *become* a human being)'.[37] Socrates is Kierkegaard's prime example of the ethical ironist, but how could Kierkegaard, or anyone for that matter, know he has made the requisite 'internal move'?

It seems likely that Rorty's version of irony was inspired by Kierkegaard, since it indeed focuses on the process of 'freely choosing what we are to become': the ironist, aware of the contingency of her final vocabulary and therefore the likelihood that it will be changed by further contingencies, seeks to take some measure of control over that process by seeking out alternative final vocabularies in the hope of finding self-transformation. But taking the hope of being different or being elsewhere as a starting point for this process is much more closely akin to Kierkegaard's 'ethical passion' than are merely epistemological doubts or knowledge. Moreover, Rorty's conception of the self renders the very idea of 'pure irony' incoherent, since that idea requires a self that can radically distance itself from its beliefs. In this way, Rorty's conception of irony, when founded on hope, extends Kierkegaard's by insisting that living ironically, as opposed merely to making ironic remarks, always involves the ethical passion Kierkegaard attributes to it. And Rorty's pragmatist version further improves on Kierkegaard's by removing the subjective element of irony, making its conditions the publicly available practical consequences for behaviour that I describe above.

In the face of criticisms like Schneewind's, many of Rorty's fellow pragmatists who have also been critical of his conceptions of irony and the public-private split might recommend simply jettisoning these ideas

---

while nevertheless hoping against hope that somehow they can manage a private conceptual revolution that results in a vocabulary that is wholly their own.

36 Bernstein, *Ironic Life*, p. 101.
37 Bernstein, *Ironic Life*, p. 97.

entirely, and Rorty occasionally writes as if they are dispensable. I would suggest that maintaining them is crucial to his argument. One sign that the very idea of private irony might not be so important to Rorty is his tendency to conflate irony with anti-foundationalism. He first does so in his introduction, where he first defines irony: 'I use "ironist" to name the sort of person who faces up to the contingency of his or her own most central beliefs and desires—someone sufficiently historicist and nominalist to have abandoned the idea that those central beliefs and desires refer back to something beyond the reach of time and chance'.[38] This definition of irony notably omits the first condition he places on it in the more detailed definition in chapter 4. But later in chapter 4, he again seems to forget about this condition, equating 'the prevalence of ironist notions among the public at large' to the increasing adoption of 'antimetaphysical, antiessentialist views about the nature of morality and rationality and human beings'.[39]

In these passages, I suspect that Rorty primarily has in mind the people he labels 'ironist theorists', the people for whom the final vocabulary they are trying to slough off is the metaphysical tradition from Plato to the present day. For those writers, irony and anti-foundationalism do amount to largely the same thing, but there are other writers Rorty discusses, most notably Proust, who are not much concerned with anti-foundationalism and hope to transcend other aspects of their final vocabularies. This also seems to be why Rorty

---

38 Rorty, CIS, p. xv.
39 Rorty, CIS, p. 85. Curtis also notes the two contradictory definitions of irony Rorty offers in CIS, but Curtis's solution is to suggest that Rorty is proposing two distinct senses of irony: 'The first sense is the civic virtue that all liberal citizens should ideally possess because it helps them be tolerant, adaptable, and just. The second sense is the more active and radical mental habit that "ironist intellectuals" exhibit as they challenge the conventional wisdoms of the cultural domains in which they work' (*Defending Rorty*, p. 93). One becomes the first sort of ironist when one 'embraces the contingency of her most deeply held beliefs' (*Defending Rorty*, p. 93), and one becomes the second sort when one adds to that the 'radical and continuing doubts' of Rorty's condition 1. The trouble with this solution is, as I have suggested, that the first sort of irony adds nothing to the anti-foundationalism that Rorty believes will become universal in his liberal utopia, so it doesn't really deserve the name of 'irony' at all. The civic virtue Curtis is really arguing for in his book is not irony but anti-foundationalism. For this reason, I think the better solution is to read Rorty's passages that confuse the two and that suggest that irony should be universal in his liberal utopia as simply unfortunate lapses.

occasionally seems to neglect this ironic function of literature, as when he writes near the end of chapter 4, 'The metaphysician's association of theory with social hope and of literature with private perfection is, in an ironist liberal culture, reversed'.[40] This passage suggests that writers like Proust, whose works are, like those of ironist theorists, 'largely irrelevant to public life and to politics',[41] will have no place in that ironist liberal culture. Rorty's suggestion that 'poetic, artistic, philosophical, scientific, or political progress results from the accidental coincidence of a private obsession with a public need' seems to ignore the account of poetic progress he draws from the work of Bloom and the example of Proust, in which progress consists of the accidental coincidence of a private obsession with other private obsessions.[42] The notion of irony, as distinct from mere anti-foundationalism and shared by everyone in Rorty's liberal utopia, serves as a necessary reminder of the valuable cultural role played by specific, private and idiosyncratic projects, even when they prove irrelevant to liberal politics.

Similarly, running together irony and anti-foundationalism creates some confusion about just how widespread irony should be in the liberal utopia imagined in CIS. After equating irony with anti-foundationalism in his introduction, Rorty writes, 'One of the aims of my book is to suggest the possibility of a liberal utopia: one in which irony, in the relevant sense, is universal'.[43] In chapter 3, he says that 'the citizens of my liberal utopia would be people who had a sense of the contingency of their language of moral deliberation, and thus of their consciences, and

---

40 Rorty, CIS, p. 94.
41 Rorty, CIS, p. 83.
42 Rorty, CIS, p. 37. Curtis echoes this passage when he says that 'a primary way in which liberal progress has been fomented was through the efforts of intellectual cultural critics who inspired social movements and taught us all to think differently, thereby reforming our public vocabulary' (*Defending Rorty*, p. 112). But in Rorty's quotation, 'political progress' is only one kind that can be achieved through such happy accidents. While Rorty would never deny that, as Curtis says, 'ideas that start out as private ironic experiments can often become crucial to the public project of liberal reform' (*Defending Rorty*, 111), this does not mean that ideas from 'poetic, philosophical, artistic, or scientific' domains cross over into the political domain nearly as often as Curtis suggests they do. This is one reason that justifications of the humanities based on their contributions to public, political projects cannot be sufficient. I will suggest some other reasons in the second half of this chapter.
43 Rorty, CIS, p. xv.

thus of their community. They would be liberal ironists…'.[44] However, as we have seen, only a few pages later Rorty seems to confine irony to a small subset of such citizens, the intellectuals: 'The sort of autonomy which self-creating ironists like Nietzsche, Derrida, or Foucault seek is not the sort of thing that *could* ever be embodied in social institutions…. It is something which certain particular human beings hope to attain by self-creation, and which a few actually do'.[45] By chapter 4, Rorty is even more emphatic about the restriction of irony to intellectuals: 'In the ideal liberal society, the intellectuals would still be ironists, although the nonintellectuals would not. The latter would, however, be commonsensically nominalist and historicist'.[46] The explanation for this obvious contradiction, I think, lies in the two different definitions of irony Rorty offers: when he suggest that irony should be universal in his liberal utopia, he is thinking of the definition in the introduction that equates irony with anti-foundationalism; when he suggests it should be confined to intellectuals, he is thinking of the definition in chapter 4 that adds the condition of 'radical and continuing doubts'.

Whether one thinks of irony as originating in doubt, as Rorty does in this definition, or whether one thinks of it as originating in hope, as I am urging, this extra condition beyond mere anti-foundationalism shows that it will be confined primarily to intellectuals. As Schneewind puts it, Rorty's conception of irony entails that 'intellectuals are just odd beings with pressing needs for sublime moments of reinvention of private vocabularies. They have no special place in the public life of utopia'.[47] While everyone is a commonsensical anti-foundationalist in Rorty's utopia, only a small subset of people will qualify as ironists because only that small subset of people in any society has experiences that lead them to fear being nothing but copies of others and to hope, therefore, that someday they will learn to talk differently and better. The vast majority will be more concerned with increasing their solidarity with others by expanding their 'we-intentions' and minimising cruelty, as the shared public vocabulary of their liberal utopia demands, all the while believing that they are merely affirming a contingent vocabulary.

---

44 Rorty, CIS, p. 61.
45 Rorty, CIS, p. 65.
46 Rorty, CIS, p. 87.
47 Schneewind, 'Rorty on Utopia and Moral Philosophy', p. 483.

At the end of chapter 4, Rorty says that 'ironist philosophers are private philosophers',[48] and the same would seem to be true of ironist literary critics, ironist historians, and all other ironist intellectuals. All the replacement of doubt with hope as the source of irony does is slightly alter the reasons for confining this special intellectual project to the private sphere. Rorty says that he 'cannot imagine a culture which socialized its youth in such a way as to make them continually dubious about their own process of socialization'.[49] But suppose this dubiousness is replaced by hope. In that case, irony is not so much antithetical to the hope of increasing solidarity through expanding 'we-intentions' and minimising cruelty, as it is, at worst, merely a distraction from that hope—you cannot do much to advance these projects when you're spending most of your time seeking out new vocabularies. A liberal utopia needs people who do both. In either case, another important reason for preserving Rorty's conception of irony is to preserve this sense of a special role for intellectuals, even in a liberal utopia.

Schneewind and Rorty are also not quite right when they deny that Rorty's conception of irony represents an advance on the projects of self-creation espoused by Montaigne, Kant and Mill. To see what is original in Rorty's conception of irony, it helps to turn to an earlier essay called 'Nineteenth-Century Idealism and Twentieth-Century Textualism' (1981), an essay that looks forward to CIS in its last sentence with its call for 'a full-scale discussion of the possibility of combining private fulfillment, self-realization, with public morality, a concern for justice'.[50] While, as always, Rorty locates the source of the poeticised culture he hopes to bring about in Romanticism, in this essay, he suggests that a step beyond Romanticism and its philosophical counterpart idealism was needed, a step represented by modernism and its philosophical counterpart textualism or pragmatism:

> Romanticism was *aufgehoben* in pragmatism, the claim that the significance of new vocabularies was not their ability to decode but their mere utility. Pragmatism is the philosophical counterpart of literary modernism, the kind of literature which prides itself on its autonomy

---

48   Rorty, CIS, pp. 94-95.
49   Rorty, CIS, p. 87.
50   Richard Rorty, 'Nineteenth-Century Idealism and Twentieth-Century Textualism', *The Monist*, 64.2 (1981), 155–74, https://doi.org/10.5840/monist198164211 (p. 158).

and novelty rather than its truthfulness to experience or its discovery of pre-existing significance.[51]

In a sense, textualism 'adds nothing save an extra metaphor to the Romanticism of Hegel and the pragmatism of James and Nietzsche':[52] where idealism claims that nothing exists save ideas, textualists claim that nothing exists save texts. However, that metaphor has a purpose, namely, to show that the romantic and pragmatist insight that everything can be redescribed 'does not need any metaphysical or epistemological or semantic back-up'.[53]

The consequences of this addition become clear in CIS, when Rorty notes the shortcomings of metaphysical idealism, which 'persisted in seeing mind, spirit, the depths of the human self, as having an intrinsic nature' and Romantics, who 'worship [...] our own deep spiritual or poetic nature, treated as one more quasi divinity'.[54] According to Schneewind, Montaigne saw the self in something like this way as well: 'His endless effort to find or make himself—like Rorty, he blurs the distinction—led him to reject as useless all previous models. He got no guidance from eternal principles or common essences either. The only essence he found was his own unique individual essence'.[55] Kant also obviously divinised the self in the form of his 'transcendental ego', and in *On Liberty*, Mill reverts to standard organicist metaphors of Romanticism in his opposition to 'wearing down into uniformity all that is individual' in people in favour of 'cultivating it and calling it forth'.[56] For Rorty, on the other hand, the textualist line of thought that runs through Blumenberg, Nietzsche, Freud and Davidson 'suggests that we try to get to the point where we no longer worship *anything*, where we treat *nothing* as a quasi divinity, where we treat *everything*—our language, our conscience, our community—as a product of time and chance'.[57] Rorty's conception of irony does add to Mill and other advocates of self-creation an original, textualist philosophical gloss on

---

51 Rorty, 'Nineteenth-Century Idealism', p. 153.
52 Rorty, 'Nineteenth-Century Idealism', p. 155.
53 Rorty, 'Nineteenth-Century Idealism', p. 154.
54 Rorty, CIS, pp. 4, 22.
55 Schneewind, 'Rorty on Utopia and Moral Philosophy', p. 490.
56 John S. Mill, *On Liberty*, ed. by Charles W. Elliott (New York: Barnes & Noble Books, 2004), p. 66.
57 Rorty, CIS, p. 22.

the process, one that is appropriate to the post-metaphysical culture he is trying to bring about.

When Rorty wrote 'Nineteenth-Century Idealism and Twentieth-Century Textualism' at the beginning of the 1980s, he believed that this poeticised culture was imminent, and he still believed that at the end of the decade when he published CIS. The forecast looks much bleaker thirty years later, but the hope that it will come about still depends on preserving and expanding a culture in which literature and the humanities have a prominent place. As much as Rorty sought to downplay the consequences of his philosophy of irony, I will spend the rest of this chapter arguing that a rehabilitated version of it can be of some use in this effort.

By now, the idea that there is a 'crisis' in the humanities, particularly in the United States, has become a cliché. Recent books on the subject like Paul Jay's *The Humanities 'Crisis' and the Future of Literary Studies* (2014) and Paul Reitter and Chad Wellmon's *Permanent Crisis: The Humanities in a Disenchanted Age* (2021) suggest that this crisis has been with us as long as the humanities themselves, but even they concede that humanistic disciplines are threatened today like never before.[58] At the heart of this crisis, of course, is the question of what function the humanities perform for society. CIS would seem to be a useful resource for stemming the tide, since it argued back in 1989 for the advantages of building a culture around the quintessentially humanistic activity of literary criticism, a culture that takes the 'strong poet' as its hero 'rather than the warrior, the priest, the sage, or the truth-seeking, "logical," "objective" scientist'.[59]

In his description of one socially useful contribution novelists can make, Rorty anticipates one of the chief defences of literary study and the humanities in general that is frequently offered today: 'Fiction like that of Dickens, Olive Schreiner, or Richard Wright gives us the details of the suffering being endured by people to whom we had not previously

---

58 See Paul Jay, *The Humanities Crisis and the Future of Literary Studies* (New York: Palgrave Macmillan US, 2014), https://doi.org/10.1057/9781137398031 and Paul Reitter and Chad Wellmon, *Permanent Crisis: The Humanities in a Disenchanted Age* (Chicago, IL: The University of Chicago Press, 2021), https://doi.org/10.7208/chicago/9780226738376.001.0001

59 Rorty, CIS, p. 53.

attended'.⁶⁰ The idea that the humanities can make us empathetic is the centrepiece of defences of the humanities in books like Martha Nussbaum's *Not for Profit: Why Democracy Needs the Humanities* (2010), and it is the function Rorty dwells on in his chapters on Orwell and Nabokov in CIS.⁶¹ However, both the immediate context of this remark and the larger project of his book make it clear that this justification of the humanities cannot take us very far. While he says that the novel is 'especially' good at serving this empathetic function, he also imputes that function to 'genres such as ethnography, the journalist's report, the comic book, [and] the docudrama'.⁶² Not all these genres could even be classified among 'the humanities', so this function cannot be the defining one for those disciplines. Moreover, it is far less clear that this function is performed nearly as well by non-narrative poetry, for example, so it is difficult to see it as the central function even of literature.

But the most important problem with taking the ability to produce empathy as the main defence of the humanities offered in CIS is that it portrays them as primarily serving the goal of public solidarity, while one of the main points of the book is to defend the existence in a liberal utopia of cultural practices that are irrelevant to or possibly even in conflict with the imperative of solidarity. A full defence of the humanities, for Rorty, requires a defence of the irony found in Proust, as well as in theorists like Nietzsche, Heidegger and Derrida. Because such irony 'is of little public use',⁶³ its justification must be its private function. Rorty's conception of irony, when reconceived as a form of hope rather than a form of doubt, is by far the most original and powerful defence of the humanities that can be derived from CIS.

Rorty's pragmatism reveals the limitations not only of defences of the humanities based on their capacity to produce empathy but also of other common defences that rely on their public functions, such as those developed in Jay's book. Jay bases his defence on the humanities' recent turn toward theory, which he believes imparts a special critical thinking skill he calls 'critique' that is 'transferable to a wide range of

---

60 Rorty, CIS, p. xvi.
61 Martha C. Nussbaum, *Not for Profit: Why Democracy Needs the Humanities*, The Public Square (Princeton, NJ: Princeton University Press, 2016), https://doi.org/10.1515/9781400883509
62 Rorty, CIS, p. xvi.
63 Rorty, CIS, p. 120.

careers outside the academy'.[64] This 'critique' consists of the effort to 'dig down to the foundations—or the absence of foundations—informing claims about value, meaning, and truth'.[65] For Rorty's pragmatism, of course, because our practices do not have theoretical foundations, this theoretical enterprise cannot make any difference to practice. Even demonstrating the absence of foundations can have no consequences for our practices—to believe otherwise would be to engage in what Stanley Fish has called 'anti-foundationalist theory hope'. Pragmatism's rejection of what Fish calls 'the fallacy of theoretical self-consciousness' and aversion to method undermines the much-cherished defence of the humanities as the source of a general critical thinking skill that other disciplines do not impart.[66]

But Jay thinks this skill allows humanists 'to track how history, philosophy, literature, and art represent the world of human experience in ways that reflect, perpetuate, or critique uneven forms of power related to gender, sexuality, class, and race', and that is why 'issues central to what it means to be human, related to gender, race, sexuality, class, subjectivity, and the politics of cultural belonging have become central in literary analyses'.[67] While Jay seems to believe that this centrality has strengthened the case for the humanities by making them more 'relevant', he seems not to realize that it has in practice made their position more precarious when he writes, 'The humanities are not threatened by irrelevancy because of the subject areas they cover, but rather, by the systematic defunding of higher education...'.[68] Perhaps in 2025 he would realise that the subject areas the humanities cover are among the causes of the systematic defunding of higher education—in particular, their progressive politics. It is undoubtedly one reason why humanities programs are targeted disproportionately for budget cuts. For almost a half century, these politics have been, at least implicitly,

---

64 Jay, *The Humanities Crisis*, p. 3.
65 Jay, *The Humanities Crisis*, p. 4.
66 For Fish's criticisms of these two ideas, see Stanley Fish, 'Anti-Foundationalism, Theory Hope, and the Teaching of Composition', in *Doing What Comes Naturally: Change, Rhetoric, and the Practice of Theory in Literary and Legal Studies* (Durham, NC: Duke UP, 1992), pp. 342–55, https://doi.org/10.1093/oso/9780198129998.003.0018, and in the same volume, 'Critical Self-Consciousness, Or Can We Know What We're Doing?', pp. 436–70, https://doi.org/10.1093/oso/9780198129998.003.0022
67 Jay, *The Humanities Crisis*, pp. 4–6.
68 Jay, *The Humanities Crisis*, p. 171.

the central argument for the relevance of the humanities—at the very least, in literary studies—and the results have not been encouraging. Nothing in Rorty's pragmatism argues for keeping politics out of the humanities classroom, nor, obviously, does it have anything against progressive politics. Rather, for pragmatic reasons, Rorty would suggest that if the humanities want to maintain the funding and the freedom that allows them to continue discussing politics in their classrooms, those politics should not be central to their rhetorical case. If making the value of the humanities depend on their public function threatens their very existence, perhaps they need to be defended in terms of a private function instead.

The more expansive story Reitter and Wellmon tell about the history of the crisis in the humanities reveals the problems with efforts like Jay's to focus their justification on their public function. According to Reitter and Wellmon, the humanities emerged out of an internal tension that looks strikingly like the tension Jay finds between humanist universalism and the professional specialisation of theory: the tension in emerging research universities between a classical dedication to *Bildung*, or the cultivation of moral character through reading and studying, and immersion in specialised disciplinary research, inspired by the growing prominence of and rivalry with the sciences. Like Jay, they note that the humanities have always defined themselves in opposition to the perceived vocationalism and instrumentality that characterise the wider culture. However, they add that the humanities in Germany remained firmly committed to an ideal of the unity of knowledge, in opposition to what they perceived as the fragmentation and overspecialisation of modernity. Their response to this 'crisis' was, in the name of the unity of knowledge, repeatedly to promise far more than they were able to deliver. Specifically, they frequently presented themselves as 'the locus of moral education and meaning in higher education',[69] playing the almost messianic role of saving from itself the very modernity that created them.

Reitter and Wellmon believe this problem persists, and they might point to Jay's defence of the humanities as a case in point. Early in his book, Jay says that 'defending the humanities must be a two-pronged

---

69 Reitter and Wellmon, *Permanent Crisis*, p. 259.

effort': one half of that effort entails touting the practical skills they inculcate, but the other half involves 'insisting on the important role the humanities play in fostering critical thinking about bottom-line values and the instrumentalization of everyday life'.[70] This is a prime instance of just the kind of overpromising Reitter and Wellmon warn against: the humanities are valuable because they are the only ones who can save us, through critique, from the forces of modernity—the very same forces German humanists opposed in the nineteenth century—that give rise to the 'crisis' that afflicts them. Jay repeats this gesture throughout the book. It is of a piece with his insistence that the humanities have a monopoly on critical and creative thinking skills and sensitivity to social justice. However, because they are themselves contingently situated members of a limited discipline, humanists cannot possibly fulfil the socially transformative role they assign to themselves, and their failure to do so will ultimately only further fuel public scepticism toward them. So, while Reitter and Wellmon echo much of what Jay says about the humanities in crisis, they also demonstrate that his defences fail to escape the pitfalls that have made the crisis in the humanities a permanent one.

If Reitter and Wellmon cannot exactly see a way beyond this permanent crisis, they do find a way forward in the work of Max Weber, who abandoned the humanists' hope for unified knowledge in favour of disciplinary pluralism. Although embracing such pluralism, Weber thought, meant disavowing the public role the humanists coveted, it would be the only way to preserve their intellectual freedom:

> Rather, he warned scholars against looking to scholarship and the university for salvation and ultimate meaning. Weber worried that if students or professors acceded to the demands and longings for a knowledge unconstrained by any disciplined practice, if they overexpected and overpromised, they risked conceding the freedom to practice scholarship and the fragile legitimacy the university still managed to maintain.[71]

This same danger is invited by recent efforts like Jay's to focus the defence of the humanities on projects of 'critique' aimed at social justice. If you make a political agenda central to your conception of the humanities,

---

70   Jay, *The Humanities Crisis*, p. 5.
71   Reitter and Wellmon, *Permanent Crisis*, p. 217.

you invite political interference, and that is exactly what we are seeing today in public universities in states like Florida, North Carolina, Texas and Wisconsin.[72]

For these reasons, Rorty's conception of private irony can serve as a far more effective defence of the humanities today. As we have seen, this conception prescribes a form of *Bildung*, but one that, like Weber, entirely abandons the idea of the unity of knowledge—in fact, it was formed in direct opposition to the effort 'to hold reality and justice in a single vision'.[73] Because politics frequently feature prominently in final vocabularies, pursuing Rorty's version of *Bildung* can still involve political advocacy; however, by acknowledging the plurality of purposes and renouncing the role of public saviour, it need not—and should not—make that advocacy the centre of the rhetorical case for the humanities. Reitter and Wellmon note one other rhetorical advantage of this approach when they consider the enthusiastic response to William Deresiewicz's book *Excellent Sheep*, which advocates for a version of *Bildung* similar to the one Rorty's irony entails: 'Even in the era of neoliberalism, the character-building ideal of *Bildung* has significant bipartisan middle-brow support'.[74] But these rhetorical advantages depend on the same rehabilitation of the conception of irony that resolves its philosophical inconsistencies: locating its source in hope rather than doubt.

While an intellectual enterprise whose goal is to produce 'anguished existentialist adolescents' will always hold an appeal for some students, no one will ever want to subsidise it. Replacing doubt with hope orients irony toward the future and toward possibility, making it more consistent with the values of both pragmatism and democracy. Apart from resolving the philosophical problems with Rorty's notion of irony as it is described in CIS, recasting it as a form of hope rather than a form

---

72 A recent article in *The Atlantic* attributes the current plight of the humanities to precisely this cause. See Tyler Austin Harper, 'The Humanities Have Sown the Seeds of Their Own Destruction', *The Atlantic* (19 December 2023), https://www.theatlantic.com/ideas/archive/2023/12/humanities-university-conservative-critics/676890/

73 Curtis also associates Rorty's ideas about self-creation with *Bildung*, as does Christopher Voparil in 'On the Idea of Philosophy as *Bildungsroman*: Rorty and His Critics', *Contemporary Pragmatism*, 2.1 (2005), 115–33, https://doi.org/10.1163/18758185-90000005

74 William Deresiewicz, *Excellent Sheep: The Miseducation of the American Elite and the Way to a Meaningful Life* (New York: Free Press, 2015), p. 75.

of doubt is crucial for preserving its power as a response to today's crisis in the humanities.

Although it never mentions irony, an essay Rorty published almost a decade after CIS as the coda to his book *Achieving Our Country* (1998) sums up the shift in thinking about this concept that I am recommending as well as its usefulness in contemporary debates about the future of the humanities. The main topic of 'The Inspirational Value of Great Works of Literature' is the opposition in contemporary literature departments between the attitude Rorty calls 'knowingness', which substitutes 'knowing theorization for awe, and resentment over the failures of the past for visions of a better future',[75] and 'inspiration', which he finds in critics who view literature (in a phrase Rorty borrows from Dorothy Allison) as 'a way to take the world by the throat and insist that there is more to this life than we have ever imagined'.[76] He attributes the former primarily to what Harold Bloom calls 'the School of Resentment', the theoretically inclined scholars motivated by social justice concerns who currently dominate the profession, and the latter to those who aspire 'to spend their teaching lives reiterating their idiosyncratic enthusiasms for their favourite prophets and demiurges' but increasingly find themselves frozen out of the profession.[77]

This distinction looks a lot like the one between theorists and humanists that Jay writes about and the one between researchers and humanists that Reitter and Wellmon write about. But it is not clear where the ironists that Rorty describes in CIS fit into this picture. His description of the 'knowing', for whom Frederic Jameson serves as his chief example, is reminiscent of some characterizations of irony, and especially of the ironist theorists he describes in CIS: 'These people have learned from Jameson and others that they can no longer enjoy "the luxury of the old-fashioned ideological critique, the indignant moral denunciation of the other". They have also learned that hero-worship is a sign of weakness, a temptation to elitism. So they substitute Stoic endurance for both righteous anger and social hope'.[78] If you think of

---

[75] Richard Rorty, *Achieving Our Country: Leftist Thought in Twentieth Century America* (Cambridge, MA: Harvard University Press, 1998), p. 127.
[76] Rorty, AOC, p. 132.
[77] Rorty, AOC, p. 134.
[78] Rorty, AOC, p. 126. Rorty is quoting Herbert Croly, *The Promise of American Life* (New York: Capricorn Books, 1964 [1909]), p. 1.

irony mostly in terms of doubt, of intellectuals who are 'never quite able to take themselves seriously because always aware [...] of the contingency and fragility of their final vocabularies, and thus of their selves',[79] then Jameson's pronouncement that 'the end of the bourgeois ego, or monad, [...] means [...] the end [...] of style, in the sense of the unique and the personal, the end of the distinctive individual brush stroke' looks like a quintessentially ironist attitude.[80] However, if, as I have argued, we should see irony as a consequence of the hope to be different, to be elsewhere, then what Rorty says the 'inspired' seek in literature looks much more like irony:

> If it is to have inspirational value, a work must be allowed to recontextualize much of what you previously thought you knew; it cannot, at least at first, be itself recontextualized by what you already believe. Just as you cannot be swept off your feet by another human being at the same time that you recognize him or her as a good specimen of a certain type, so you cannot simultaneously be inspired by a work and be knowing about it.[81]

It is difficult to tell which is the real ironist in this essay, and I believe that is a symptom of Rorty's own somewhat conflicting views on irony in CIS.

In this chapter, I have argued that the best way to render Rorty's conception of irony coherent is to associate it with hope rather than doubt, and thus with inspiration rather than knowingness. Moreover, I have urged that we think of this version of irony founded on hope as the best way to characterise what the humanities produce if we hope to relieve the current crisis that afflicts them. In 'The Inspirational Value of Great Works of Literature', Rorty associates inspiration with 'the hope for a religion of literature, in which works of the secular imagination replace Scripture as the principal source of inspiration and hope for each new generation'.[82] In this context, it is helpful to remember that Nietzsche's 'desire to be different, to be in a different place' originally described the motive for religion in *On the Genealogy of Morals*, although Bloom repurposed it in *Agon* as the motive for literature. While Rorty says that 'a humanistic discipline is in good shape only when

---

79 Rorty, CIS, p. 74.
80 Qtd. in Rorty, AOC, p. 123.
81 Rorty, AOC, p. 133.
82 Rorty, AOC, p. 136.

it produces both inspiring works and works which contextualize', he goes on to note that 'within the academy, the humanities have been a refuge for enthusiasts. If there is no longer a place for them within either philosophy or literature departments, it is not clear where they will find shelter in the future'.[83] Rorty has much to say against professionalism in this essay, but he is actually making a more original suggestion than the ones attributed to the 'mandarin' defenders of humanism by both Jay's book and Reitter and Wellmon's: he is overcoming the divide between humanism and professionalism by defining a scholarly profession that emphasises hope over knowledge, a profession defined by irony.

And what bridges this divide turns out to be precisely the acceptance of contingency that leads to irony. Rorty defends the humanistic-sounding value he invests in 'great works of literature' by contrasting the humanists' universalist and essentialist notion of the canon with his own 'pragmatist functionalist' version: 'Where essentialists take canonical status as indicating the presence of a link to eternal truth, and lack of interest in a canonical work as a moral flaw, functionalists take canonical status to be as changeable as the historical and personal situations of readers'.[84] Near the end of the essay, he portrays efforts to restore inspiration to the study of literature as attempts to resist philosophers' attempts to gain supremacy over literature. He says that resistance requires embracing contingency the way ironist hope does: 'But I do not think that literature will succeed in resisting philosophy unless literary critics think of it [...] as having nothing to do with eternity, knowledge, or stability, and everything to do with futurity and hope—with taking the world by the throat and insisting that there is more to this life than we have ever imagined'.[85]

Even though Rorty's conception of inspiration in this essay remains in the private sphere as defined by CIS, involving as it does 'reiterating idiosyncratic enthusiasms', he closes his essay by linking it to the public project of solidarity, and specifically his project of bringing about his liberal utopia, when he says that 'it is only those who still read for inspiration who are likely to be of much use in building a cooperative

---

83 Rorty, AOC, pp. 134–35.
84 Rorty, AOC, p. 137.
85 Rorty, AOC, p. 138.

commonwealth'.⁸⁶ Replacing a conception of irony based on doubt with one based on hope shows why a liberal utopia goes hand in hand with a literary culture of irony: by fostering a culture of hope in general, the hope for the transformation of society and the hope for the transformation of the self can not only coexist but can mutually reinforce one another, even when the latter projects do not directly advance the former.⁸⁷ Such a modest and indirect⁸⁸ benefit of irony to the public sphere might not be sufficient for many humanistic intellectuals—including defenders of Rorty like Curtis—who still dream of a more direct, messianic role, but we have seen that it could inspire a more coherent and appealing defence of the humanities than the ones they have offered. Substituting hope for doubt is not only the best way to save Rorty's conception of irony, but even if it denies humanistic intellectuals the hope of saving the world, it just might be their best hope of saving themselves.

---

86   Rorty, AOC, p. 140.
87   'Inspiration' is also a good word for thinking about the role the humanities, understood in terms of a rehabilitated conception of irony, play in supporting liberal democracy. They support it not necessarily because they instil us with virtues that make us better citizens—because if the irony they cultivate is a virtue, it is a private one—and not necessarily because they are a source of political ideas or programs—because they play that role only occasionally and serendipitously—but because they inspire us to hope for a better future, both for ourselves and for our society. This is what Rorty means when he says his liberal utopia would take the strong poet as one of its primary culture heroes.
88   This benefit to liberal democracy is indirect in the sense that it only directly benefits the humanities, which existed in one form or another long before modern democracies. But the humanities, especially as institutionalized in modern universities, have benefits to liberal democracy beyond occasionally and accidentally producing socially useful ideas. As I suggest in my book *Reconstruction in Literary Studies: An Informalist Approach* (New York: Palgrave MacMillan, 2014), https://doi.org/10.1057/9781137428837, universities are useful to democracy because they teach students how to participate in a culture in which power depends on persuasion rather than force. I argue furthermore that the humanities, as disciplines that do not necessarily aim at consensus, teach students how to live in a society in which people disagree on fundamental matters—how to engage in conversations that sometimes require us to agree to disagree.

Works Cited

Abramson, Kate, 'Turning Up the Lights on Gaslighting', *Philosophical Perspectives*, 28 (2014), 1–30, https://doi.org/10.1111/phpe.12046

Albrecht, Don, 'Vaccination, Politics and COVID-19 Impacts', *BMC Public Health*, 22.96 (2022), https://doi.org/10.1186/s12889-021-12432-x

Allen, Amy, *Critique on the Couch: Why Critical Theory Needs Psychoanalysis* (New York: Columbia University Press, 2021), https://doi.org/10.7312/alle19860

Allen, Barry 'The Rorty-Deleuze *Pas de Deux*', in *Deleuze and Pragmatism*, ed. by S. Bowden, S. Bignalli and P. Patton (New York: Routledge, 2015), pp. 163–79.

Anderson, John P., 'Achieving Rorty's New Private-Public Divide', in *Handbuch Richard Rorty* , ed. by Martin Müller (Wiesbaden: Springer Fachmedien Wiesbaden, 2022), pp. 865–82, https://doi.org/10.1007/978-3-658-16260-3_51-1

Bacon, Michael and Rutherford, Nat, 'Rorty, Habermas, and Radical Social Criticism', in *The Ethics, Epistemology, and Politics of Richard Rorty*, ed. by Giancarlo Marchetti (New York and London: Routledge, 2021), pp. 191–208, https://doi.org/10.4324/9780429324734-14

Bacon, Michael, 'A Defence of Liberal Ironism', *Res Publica*, 11 (2005), 403–23, https://doi.org/10.1007/s11158-005-5761-0

Bacon, Michael, 'Rorty, Irony and the Consequences of Contingency for Liberal Society', *Philosophy and Social Criticism*, 43.9 (2017), 953–65, https://doi.org/10.1177/0191453716688365

Bacon, Michael, *Richard Rorty: Pragmatism and Political Liberalism* (Lanham, Plymouth: Lexington Books, 2007).

Guido Baggio, 'Narrazione e cosmopolitismo etnocentrico', in *La filosofia di Rorty. Epistemologia, etica e politica*, ed. by Giancarlo Marchetti (Milano: Mimesis, 2022), pp. 139–51.

Barreto, José-Manuel, 'Rorty and Human Rights: Contingency, Emotions and How to Defend Human Rights Telling Stories', *Utrecht Law Review*, 7 (2011), 93–112, https://doi.org/10.18352/ulr.164

Baruchello, Giorgio, 'Rorty's Painful Liberalism', *Bijdragen*, 63 (2002), 22–45, https://doi.org/10.2143/BIJ.63.1.795

Bella, Michela, 'Novelty and Causality in William James's Pluralistic Universe', *European Journal of Pragmatism and American Philosophy*, 11.2 (2019), https://doi.org/10.4000/ejpap.1668

Benesch, Klaus, 'Is Truth to Post-Truth what Modernism Is to Postmodernism? Heidegger, the Humanities, and the Demise of Common-Sense', *European Journal of American Studies*, 15.1 (2020), https://doi.org/10.4000/ejas.15619

Berenstain, Nora, 'Epistemic Exploitation', *Ergo*, 3 (2016), 569–90.https://doi.org/10.3998/ergo.12405314.0003.022

Berlin, Isiah, *Four Essays on Liberty* (Oxford University Press, 1969).

Bernstein, Jay M., *Torture and Dignity: An Essay on Moral Injury* (Chicago, IL: University of Chicago Press, 2015), pp. 75–76, https://doi.org/10.7208/chicago/9780226266466.001.0001

Bernstein, Richard J., 'A Reply to Heidi Salaverría', in *Confines of Democracy. The Social Philosophy of Richard Bernstein: Essays on the Philosophy of Richard Bernstein*, ed. by Ramón del Castillo, Ángel M. Faerna and Larry A. Hickman (New York: Brill/Rodopi, 2015), pp. 169–70, https://doi.org/10.1163/9789004301207_019

Bernstein, Richard J., *Ironic Life* (Cambridge and Malden: Polity, 2016).

Bernstein, Richard J., *The Abuse of Evil: the Corruption of Politics and Religion since 9/11* (Malden, MA: Polity Press, 2005).

Bernstein, Richard J., *The New Constellation: The Ethical-Political Horizons of Modernity/Postmodernity* (Cambridge: Polity Press, 1991).

Bernstein, Richard J., 'Richard Rorty's Deep Humanism', *New Literary History*, 39 (2008), 13–27, https://doi.org/10.1353/nlh.0.0012

Bernstein, Richard J., 'Rorty's Inspirational Liberalism', in *Richard Rorty*, ed. by Charles Guignon and David R. Hiley (Cambridge: Cambridge University Press, 2003), pp. 124–38, https://doi.org/10.1017/cbo9780511613951.007

Bernstein, Richard J., 'What Is the Difference That Makes a Difference? Gadamer, Habermas, and Rorty', *Proceedings of the Biennial Meeting of the Philosophy of Science Association*, 1982 (1983), 331–59, p. 351, https://doi.org/10.1086/psaprocbienmeetp.1982.2.192429

Best, Susan, *Reparative Aesthetics: Witnessing in Contemporary Art Photography* (New York: Bloomsbury, 2016), https://doi.org/10.5040/9781474277839

Bettcher, Talia M., 'Trans Women and the Meaning of "Woman"', in *Philosophy of Sex: Contemporary Readings (Sixth Edition)*, ed. by N. Power, R. Halwani and A. Soble (New York: Rowan and Littlefield, 2012), pp. 233–50.

Bilgrami, Akeel, 'Is Truth a Goal of Inquiry?: Rorty and Davidson on Truth', in *Rorty and His Critics*, ed. by Robert B. Brandom, Philosophers and Their Critics 9 (Malden, MA, Oxford: Blackwell, 2000), pp. 242–62.

Bloom, Harold, *Agon: Towards a Theory of Revisionism* (Oxford: Oxford University Press, 1982).

Boncompagni, Anna, *Wittgenstein and Pragmatism* (London: Palgrave Macmillan, 2016), https://doi.org/10.1057/978-1-137-58847-0

Borges, J. L., *Ficciones*, trans. by Anthony Kerrigan (New York: Grove Press, 1962).

Bourdieu, Pierre, *Distinction. A Social Critique of the Judgment of Taste* (Cambridge, MA: Harvard University Press, 1984).

Brandom, Robert B. (ed.), *Rorty and His Critics*, Philosophers and Their Critics 9 (Malden, MA, Oxford: Blackwell, 2000).

Brandom, Robert B., 'Achieving the Enlightenment', in *Pragmatism as Anti-Authoritarianism*, ed. by Eduardo Mendieta (Cambridge, MA: Harvard University Press, 2021), pp. vii–xxvi, https://doi.org/10.4159/9780674270077-001

Brandom, Robert B., 'Introduction', in *Rorty and His Critics*, ed. by Robert B. Brandom, Philosophers and Their Critics 9 (Malden, MA, Oxford: Blackwell, 2000), pp. ix–xx.

Brandom, Robert B., *Tales of the Mighty Dead: Historical Essays in the Metaphysics of Intentionality* (Cambridge, MA: Harvard University Press, 2002).

Brandom, Robert B., 'Vocabularies of Pragmatism: Synthesizing Naturalism and Historicism', in *Rorty and His Critics*, ed. by Robert B. Brandom, Philosophers and Their Critics 9 (Malden, MA, Oxford: Blackwell, 2000), pp. 156–83.

https://doi.org/10.4000/ejpap.1668Brioschi, Maria Regina, *Creativity Between Experience and Cosmos: C.S. Peirce and A.N. Whitehead on Novelty* (München: Verlag Karl Alber, 2020), https://doi.org/10.5771/9783495823958

Brunkhorst, Hauke, 'Not Just A Liberal–Social Philosophy as Antiauthoritarian and Utopian Social Criticism: Richard Rorty's *Achieving Our Country* Today', *Philosophy & Social Criticism*, 48 (2022), 1353–68, https://doi.org/10.1177/01914537221122270

Butler, Judith, *The Force of Nonviolence: An Ethico-Political Bind* (Verso: London/New York, 2021).

Calcaterra, Rosa Maria, *Contingency and Normativity. The Challenges of Richard Rorty* (Leiden and Boston, MA: Brill Rodopi, 2019), https://doi.org/10.1163/9789004393837

Castro, Susana de, 'Can We Avoid Cruelty?', *Contemporary Pragmatism*, 11 (2014), 143–52, https://doi.org/10.1163/18758185-90000282

Cavell, Stanley, *The Claim of Reason* (Oxford: Clarendon Press, 1979).

Chin, Clayton, *The Practice of Political Theory: Rorty and Continental Thought*, New Directions in Critical Theory (New York: Columbia University Press, 2018), https://doi.org/10.7312/chin17398

Clough, Sharyn, 'Rorty as Liberal Ironist Peace Warrior', in *The Ethics, Epistemology, and Politics of Richard Rorty*, ed. by Giancarlo Marchetti (New York and London: Routledge, 2021), pp. 29–49, https://doi.org/10.4324/9780429324734-3

Coates, Ta-Nehisi, *Interview with Oprah Winfrey on The Water Dancer* (Oprah's Book Club: Club Apple TV, 2019).

Colapietro, Vincent Michael, 'Toward a Pragmatic Conception of Practical Identity', in *Transactions of the Charles S. Peirce Society*, 42.2 (2006), 173–205, https://doi.org/10.1353/csp.2006.0019

Conant, James, 'Freedom, Cruelty, and Truth: Rorty versus Orwell', in *Rorty and His Critics*, ed. by Robert B. Brandom, Philosophers and Their Critics 9 (Malden, MA, Oxford: Blackwell, 2000), pp. 268–342.

Croly, Herbert, *The Promise of American Life* (New York: Capricorn Books, 1964 [1909]).

Curtis, William, *Defending Rorty: Pragmatism and Liberal Virtue* (Cambridge: Cambridge University Press, 2015), https://doi.org/10.1017/cbo9781316272145

Davidson, Donald, 'Paradoxes of Irrationality', in *Problems of Rationality* (Oxford: Oxford University Press, 2004), pp. 169–88, https://doi.org/10.1093/0198237545.003.0011

Davis, Emmalon, 'Typecasts, Tokens, and Spokespersons: A Case for Credibility Excess as Testimonial Injustice', *Hypatia*, 31 (2016), 485–501, https://doi.org/10.1111/hypa.12251

Deleuze, Gilles and Guattari, Félix, *What is Philosophy?*, trans. by H. Tomlinson and G. Burchill (London: Verso, 1994).

Dennett, Daniel C., 'Postmodernism and Truth', *The Proceedings of the Twentieth World Congress of Philosophy*, 8 (2000), 93–103.

Deresiewicz, William, *Excellent Sheep: The Miseducation of the American Elite and the Way to a Meaningful Life* (New York: Free Press, 2015).

Dewey, John, *Liberalism and Social Action* (New York: Capricorn Books, 1939).

Dewey, John, *The Quest for Certainty. A Study of the Relation of Knowledge and Action*, The Later Works of J. Dewey, 1925–1953, vol. 4, ed. by J. A. Boydston (Carbondale and Edwardsville, IL: Southern Illinois University Press, 1984).

Dewey, John, 'William James as Empiricist', in *The Later Works of John Dewey, 1925-1953*, vol. 15, ed. by Jo Ann Boydston (Carbondale, IL: Southern Illinois University Press, 1989), pp. 9–17.

Diamond, Cora, 'Losing Your Concepts', *Ethics*, 98 (1988), 255–77, https://doi.org/10.1086/292940

Dieleman, Susan, 'Defending Rorty: Pragmatism and Liberal Virtue, Written by William M. Curtis', *Contemp. Pragmatism.*, 13.4 (2016), 441–44, https://doi.org/10.1163/18758185-01304006

Dieleman, Susan, 'Realism, Pragmatism, and Critical Social Epistemology', in *Pragmatism and Justice*, ed. by Susan Dieleman, David Rondel, and Christopher Voparil (Oxford: Oxford University Press, 2017), pp. 130–43, https://doi.org/10.1093/acprof:oso/9780190459239.003.0008

Dieleman, Susan, 'Revisiting Rorty: Contributions to a Pragmatist Feminism', *Hypatia*, 25 (2010), 891–908, https://doi.org/10.1111/j.1527-2001.2010.01133.x

Donatelli, Piergiorgio, 'Rorty and Democracy', *Iride*, 32 (2019), 617–30, https://doi.org/10.1414/95827

Dotson, Kristie, 'A Cautionary Tale: On Limiting Epistemic Oppression', *Frontiers: A Journal of Women Studies*, 33 (2012), 24–47, https://doi.org/10.1353/fro.2012.a472779

Dotson, Kristie, 'Tracking Epistemic Violence, Tracking Practices of Silencing', *Hypatia*, 26 (2011), 236–57, https://doi.org/10.1111/j.1527-2001.2011.01177.x

Elshtain, Jean B., 'Don't Be Cruel: Reflections on Rortyan Liberalism', in *Richard Rorty*, ed. by Charles Guignon and David R. Hiley (Cambridge: Cambridge University Press, 2003), pp. 139–57, https://doi.org/10.1017/cbo9780511613951.008

Ferraris, Maurizio, *Postverità e altri enigmi* (Bologna: Il Mulino, 2017).

Festenstein, Matthew, 'Politics and Acquiescence in Rorty's Pragmatism', *Theoria: A Journal of Social and Political Theory*, 101 (2003), 1–24.

Fish, Stanley, 'Anti-Foundationalism, Theory Hope, and the Teaching of Composition', in *Doing What Comes Naturally: Change, Rhetoric, and the Practice of Theory in Literary and Legal Studies* (Durham, NC: Duke UP, 1992), pp. 342–55, https://doi.org/10.1093/oso/9780198129998.003.0018

Fish, Stanley, 'Critical Self-Consciousness, Or Can We Know What We're Doing?', in *Doing What Comes Naturally: Change, Rhetoric, and the Practice of Theory in Literary and Legal Studies* (Durham, NC: Duke UP, 1992), pp. 436–70, https://doi.org/10.1093/oso/9780198129998.003.0022

Follett, Mary Parker, *Creative Experience* (New York: Longmans, Green and Co., 1924).

Foucault, Michel, M. *The Foucault Reader*, ed. by P. Rabinow (New York: Pantheon, 1984).

Fraser, Nancy, 'From Irony to Prophecy to Politics', in *Feminist Interpretations of Richard Rorty*, ed. by Marianne Janack, Re-reading the Canon (University Park, PA: Pennsylvania State University Press, 2010), pp. 47-55.

Fricker, Miranda, *Epistemic Injustice: Power and the Ethics of Knowing* (Oxford: Oxford University Press, 2007), https://doi.org/10.1093/acprof:oso/9780198237907.001.0001

Frye, Marilyn, *Politics of Reality* (Trumansburg/New York: The Crossing Press, 1983).

Gander, Eric M., *The Last Conceptual Revolution: A Critique of Richard Rorty's Political Philosophy* (Albany, NY: State University of New York Press, 1999).

Gascoigne, Neil, *Richard Rorty: Liberalism, Irony and the Ends of Philosophy*, Key Contemporary Thinkers (Cambridge: Polity, 2008).

Geuss, Raymond, *The Idea of a Critical Theory* (Cambridge: Cambridge University Press, 1981).

Giladi, Paul, 'Epistemic Exploitation and Ideological Recognition', in *Epistemic Injustice and the Philosophy of Recognition*, ed. by P. Giladi and N. McMillan (New York: Routledge, 2022), pp. 138–70, https://doi.org/10.4324/9780429435133-8

Giladi, Paul, 'Epistemic Injustice: A Role for Recognition?', *Philosophy & Social Criticism*, 44 (2018), 141–58, https://doi.org/10.1177/0191453717707237

Giladi, Paul, 'The Agent in Pain: Alienation and Discursive Abuse', *International Journal of Philosophical Studies*, 28 (2020), 692–712, https://doi.org/10.1080/09672559.2020.1784534

Gili, Guido, and Mangone, Emiliana, 'Is a Sociology of Hope Possible? An Attempt to Recompose a Theoretical Framework and a Research Programme', *The American Sociologist* 54.6 (2022), https://doi.org/10.1007/s12108-022-09539-y

Goldman, Emma, 'Anarchism: What It Really Stands For' (1910), *Digital History*, http://www.digitalhistory.uh.edu/disp_textbook.cfm?smtID=3&psid=1339

Gooding-Williams, Robert, *Look, a Negro!: Philosophical Essays on Race, Culture and Politics* (New York: Routledge, 2006), https://doi.org/10.4324/9781315870618

Green, Joshua, *Moral Tribes: Emotion, Reason, and the Gap Between Us and Them* (New York: Penguin, 2013).

Habermas, Jürgen, *Ein neuer Strukturwandel der Öffentlichkeit und die deliberative Politik* (Berlin: Suhrkamp Verlag, 2022).

Habermas, Jürgen, *The Philosophical Discourse of Modernity: Twelve Lectures*, trans. by F. Lawrence (Cambridge: Polity Press, 1987).

Haffenden, John, *The Life of John Berryman* (London: Routledge and Kegan Paul, 1982).

Haliburton, Rachel, 'Richard Rorty and the Problem of Cruelty', *Philosophy & Social Criticism*, 23 (1997), 49–69, https://doi.org/10.1177/019145379702300104

Harper, Tyler Austin, 'The Humanities Have Sown the Seeds of Their Own Destruction', *The Atlantic* (19 December 2023), https://www.theatlantic.com/ideas/archive/2023/12/humanities-university-conservative-critics/676890/

Heins, Volker M., '"More Modest and More Political": From the Frankfurt School to the Liberalism of Fear', in *Between Utopia and Realism: The Political Thought of Judith N. Shklar*, ed. by S. Ashenden and A. Hess (Philadelphia, PN: University of Pennsylvania Press, 2019), pp. 179–97, https://doi.org/10.9783/9780812296525-010

Honneth, Axel, *Reification: A New Look at an Old Idea—with Commentaries by Judith Butler, Raymond Geuss, and Jonathan Lear* (Oxford: Oxford University Press, 2008), https://doi.org/10.1093/acprof:oso/9780195320466.001.0001

Honneth, Axel, *The Struggle for Recognition: The Moral Grammar of Social Conflicts*, trans. by J. Anderson (Cambridge, MA: MIT Press, 1995).

Horkheimer, Max, 'Traditional and Critical Theory', in *Critical Theory: Selected Writings*, trans. by M. O'Connell (New York: Continuum, 2002).

Huckerby, Elin D. (forthcoming), 'False Starts and Poetic Ends: Edifying Philosophy, Literary Culture, and Rortyan Pragmatism as Poeticism', in *Philosophy and the Mirror of Nature at 45*, ed. by David Rondel (Cambridge: Cambridge University Press, 2026).

Huckerby, Elin D., 'Finely Aware and Ironically Responsible: Rorty and the Functions of Literature', *Studium Ricerca*, 120.2 (2024), 22–37, https://www.edizionistudium.it/riviste/studium-ricerca-n-2-2024

Huckerby, Elin D., 'The Takeover by a Literary Culture: Richard Rorty's Philosophy of Literature' (Doctoral Thesis, University of Cambridge, 2021), https://doi.org/10.17863/CAM.76906

Huetter-Almerigi, Yvonne, 'Two Forms of Realism', *ejpap*, 12.1 (2020), https://doi.org/10.4000/ejpap.1868

Izzard, Eddie, 'Eddie Izzard at the 2022 Equality Utah Allies Gala', *YouTube* (31 January 2023), https://www.youtube.com/watch?v=nOyye_ldJoA

James, William, *Pragmatism* (Cambridge, MA, and London: Harvard University Press, 1975).

James, William, *Some Problems of Philosophy* (Cambridge, MA, and London: Harvard University Press, 1979).

James, William, *The Meaning of Truth* (Cambridge, MA, and London: Harvard University Press, 1975).

James, William, *The Writings of William James a Comprehensive Edition*, ed. by John J. McDermott (Chicago, IL: University of Chicago Press, 1977).

James, William, 'On a Certain Blindness in Human Beings', in *Talks to Teachers on Psychology. And to Students on Some of Life's Ideals* (Cambridge, MA, and London: Harvard University Press, 1983), pp. 132–49.

Janack, Marianne (ed.), *Feminist Interpretations of Richard Rorty* (University Park, PA: Pennsylvania State University Press, 2010).

Janack, Marianne, 'Introduction', in *Feminist Interpretations of Richard Rorty*, ed. by Marianne Janack, Re-reading the Canon (University Park, PA: Pennsylvania State University Press, 2010), pp. 1–17.

Jay, Paul, *The Humanities Crisis and the Future of Literary Studies* (New York: Palgrave Macmillan US, 2014), https://doi.org/10.1057/9781137398031

Jeffries, Stuart, 'How to Make Philosophers Telegenic', *The Guardian*, 3 November 2003, https://www.theguardian.com/media/2003/nov/03/broadcasting.artsandhumanities

Jeffries, Stuart, 'Richard Rorty: The Man Who Killed Truth' (BBC). Recorded off-air from BBC4 on 16/12/2003. Repeat: original airing date 04/12/2003.

Jiang, Julie, Ren, Xiang and Ferrara, Emilio, 'Social Media Polarization and Echo Chambers in the Context of COVID-19: Case Study', *JMIRx Med*, 2.3 (2021), https://doi.org/10.2196/29570

Kekes, John, 'Cruelty and Liberalism', *Ethics*, 106 (1996), 834–44, https://doi.org/10.1086/233675

Klein, Melanie, 'Notes on Some Schizoid Mechanisms', in *The Writings of Melanie Klein*, ed. by Roger Money-Kyrle, 5 vols (New York: The Free Press, 1984), III, 1–24.

Koopman, Colin, 'The Will, the Will to Believe, and William James: An Ethics of Freedom as Self-Transformation', *Journal of the History of Philosophy* 55, 3 (2017), 491–512, https://doi.org/10.1353/hph.2017.0051

Korsgaard, Christine M., *The Sources of Normativity* (Cambridge: Cambridge University Press, 1996).

Kraugerud, Hanne Andrea and Ramberg, Bjørn T., 'The New Loud: Richard Rorty, Quietist?', *Common Knowledge*, 16.1 (2010), 46–85, https://doi.org/10.1215/0961754X-2009-060

Kremer, Alexander, 'Rorty and Normativity', *Human Affairs*, 17 (2007), 71–77, https://doi.org/10.2478/v10023-007-0007-8

Lear, Jonathan, *A Case for Irony*, Tanner Lectures on Human Values (Cambridge, MA, and London: Harvard University Press, 2011), https://doi.org/10.4159/harvard.9780674063143

Lessenich, Stephan, *Living Well at Others' Expense: The Hidden Costs of Western Prosperity* (Oxford: Polity Press, 2019).

Levitas, Ruth, *The Concept of Utopia: Reissue with New Preface by the Author*, Ralahine Utopian Studies 3 (Oxford: Peter Lang AG, Internationaler Verlag der Wissenschaften, 2011), https://doi.org/10.3726/978-3-0353-0010-9

Levitas, Ruth, *Utopia as Method: The Imaginary Reconstitution of Society* (Basingstoke: Palgrave Macmillan, 2013), https://doi.org/10.1057/9781137314253

Levitas, Ruth, '3 For Utopia: The (Limits of the) Utopian Function in Late Capitalist Society', in *The Philosophy of Utopia*, ed. by Barbara Goodwin (London, Portland, OR: Frank Cass, 2001), https://doi.org/10.4324/9780203045565, 25–43.

Levitas, Ruth, 'Pragmatism, Utopia and Anti-Utopia', *Critical Horizons*, 9.1 (2008), 42–59, https://doi.org/10.1558/crit.v9i1.42

Livingston, Alexander, *Damn Great Empires! William James and the Politics of Pragmatism* (New York: Oxford University Press, 2016), https://doi.org/10.1093/acprof:oso/9780190237158.001.0001

Llanera, Tracy, *Richard Rorty: Outgrowing Modern Nihilism* (New York: Palgrave, 2020), https://doi.org/10.1007/978-3-030-45058-8

Lorusso, Anna Maria, *Postverità. Fra reality tv, social media e storytelling* (Rome: Laterza, 2018), https://hdl.handle.net/11585/626637

Lyotard, Jean-François, *Postmodern Fables* (Minneapolis, MN: University of Minnesota Press, 1999).

Lyotard, Jean-François, *The Inhuman: Reflections on Time* (Stanford, CA: Stanford University Press, 1991).

Lyotard, Jean-François, *The Postmodern Condition: A Report on Knowledge*, trans. by G. Bennington and B. Massumi (Manchester: Manchester University Press, 1984)

Macarthur, David and Price, Huw, 'Pragmatism, Quasi-realism, and the Global Challenge', in Misak, Cheryl (ed.), *New Pragmatists* (Oxford: Clarendon Press, 2007), pp. 91–121, https://doi.org/10.1093/oso/9780199279975.003.0006

MacIntyre, Alasdair, *After Virtue* (Notre Dame, IN: Notre Dame University Press, 1981).

Maddalena, Giovanni and Gili, Guido, 'After Post-Truth Communication', *European Journal of Pragmatism and American Philosophy*, 14.1 (2022), https://doi.org/10.4000/ejpap.2795

Maddalena, Giovanni and Gili, Guido, *The History and Theory of Post-Truth Communication* (Cham: Palgrave Macmillan, 2020), https://doi.org/10.1007/978-3-030-41460-3

Malachowski, Alan, *Richard Rorty* (New York: Routledge, 2002), https://doi.org/10.1017/UPO9781844653140

Malachowski, Alan, 'Imagination over Reason: Rorty's Romance with Contingency', in *Handbuch Richard Rorty*, ed. by Martin Müller (Wiesbaden: Springer Fachmedien Wiesbaden, 2022), pp. 799–813, https://doi.org/10.1007/978-3-658-16253-5_48

Malcolm, Dominic, 'Post-Truth Society? An Eliasian Sociological Analysis of Knowledge in the 21st Century', *British Sociological Association*, 55.6 (2021), 1063–79, https://doi.org/10.1177/0038038521994039

Marchetti, Giancarlo, 'The Philosophy of Richard Rorty', in *The Ethics, Epistemology, and Politics of Richard Rorty*, ed. by Giancarlo Marchetti, (New York and London: Routledge, 2021), pp. 1–26, https://doi.org/10.4324/9780429324734-1

Marchetti, Sarin, *Ethics and Philosophical Critique in William James* (London: Palgrave Macmillan, 2015), https://doi.org/10.1057/9781137541789

Marchetti, Sarin, 'Irony and Redescription', *Iride*, 32 (2019), 631–43.

Marcuse, Herbert, *One-Dimensional Man* (London/New York: Routledge, 2002).

Marx, Karl, 'Excerpt-Notes of 1844', in *Writings of the Young Marx on Philosophy and Society*, ed. by L. D. Easton and K. H. Guddat (Garden City, NY: Doubleday and Co, 1967).

McIntyre, Lee, *Post-Truth* (Cambridge, MA: MIT Press, 2018), https://doi.org/10.7551/mitpress/11483.001.0001

Medina, José, *The Epistemology of Resistance: Gender and Racial Oppression, Epistemic Injustice, and Resistant Imaginations* (Oxford: Oxford University Press, 2013), https://doi.org/10.1093/acprof:oso/9780199929023.001.0001

Medina, José, 'Misrecognition and Epistemic Injustice', *Feminist Philosophy Quarterly*, 4 (2018), 1–16, https://doi.org/10.5206/fpq/2018.4.6233

Mendieta, Eduardo, *Take Care of Freedom and Truth Will Take Care of Itself: Interviews with Richard Rorty, Cultural Memory in the Present* (Stanford, CA: Stanford University Press, 2006), https://doi.org/10.1515/9781503620391

Mendieta, Eduardo, 'Introduction', *Take Care of Freedom and Truth Will Take Care of Itself: Interviews with Richard Rorty, Cultural Memory in the Present* (Stanford, CA: Stanford University Press, 2006), pp. xi–xxx, https://doi.org/10.1515/9781503620391

Mill, John S., *On Liberty*, ed. by Charles W. Elliott (New York: Barnes & Noble Books, 2004).

Mills, Charles W., *The Racial Contract* (Ithaca, NY: Cornell University Press, 1997).

Montaigne, Michel de, *The Complete Essays*, trans. by M. A. Screech (London and New York: Penguin, 1993).

Morrison, Toni, *The Bluest Eye* (New York: Vintage International, 2007).

Mouffe, Chantal (ed.), *Deconstruction and Pragmatism: Simon Critchley, Jacques Derrida, Ernesto Laclau and Richard Rorty* (London, New York: Routledge, 1996).

Murdoch, Iris, 'Against Dryness: A Polemical Sketch', *Encounter*, 16 (1961), 16–20.

Myers, Gerald, 'James and Freud', *The Journal of Philosophy*, 11 (1990), 593–99, https://doi.org/10.5840/jphil1990871113

Müller, Martin, *Private Romantik, öffentlicher Pragmatismus?: Richard Rortys transformative Neubeschreibung des Liberalismus*, Edition Moderne Postmoderne (Bielefeld: Transcript, 2014).

Müller, Martin, *Richard Rorty: A Short Introduction* (Wiesbaden: Springer VS, 2022), https://doi.org/10.1007/978-3-658-38838-6

Müller, Martin, 'General Introduction to the Handbuch Richard Rorty', in *Handbuch Richard Rorty*, ed. By Martin Müller (Wiesbaden: Springer Fachmedien Wiesbaden, 2022), pp. 1–30, https://doi.org/10.1007/978-3-658-16260-3_80-1

Nelson, Maggie, *On Freedom. Four Songs on Care and Constraint* (New York: Vintage, 2021).

Nicholson, Carol, 'Education and the Pragmatic Temperament', in *The Cambridge Companion to Pragmatism*, ed. by Alan Malachowski, Cambridge Companions to Philosophy (Cambridge: Cambridge University Press, 2013), pp. 249–71, https://doi.org/10.1017/cco9781139022132

Nietzsche, Friedrich, *Basic Writings of Nietzsche*, ed. by Walter Kaufman, Modern Library Classics (New York: Modern Library, 1968).

Nietzsche, Friedrich, *The Gay Science*, trans. by J. Nauckhoff (New York: Cambridge University Press, 2001), https://doi.org/10.1017/CBO9780511812088

Nussbaum, Martha C., *Not for Profit: Why Democracy Needs the Humanities*, The Public Square (Princeton, NJ: Princeton University Press, 2016), https://doi.org/10.1515/9781400883509

Nussbaum, Martha C., '"Finely Aware and Richly Responsible": Moral Attention and the Moral Task of Literature', *The Journal of Philosophy*, 82.10 (1985), 516–29, https://doi.org/10.2307/2026358

Oakes, James, 'What's Wrong with "Negative Liberty": Commentary', *Law & Social Inquiry* 21.1 (1996), 79–82, https://doi.org/10.1111/j.1747-4469.1996.tb00010.x

Oliver, Kelly, 'Gaslighting: Pathologies of Recognition and the Colonisation of Psychic Space', in *Epistemic Injustice and the Philosophy of Recognition*, ed. by P. Giladi and N. McMillan (New York: Routledge, 2022), pp. 138–70, https://doi.org/10.4324/9780429435133-7

Orwell, George, *Nineteen Eighty-Four* (London: Plume, 2003).

Owen, David, 'The Avoidance of Cruelty: Joshing Rorty on Liberal Irony', in *Richard Rorty: Critical Dialogues*, ed. by M. Festenstein and S. Thompson (Cambridge: Polity Press, 2001), pp. 93–110.

Pariser, Eli, *The Filter Bubble: What the Internet Is Hiding from You* (New York and London: Penguin Books, 2011), https://doi.org/10.3139/9783446431164

Peirce, Charles Sanders, *The Collected Papers of C.S. Peirce*, 8 vols, ed. by C. Harsthorne, P. Weiss and A. Burks, (Cambridge, MA: Harvard University Press, 1938–59).

Peirce, Charles Sanders, 'The Fixation of Belief', in *Charles Sanders Peirce: Selected Writings (Values in a Universe of Chance)*, ed. by Philip P. Wiener (New York: Dover, 1958), pp. 91–112.

Pettegrew, John (ed.), *A Pragmatist's Progress?: Richard Rorty and American Intellectual History*, American Intellectual Culture (Lanham, MD: Rowman and Littlefield, 2000).

Putnam, Hilary, *Realism with a Human Face*, ed. by James Conant (Cambridge, MA: Harvard Univ. Press, 1992).

Putnam, Hilary, *Words and Life*, ed. by James Conant (Cambridge, MA: Harvard University Press, 1994).

Raekstad, Paul, and Gradin, Sofa Saio, *Prefigurative Politics: Building Tomorrow Today* (Cambridge: Polity Press, 2020).

Ramberg, Bjørn T., 'Irony's Commitment: Rorty's Contingency, Irony and Solidarity', *The European Legacy*, 19 (2014), 144–62, https://doi.org/10.1080/10848770.2014.876197

Ramberg, Bjørn T., 'Strategies for Radical Rorty ("... but is it progress?")', *Canadian Journal of Philosophy*, 23, Supplementary Volume 19: New Essays on Metaphilosophy (1993), 223–46, https://doi.org/10.1080/00455091.1993.10717349

Rancière, Jacques, 'The Sublime from Lyotard to Schiller: Two Readings of Kant and their Political Significance', *Radical Philosophy*, 126 (2004), 8–15.

Reitter, Paul, and Wellmon, Chad, *Permanent Crisis: The Humanities in a Disenchanted Age* (Chicago, IL: The University of Chicago Press, 2021), https://doi.org/10.7208/chicago/9780226738376.001.0001

Rivera, Jeffrey, 'The Irony of Ironism: A Critique of Rorty's Postmetaphysical Utopia', *Macalester Journal of Philosophy*, 20 (2012), 61–76.

Roberts, David, 'Donald Trump and the Rise of Tribal Epistemology', *Vox* (19 May 2017), https://www.vox.com/policy-and-politics/2017/3/22/14762030/donald-trump-tribal-epistemology

Voparil, Christopher, 'On the Idea of Philosophy as *Bildungsroman*: Rorty and His Critics', *Contemporary Pragmatism*, 2.1 (2005), 115–33, https://doi.org/10.1163/18758185-90000005

Rorty, Richard (n.d.),'Rational Beauty, Non-discursive Sublimity, and the Community of Philosophers', *drafts 1988 and undated* (Special Collections and Archives, The UC Irvine Libraries, Irvine, California. 30.08.2023), box 11, folder 8, Richard Rorty Papers. MS-C017.

Rorty, Richard, *Achieving our Country. Leftist Thought in Twentieth-Century America* (Cambridge, MA: Harvard University Press, 1989).

Rorty, Richard, *Consequences of Pragmatism: (Essays: 1972-1980)* (Minneapolis, MN: University of Minnesota Press, 1982).

Rorty, Richard, *Contingency, Irony and Solidarity* (Cambridge: Cambridge University Press, 1989), https://doi.org/10.1017/cbo9780511804397

Rorty, Richard, 'Deconstruction and Circumvention', *Critical Inquiry*, 11.1 (1984), 1–23, https://doi.org/10.1086/448273

Rorty, Richard, *Die Schönheit, die Erhabenheit und die Gemeinschaft der Philosophen* (Frankfurt/Main: Suhrkamp, 2000).

Rorty, Richard, 'Erwiderung auf Ulrich Baltzer', in *Hinter den Spiegeln: Beiträge zur Philosophie Richard Rortys mit Erwiderungen von Richard Rorty*, ed. by Thomas Schäfer, Udo Tietz and Rüdiger Zill, Suhrkamp Taschenbuch Wissenschaft, 1522, 1st edn (Frankfurt am Main: Suhrkamp, 2001), pp. 49–55.

Rorty, Richard, *Essay on Heidegger and Others* (Cambridge: Cambridge University Press, 1991), https://doi.org/10.1017/CBO9780511609039

Rorty, Richard, 'Feminism and Pragmatism', in *The Rorty Reader*, ed. by Christopher J. Voparil and Richard J. Bernstein (Malden: Wiley-Blackwell, 2010), pp. 330–51.

Rorty, Richard, 'Feminism and Pragmatism', in *Truth and Progress* (Cambridge: Cambridge University Press, 1998), pp. 202–27, https://doi.org/10.1017/cbo9780511625404.012

Rorty, Richard, 'Freud and Moral Reflection', in *Pragmatism's Freud: The Moral Disposition of Psychoanalysis*, ed. by Joseph H. Smith and William Kerrigan (Baltimore, MD: Johns Hopkins University Press, 1986), pp. 1–27.

Rorty, Richard, 'Freud and Moral Reflection', in *Essays on Heidegger and Others* (Cambridge: Cambridge University Press, 2010 [1991]), pp. 143–63, https://doi.org/10.1017/cbo9780511609039.010

Rorty, Richard, 'Freud and Moral Reflection', in *The Rorty Reader*, ed. by Christopher J. Voparil and Richard J. Bernstein (Malden: Wiley-Blackwell, 2010), pp. 259–79.

Rorty, Richard, 'Grandeur, Profundity, and Finitude', in *Philosophy as Cultural Politics* (Cambridge: Cambridge University Press 2007), pp. 73–89, https://doi.org/10.1017/cbo9780511812835.006

Rorty, Richard, 'Habermas and Lyotard on Postmodernity', in Richard Rorty, *Essays on Heidegger and Others* (Cambridge: Cambridge University Press, 1991), pp. 164–76, https://doi.org/10.1017/cbo9780511609039.011

Rorty, Richard, 'Habermas, Derrida, and the Functions of Philosophy', in *Truth and Progress* (Cambridge: Cambridge University Press, 1998), pp. 307–26.

Rorty, Richard, 'Heidegger, Kundera, and Dickens', in *Essays on Heidegger and Others* (Cambridge: Cambridge University Press, 2010 [1991]), pp. 66–82, https://doi.org/10.1017/cbo9780511609039.005

Rorty, Richard, 'Hilary Putnam and the Relativist Menace', in *Truth and Progress* (Cambridge: Cambridge University Press, 1998), pp. 43–62, https://doi.org/10.1017/cbo9780511625404.003

Rorty, Richard, 'Idealizations, Foundations, and Social Practices', in *Democracy and Difference*, ed. by S. Benhabib (Princeton, NJ: Princeton University Press, 1996).

Rorty, Richard, *Is "Post-Modernism" Relevant to Politics?: Spinoza Lectures* (Assen: Van Gorcum, 1997), https://doi.org/10.1017/CBO9781139173643

Rorty, Richard, 'Is Natural Science a Natural Kind?', in *Objectivity, Relativism, and Truth* (Cambridge: Cambridge University Press, 1990), pp. 46–62, https://doi.org/10.1017/cbo9781139173643.004

Rorty, Richard, 'Nineteenth-Century Idealism and Twentieth-Century Textualism', *The Monist*, 64.2 (1981), 155–74, https://doi.org/10.5840/monist198164211

Rorty, Richard, *Objectivity, Relativism, and Truth* (Cambridge: Cambridge University Press, 1990),

Rorty, Richard, 'On Ethnocentrism: A Reply to Clifford Geertz', in *Objectivity, Relativism, and Truth* (Cambridge: Cambridge University Press, 1990), pp. 203–10, https://doi.org/10.1017/cbo9781139173643.014

Rorty, Richard, *On Philosophy and Philosophers: Unpublished Papers, 1960-2000*, ed. by W. P. Małecki and Christopher Voparil (Cambridge: Cambridge University Press, 2020), https://doi.org/10.1017/9781108763967

Rorty, Richard, *Philosophy and Social Hope* (London and New York: Penguin, 1999).

Rorty, Richard, *Philosophy and the Mirror of Nature* (Princeton, NJ: Princeton University Press, 1979).

Rorty, Richard, 'Philosophy as a Kind of Writing: An Essay on Derrida', *New Literary History*, 10.1 (1978), 141–60, https://doi.org/10.2307/468309

Rorty, Richard, 'Philosophy as a Transitional Genre', in *Pragmatism, Critique, Judgment: Essays for Richard J. Bernstein*, ed. by Richard J. Bernstein, Seyla Benhabib and Nancy Fraser (Cambridge, MA: MIT Press, 2004), pp. 3–28.

Rorty, Richard, *Philosophy as Cultural Politics* (Cambridge: Cambridge University Press, 2007), https://doi.org/10.1017/CBO9780511812835

Rorty, Richard, *Philosophy as Poetry* (Charlottesville, VA, and London: University of Virginia Press, 2016).

Rorty, Richard, 'Postmodernist Bourgeois Liberalism', *The Journal of Philosophy*, 80.10 (1983), 583, https://doi.org/10.2307/2026153

Rorty, Richard, 'Pragmatism as Anti-authoritarianism', in *A Companion to Pragmatism*, ed. by J. R. Shook and J. Margolis (Oxford: Blackwell Publishing, 2006), pp. 257–66, https://doi.org/10.1002/9780470997079.ch26

Rorty, Richard, *Pragmatism as Anti-Authoritarianism*, ed. by Eduardo Mendieta, Robert Brandom (Cambridge, MA: Harvard University Press, 2021), https://doi.org/10.2307/j.ctv33mgbns

Rorty, Richard, 'Pragmatism, Relativism, and Irrationalism,' in *The Rorty Reader*, ed. by Christopher J. Voparil and Richard J. Bernstein (Malden: Wiley-Blackwell, 2010) pp. 111–22.

Rorty, Richard, 'Pragmatism, Relativism, and Irrationalism', in *Consequences of Pragmatism: (Essays: 1972-1980)* (Minneapolis, MN: University of Minnesota Press, 1982), pp. 160–75.

Rorty, Richard, 'Pragmatism, Relativism, and Irrationalism', *Proceedings and Addresses of the American Philosophical Association*, 53.6 (1980), 719–38.

Rorty, Richard, 'Professionalized Philosophy and Transcendentalist Culture', *The Georgia Review*, 30.4 (1976), 757–69.

Rorty, Richard, 'Redemption from Egotism: James and Proust as Spiritual Exercises', in *The Rorty Reader*, ed. by Christopher Voparil and Richard J. Bernstein (Malden, MA: Wiley-Blackwell, 2010), pp. 389–406.

Rorty, Richard, 'Reply to J. B. Schneewind', in *The Philosophy of Richard Rorty: The Library of Living Philosophers, Volume XXXII*, ed. by Randall E. Auxier and Lewis E. Hahn (Chicago and Lasalle, IL: Open Court, 2010), pp. 506–09.

Rorty, Richard, 'Response to Dennett', in *Rorty and His Critics*, ed. by Robert B. Brandom, Philosophers and Their Critics 9 (Malden, MA, Oxford: Blackwell, 2000), pp. 101–08.

Rorty, Richard, 'Science as Solidarity', in *Objectivity, Relativism, and Truth* (Cambridge: Cambridge University Press, 1990), pp. 35–45, https://doi.org/10.1017/CBO9781139173643.003

Rorty, Richard, 'Solidarity or Objectivity?', *Nanzan Review of American Studies*, 6 (1984), 1–18.

Rorty, Richard, 'Texts and Lumps', *New Literary History*, 17.1 (1985), 1–16, https://doi.org/10.2307/468973

Rorty, Richard, 'The Contingency of Selfhood', *London Review of Books*, 8.8 (1986).

Rorty, Richard, 'The Inspirational Value of Great Works of Literature', in *Achieving our Country. Leftist Thought in Twentieth-Century America* (Cambridge, MA: Harvard University Press, 1989).

Rorty, Richard, 'The Pragmatist's Progress', in *Interpretation and Overinterpretation*, ed. by Stefan Collini (Cambridge: Cambridge University Press, 1992), pp. 89–108, https://doi.org/10.1017/CBO9780511627408.005

Rorty, Richard, 'The Priority of Democracy to Philosophy', in *Objectivity, Relativism, and Truth* (Cambridge: Cambridge University Press, 1990), https://doi.org/10.1017/CBO9781139173643 , pp. 175–96.

Rorty, Richard, 'Thugs and Theorists: A Reply to Bernstein', *Political Theory*, 15 (1987), 564–80, https://doi.org/10.1177/0090591787015004004

Rorty, Richard, 'Trotsky and the Wild Orchids', *Common Knowledge*, 1.3 (1992).

Rorty, Richard, *Truth and Progress* (Cambridge: Cambridge University Press, 1998), https://doi.org/10.1017/CBO9780511625404

Rorty, Richard, 'Universality and Truth', in *Rorty and His Critics*, ed. by Robert B. Brandom, Philosophers and Their Critics 9 (Malden, MA, Oxford: Blackwell, 2000), pp. 1–30.

Rorty, Richard, 'Words or Worlds Apart? The Consequences of Philosophy for Literary Studies', *Philosophy and Literature*, 26 (2002), 369–96, https://doi.org/10.1353/phl.2003.0015

Rothwell, Jonathan T., Makridis, Christos A., Ramirez, Christina M., and Desai, Sonal 'Information, Partisanship, and Preferences in a Pandemic', *Frontiers in Public Health*, 11 (2023), https://doi.org/10.3389/fpubh.2023.1019206

Salaverría, Heidi, 'The Beauty of Doubting', in *Between the Ticks of the Watch. Exhibition Catalogue*, ed. by Solveig Øvstebo and Karsten Lund (Chicago, IL: The Renaissance Society at the University of Chicago,2017), pp. 153–83.

Salaverría, Heidi, 'Enjoying the Doubtful. On Transformative Suspensions in Pragmatist Aesthetics', *European Journal of Pragmatism and American Philosophy*, 4.1 (2012), https://doi.org/10.4000/ejpap.791

Salaverría, Heidi, 'Prophetische Zweifel und der "dunkel erahnte Zusammenhang von Kunst und Folter"–zur politischen Ästhetik Rortys', in *Handbuch Richard Rorty*, ed. by Martin Müller (Wiesbaden: Springer Fachmedien Wiesbaden, 2022), pp. 933–47, https://doi.org/10.1007/978-3-658-16253-5_57

Salaverría, Heidi, *Spielräume des Selbst. Pragmatismus und kreatives Handeln* (Akademie-Verlag: Berlin, 2007), pp. 167–90, https://doi.org/10.1524/9783050047232

Salaverría, Heidi, 'Vague Certainty, Violent Derealization, Imaginative Doubting. Reflections on Common Sense and Critique in Peirce and Butler', *European Journal of Pragmatism and American Philosophy*, 12.2 (2020), https://doi.org/10.4000/ejpap.2102

Sandbothe, Mike, 'Davidson and Rorty on Truth', in *A House Divided: Comparing Analytic and Continental Philosophers*, ed. by Carlos Prado (Amherst: Humanities Press, 2003), pp. 235–58.

Sartwell, Crispin, 'The Provocateur's Philosopher', *Los Angeles Times* (12 June 2007), https://www.latimes.com/archives/la-xpm-2007-jun-12-oe-sartwell12-story.html

Scarry, Elaine, *The Body in Pain: The Making and Unmaking of the World* (Oxford: Oxford University Press, 1985).

Schneewind, J. B., 'Rorty on Utopia and Moral Philosophy', in *The Philosophy of Richard Rorty: The Library of Living Philosophers, Volume XXXII*, ed. by Randall E. Auxier and Lewis E. Hahn (Chicago and Lasalle, IL: Open Court, 2010), pp. 479–505.

Scruton, Roger, *Sexual Desire: A Philosophical Investigation* (London: Phoenix Press, 2001).

Sedgwick, Eve Kosofsky, 'Paranoid Reading and Reparative Reading, or, You're So Paranoid, You Probably Think this Essay is About You', in *Touching Feeling. Affect, Pedagogy, Performativity* (Durham, NC: Duke University Press, 2003), pp. 123–51, https://doi.org/10.2307/j.ctv11smq37.9

Sellars, Wilfrid, *Empiricism and the Philosophy of Mind*, Minnesota Studies in the Philosophy of Science 1 (Cambridge, MA: Harvard University Press, 1997).

Sellars, Wilfrid, 'Empiricism and the Philosophy of Mind', in *Minnesota Studies in the Philosophy of Science*, ed. by Herbert Feigl and Michael Scrive (Minneapolis, MN: University of Minnesota Press, 1956), pp. 253–329.

Shklar, Judith N., 'Liberalism and Fear', in *Liberalism and the Moral Life*, ed. by N. L. Rosenblum (Cambridge, MA: Harvard University Press, 1989), pp. 21–38.

Shklar, Judith N., 'Putting Cruelty First', *Daedalus*, 111 (1982), 17–27.

Shusterman, Richard, *Practicing Philosophy: Pragmatism and the Philosophical Life* (London: Routledge, 1997).

Spelman, Elizabeth V., *Inessential Woman: Problems of Exclusion in Feminist Thought* (Boston, MA: Beacon Press, 1988).

Spencer, Philip, '"Putting Cruelty First": The *Summum Malum*, Genocide, and Crimes Against Humanity', in *Between Utopia and Realism: The Political Thought of Judith N. Shklar*, ed. by S. Ashenden and A. Hess (Philadelphia, PN: University of Pennsylvania Press, 2019), pp. 179–97, https://doi.org/10.9783/9780812296525-011

Stanovich, Keith E., *The Bias That Divides Us: The Science and Politics of Myside Thinking* (Cambridge, MA/London: MIT Press, 2021), https://doi.org/10.7551/mitpress/13367.001.0001

Stullerova, Kamila, 'Cruelty and International Relations', in *Between Utopia and Realism: The Political Thought of Judith N. Shklar*, ed. by S. Ashenden and A. Hess (Philadelphia, PN: University of Pennsylvania Press, 2019), pp. 67–85, https://doi.org/10.9783/9780812296525-004

Sunstein, Cass R., *#Republic: Divided Democracy in the Age of Social Media* (Princeton, NJ: Princeton University Press, 2017), https://doi.org/10.1515/9781400884711

Vaid-Menon, Alok, in conversation with Jamie Lee Curtis, Upfront Ventures, 'Jamie Lee Curtis Interviews ALOK on the World Beyond the Gender Binary 2023 Upfront Summit', *YouTube* (10 March 2023), https://youtu.be/hWAs_2oGNB8?t=2

Vescio, Bryan *Reconstruction in Literary Studies: An Informalist Approach* (New York: Palgrave MacMillan, 2014), https://doi.org/10.1057/9781137428837

Voparil, Christopher, *Reconstructing Pragmatism: Richard Rorty and the Classical Pragmatists* (New York, NY: Oxford University Press, 2021), https://doi.org/10.1093/oso/9780197605721.001.0001

Voparil, Christopher, 'Rorty and James on Irony, Moral Commitment, and the Ethics of Belief', *William James Studies*, 12.2 (2016), 1–30.

Voparil, Christopher, 'Rorty's Ethics of Responsibility', in *A Companion to Rorty*, ed. by Alan Malachowski, Blackwell Companions to Philosophy 73 (Hoboken, NJ: Wiley Blackwell, 2020), pp. 490–504, https://doi.org/10.1002/9781118972199.ch30

Voparil, Christopher, 'The Truth Doesn't Matter', *The Boston Globe* (7 June 2017), https://www.bostonglobe.com/ideas/2017/06/07/the-truth-doesn-matter/I4fY2nu99KnViMINTkIOCP/story.html

Wallace, R. Jay, 'Recognition and the Moral Nexus', *European Journal of Philosophy*, 29 (2021), 634–45, https://doi.org/10.1111/ejop.12677

Williams, Michael, 'Rorty on Knowledge and Truth', in *Richard Rorty*, ed. by Charles Guignon and David R. Hiley (Cambridge: Cambridge University Press, 2003), pp. 61–80.

Wittgenstein, Ludwig, *The Blue and Brown Books: Preliminary Studies for the 'Philosophical Investigations'* (Oxford: Blackwell, 1958).

Wittgenstein, Ludwig, *Philosophische Untersuchungen. Philosophical Investigations*, trans. by G. E. M. Anscombe (New York: The Macmillan Company, 1953).

Index

agonism 106
anti-authoritarianism 4, 7–8, 46, 53–54, 60, 92, 96, 108–109, 111, 120, 125, 131, 134–136, 145, 158, 164–165, 168–169
anti-essentialism 8, 58–61, 67–68, 71, 73, 75, 88–91, 135, 164, 186
anti-foundationalism 4, 27, 29, 150–151, 156–158, 161, 163, 165, 168, 173–174, 178, 180–181, 183, 186–188, 193
anti-representationalism 27, 29, 34, 57, 71, 80, 85, 87, 97, 108–109, 128, 151
anti-utopianism 64–65
artefact 71–72, 74, 76, 79, 81–82, 171
authorial intention 13, 15–16, 18
autonomy 6, 24, 80, 123, 125–127, 136–138, 140–142, 152–153, 161–162, 180, 184, 188–189

Bacon, Michael 5, 30, 55, 57–63, 66–68, 73, 75, 85–87, 90–91, 130–131, 156, 159, 161, 163
Bernstein, Richard J. 5, 27, 37, 41, 54, 87, 131, 149–150, 156–162, 173, 183–185
Bildung 152, 194, 196
Black Lives Matter (BLM) 50–51, 134
Borges, Jorge Luis 23
Bourdieu, Pierre 137–138
bullshitters 169–170
Butler, Judith 124, 143

capitalism 3, 34–35, 38, 48, 55, 63, 67
care 17, 40–41, 50, 74
Cartesian doubt/scepticism 159–160

certainty 113, 125, 131, 134–136, 138, 141, 143–145, 149, 162, 164, 176
  authoritarian certainty 125, 131, 143–144
change, revolutionary versus reformist 3, 19, 23, 53, 63, 66–67, 83–84, 118
civic virtue 7, 107, 114, 148, 150–151, 155–157, 172–173, 176, 186
commensurability 98, 105
common sense 71, 87–88, 90, 113, 155, 163, 166–167, 174, 178–179, 188
conceptual loss 26, 46–47
conciliatory attitude 4, 6, 103–105, 108, 117, 120
contingency
  contingency of communities 30, 44, 73, 96, 106–118
  contingency of self 73, 96, 100–106, 151, 153
  linguistic contingency 24, 34, 39, 42, 73, 96–100, 151
contradictory descriptions 103–104
conversability 7, 147–148, 150–151, 157, 167, 169–170, 172–174
Covid-19 pandemic 1, 115
creative doubt. *See* doubt: creative or imaginative doubt
crisis in the humanities. *See* humanities: crisis in
critical theory 60, 90, 124, 166
cruelty 3–4, 8, 15–16, 26–27, 31–32, 37–39, 41–45, 49–50, 53–54, 70, 73, 75, 84, 89, 117–118, 123, 125–126, 134–135, 141, 152–153, 188–189
cultural politics 75, 166

curiosity 6–7, 96, 110, 117, 120, 123, 143, 170
Curtis, William 114, 149–150, 155–157, 176–177, 186–187, 200

democratic
  backsliding 3
  culture 1, 74, 165, 169
  discourse 7, 148, 165, 170
  practice 165
  virtue 7, 169–170, 172
dependence/dependency 6, 125–126, 140–141, 143–144
Dewey, John 13, 39, 55, 85, 95, 105–106, 108, 112, 114, 129, 131–132, 134–135, 163–164, 176
Diamond, Cora 26, 46
disciplinary pluralism. *See* pluralism/plurality: disciplinary
discourse, 'abnormal' or 'normal' 19, 23, 75, 78, 81, 88, 171
discursive abuse 25
discursive pluralism. *See* pluralism/plurality: discursive
doublethink 140–141, 145, 176
doubt 4, 6–7, 11, 13, 31, 33, 90, 101, 124–126, 128–135, 140, 142–145, 150, 157–162, 167–168, 173, 176–186, 188–189, 192, 196–198, 200
  authoritarian doubt 125, 133–134, 140, 145
  creative or imaginative doubt 6–7, 124–126, 128–130, 132, 134, 145
  'radical and continuing' doubt 31, 101, 133, 157, 159–161, 177–178, 181, 183, 186, 188
  self-doubt 6, 125, 129, 132–134, 143

Eco, Umberto 13–15, 18
edification 88, 119, 152, 167
education 18, 28, 38, 41, 57, 66, 74, 76, 82, 88, 172, 176–177, 193–194
  liberal arts 176
  of hope 57, 66, 76
egotism 6, 128–130, 142, 170

eirenism 6, 93–96, 98–100, 103–109, 114–121
emotions/feelings 22, 38, 40, 52, 96, 110–114, 117, 119
  versus reason 96–97, 119
empathy 18, 28, 38, 40, 124, 141–143, 192
energetic versus hermeneutic 93, 103–104
Enlightenment 24, 30, 47, 73, 90, 112
epistemic injustice/exploitation 5, 26, 44
essentialism 3, 67–68, 89, 150, 157–158, 163, 166, 173–174
existentialism 129–130, 156, 159, 161–163, 167, 180, 196

fallibilism 7, 39, 65, 108, 120, 147, 149–151, 156–160, 162–163, 173–174, 176, 180
  as virtue 149, 151, 156
  serene 7, 147, 150–151, 157–158, 173
feminism 4, 11–14, 19–24, 29, 32, 40, 94, 129
  and pragmatism 12, 14
fiction 16, 18–19
final vocabulary. *See* vocabulary: final vocabulary
finitude 9, 72, 87, 151, 159, 163
fragmentation 1, 85, 91, 115, 147–148, 151, 169–171, 174, 194
  epistemic 91
  in the public sphere 147–148, 151, 169, 171, 174
Fraser, Nancy 14
Freud, Sigmund 93, 97, 100, 102–105, 114, 116, 123, 126, 128, 134–135, 143, 162, 190

gaslighting 44, 52–53
Geertz, Clifford 17, 19, 23
'great works of literature' 199

historicism 30, 39, 42, 76, 80, 88, 105–107, 112–114, 128, 152, 155, 164, 186, 188
holism 15, 66, 68, 114, 132

humanities
  crisis in 176, 191, 194–195, 197–198
  defence of 7, 177, 192–196, 200
  future of 197
humiliability 125–126
humiliation 6, 26, 30, 32, 37–41, 44, 84, 106, 113, 119, 123, 125, 128, 133–136, 138–145, 152–153, 167

Ideologiekritik 33–34, 36
incommensurability 6, 33, 83, 105, 118, 121, 136–137, 170–171
inspiration 62, 71, 79–81, 145, 150, 197–199
  versus knowingness 80–82, 86, 197–198
inspirational value of literature 197–198
interpretations 12–14, 16, 19, 23, 35, 70, 80, 147, 161, 183
ironism/irony 4, 6, 8, 17, 24, 28–32, 36, 39–41, 43, 53, 61, 79–80, 84, 88–92, 94, 98, 101, 110, 113, 117–118, 121, 125, 129, 131, 136, 143, 147–148, 150–168, 170, 172–175, 177–187, 189, 197–199
  and cruelty 31, 188–189
  and solidarity 107, 150, 154, 161, 173–174
  as awareness of contingency 147, 150–151, 158, 173
  as hope 4, 7, 182, 184
  as virtue 152
  privatisation of 153, 155, 167
  the ironist 28, 30, 32, 39, 43, 84, 88, 150, 152, 155, 157–164, 166–168, 172–174, 178–181, 183–185, 197
  two senses of 140, 150–151, 155–157, 173
ironist theory 186–187, 197

James, William 94–98, 100–103, 106–108, 112, 114, 116, 119–120, 140, 168, 178, 190

justification 7, 18, 28–29, 140, 151, 159, 165, 168, 171–174, 187, 192, 194

Kierkegaard, Søren 183–185
Klein, Melanie 124, 126, 133, 135–136, 139–141
knowingness. *See* inspiration: versus knowingness

leftism 33–34, 66, 173
Levitas, Ruth 5–6, 57–60, 62–68, 71–72, 74, 76–79, 82–83, 85–86, 90
liberal ironism 17, 24, 36, 41, 113–114, 118, 125, 129, 147–148, 150–155, 158, 163–164, 167–168, 170, 172–174, 180, 184, 188
liberalism 3, 8, 27, 32, 34, 38, 53–55, 58, 60–63, 67, 77, 86–87, 89, 91, 94, 112, 149–150, 154, 164–165, 172, 178, 182, 184
liberal virtue ethics 149
literary culture 47, 71, 120, 200
literature 4, 23–24, 39–41, 81, 120, 164, 181, 187, 189, 191–193, 197–199

Marxism 33, 60, 66, 85
Marx, Karl 26, 33–34, 47–48, 60, 62, 66, 128
mental pain 25–26, 48
metaphysics 3, 14, 23, 27–29, 33, 36, 48–49, 60, 62, 74, 80, 85, 88, 97, 114, 118, 132, 135–137, 151–152, 163, 166–167, 186, 190–191
myside bias 148, 167, 174
myside society 148

Nabokov, Vladimir 15–17, 19, 23, 45, 80, 141, 192
  Lolita 15–16
  Pale Fire 15
naturalism 29–30
Nelson, Maggie 124, 133
Nietzsche, Friedrich 11, 100, 102–103, 117, 139, 148, 162, 181, 188, 190, 192, 198

nominalism 30, 39, 42, 80, 88, 106–107, 113–114, 152, 155, 164, 186, 188
novels 15–17, 27, 40, 75, 101
Nussbaum, Martha 15–16, 192

open-mindedness 7, 150, 156, 158, 167, 170, 173–174
openness 7–8, 66, 78, 85–86, 120, 148, 157, 160, 166, 168
Orwell, George 15–17, 19, 22–23, 45, 48, 76, 140, 192
  1984 15, 22, 26, 44–45, 49, 140
  Animal Farm 15, 18

paranoid reading/position 124, 126–128, 130, 134, 136–137, 139–141, 144
pluralism/plurality 8, 45, 64, 78, 88, 153–154, 160, 165, 183, 195–196
  disciplinary 195
  discursive 165
poeticised culture 6, 70–71, 91, 181, 189, 191
polarisation 3, 7, 110–112, 115, 119
populism 90, 173
post-truth society 4, 6–7, 93–95, 108–112, 114–116, 118–120, 148, 169, 171
pragmatism as anti-authoritarianism 60
private versus public distinction 69–70, 130, 154–155, 173, 175, 177, 180
professionalism 22, 199
pure irony (Kierkegaardian) 184–185
purification 134–136, 141–142, 145
purity 117, 135–138, 142, 155, 184–185

racism 7, 37, 40, 42–44, 50, 53, 127, 134
radical and continuing doubt.
  See doubt: 'radical and continuing' doubt
radical, definition of 83
Radical Rorty 5, 26, 32, 41, 44–45, 53–55, 59–60, 73, 86, 90

Ramberg, Bjørn T. 5, 26, 41, 44, 59, 61, 68, 72–73, 85, 87, 90, 128, 131, 134, 156, 159–161, 164, 167
reason. *See* emotions/feelings: versus reason
reconstruction 177
recontextualisation 86, 182, 198
redescription 4, 8, 20, 28–31, 33, 39, 41–43, 68, 80, 84, 100, 102, 106, 119, 128, 130, 132, 134, 137–138, 140, 144, 147–148, 150–151, 153, 157–158, 161–167, 169–170, 173–174, 180, 182, 190
reformism 23, 35–36, 56, 63, 66, 75, 83, 118, 154
relationality 6, 51, 70, 124, 126, 135
  relational dependence 126
relativism 68, 78, 82, 107, 110, 117, 142, 156–157, 169
reparative aesthetics 6
reparative critique 123–125
reparative solidarity. *See* solidarity: reparative
representationalism 3, 28–29, 36, 54, 97, 100, 120, 168
revolutionary change versus reform. *See* change, revolutionary versus reformist
Rich, Adrienne 12, 19, 21
Romanticism 30, 47, 77, 114, 142, 153, 163, 189–190
Rutherford, Nat 5, 9, 55, 57–63, 66–68, 73, 75, 85–87, 90–91

scepticism 15, 76, 125, 131, 150, 157–159, 173, 195
Schneewind, J.B. 129, 133, 147–148, 158, 162–163, 175, 177–185, 188–190
Sedgwick, Eve Kosofsky 124, 127–128, 130, 137, 144
self-creation 16, 89, 107, 123–126, 128–130, 132, 134, 137–139, 141, 152–154, 156, 161–163, 167, 179–180, 184, 188–190, 196
sensitivity 40, 101, 106, 116, 119, 131, 143, 195

serene fallibilism. *See* fallibilism: serene
shame 7, 111, 133–135, 141
Shklar, Judith 27, 37–38, 53, 140, 152
social change 4, 14, 19, 22–24, 57, 67, 76, 94, 108, 117, 164
social justice 58, 90, 117, 195, 197
social media 111, 114–115, 120, 170
  effects on public sphere 115, 170
solidarity 7–9, 16, 18, 28, 30, 39, 41, 72, 75, 84–85, 94, 105–107, 110, 117, 123, 125, 128–129, 134, 137, 140, 142–143, 145, 150–151, 154, 161, 168, 171–174, 177, 184, 188–189, 192, 199
  reparative 142–145
status quo 5, 8, 26, 36, 51–52, 54–56, 58–59, 63, 87, 124
strong poet/poetry 39–40, 78–80, 82, 85–86, 127, 138, 143, 153, 155, 162–164, 184, 191, 200

Tanner Lectures 12–14, 17, 32, 40, 45, 166
  Rorty's 12–14, 32, 40, 45
teleology 99–100
trans rights/movement 44, 89–90, 126
tribal epistemology 170
Truth 4, 7, 9, 21, 24, 29, 72, 74, 80, 90, 91, 110, 148, 150, 151, 164, 169, 170, 174. *See also* post-truth society
uncertainty 3, 9, 70, 74, 138
utopianism 4–6, 22–23, 28, 35, 37–39, 55, 57–59, 62–68, 70–79, 82–83, 85–86, 89–91, 113, 120, 138, 150–152, 154–155, 163–164, 167, 174, 176–178, 180–181, 186–189, 192, 199–200

vaccine 115
violence 35–37, 43, 96, 109, 117–118, 120, 124, 128, 133, 135–136, 144
vocabulary 6, 14, 24, 28–32, 34–36, 38–40, 42–43, 50, 61, 68, 71, 73–74, 76, 78, 80–81, 84, 87–90, 94, 96–103, 105–107, 110, 112, 114, 116–119, 121, 127, 129, 134, 136, 143, 152, 154, 157–168, 170–171, 173–174, 177–179, 181–189, 196, 198
  final vocabulary 31–32, 73, 84, 87–88, 101, 110, 114, 117–119, 152, 154, 157–164, 166–168, 170, 173, 177–179, 181–186, 196, 198
  Rorty's 'vocabulary vocabulary' 179
Voparil, Christopher 94–95, 101, 107–108, 116, 144, 156, 167, 171

we-intentions 142, 188–189
white supremacism 42, 127

About the Team

Alessandra Tosi was the managing editor for this book.

Adèle Kreager proof-read this manuscript and compiled the index.

Jeevanjot Kaur Nagpal designed the cover. The cover was produced in InDesign using the Fontin font.

Annie Hine typeset the book in InDesign. The main text font is Tex Gyre Pagella and the heading font is Californian FB.

Jeremy Bowman produced the PDF, paperback, and hardback editions and created the EPUB.

The conversion to the HTML edition was performed with epublius, an open-source software which is freely available on our GitHub page at https://github.com/OpenBookPublishers

Laura Rodríguez was in charge of marketing.

This book was peer-reviewed by Prof. Emil Višňovský, Comenius University (Bratislava), and an anonymous referee. Experts in their field, these readers give their time freely to help ensure the academic rigour of our books. We are grateful for their generous and invaluable contributions.

This book need not end here...

Share

All our books — including the one you have just read — are free to access online so that students, researchers and members of the public who can't afford a printed edition will have access to the same ideas. This title will be accessed online by hundreds of readers each month across the globe: why not share the link so that someone you know is one of them?

This book and additional content is available at
https://doi.org/10.11647/OBP.0487

Donate

Open Book Publishers is an award-winning, scholar-led, not-for-profit press making knowledge freely available one book at a time. We don't charge authors to publish with us: instead, our work is supported by our library members and by donations from people who believe that research shouldn't be locked behind paywalls.

Join the effort to free knowledge by supporting us at
https://www.openbookpublishers.com/support-us

We invite you to connect with us on our socials!

BLUESKY
@openbookpublish
.bsky.social

MASTODON
@OpenBookPublish
@hcommons.social

LINKEDIN
open-book-publishers

Read more at the Open Book Publishers Blog
https://blogs.openbookpublishers.com

You may also be interested in:

Knowledge
A Human Interest Story
Brian Weatherson
https://doi.org/10.11647/OBP.0425

Forms of Life and Subjectivity
Rethinking Sartre's Philosophy
Daniel Rueda Garrido
https://doi.org/10.11647/OBP.0259

Troubled People, Troubled World
Psychotherapy, Ethics and Society
Michael Briant
https://doi.org/10.11647/OBP.0416

Hanging on to the Edges
Essays on Science, Society and the Academic Life
Daniel Nettle
https://doi.org/10.11647/OBP.0155

www.ingramcontent.com/pod-product-compliance
Lightning Source LLC
Chambersburg PA
CBHW050523170426
43201CB00013B/2057